CIRCULATING CULTURE

New World Diasporas

UNIVERSITY PRESS OF FLORIDA

Florida A&M University, Tallahassee
Florida Atlantic University, Boca Raton
Florida Gulf Coast University, Ft. Myers
Florida International University, Miami
Florida State University, Tallahassee
New College of Florida, Sarasota
University of Central Florida, Orlando
University of Florida, Gainesville
University of North Florida, Jacksonville
University of South Florida, Tampa
University of West Florida, Pensacola

Circulating Culture

Transnational Cuban Networks of Exchange

Jennifer Cearns

UNIVERSITY PRESS OF FLORIDA

Gainesville/Tallahassee/Tampa/Boca Raton
Pensacola/Orlando/Miami/Jacksonville/Ft. Myers/Sarasota

Publication of this work made possible by a Sustaining the Humanities through the American Rescue Plan grant from the National Endowment for the Humanities.

Copyright 2023 by Jennifer Cearns
All rights reserved
Published in the United States of America.

28 27 26 25 24 23   6 5 4 3 2 1

A record of the cataloging-in-publication data is available at the Library of Congress.
ISBN 978-0-8130-6976-0 (cloth)   ISBN 978-0-8130-8008-6 (paper)

The University Press of Florida is the scholarly publishing agency for the State University System of Florida, comprising Florida A&M University, Florida Atlantic University, Florida Gulf Coast University, Florida International University, Florida State University, New College of Florida, University of Central Florida, University of Florida, University of North Florida, University of South Florida, and University of West Florida.

University Press of Florida
2046 NE Waldo Road
Suite 2100
Gainesville, FL 32609
http://upress.ufl.edu

Contents

List of Figures vii
Acknowledgments ix
Chronology xi

Introduction 1

Part I. Creating Value

1. "Fake It to Make It": Conspicuously Consuming Fantasy in Hialeah and Havana 33
2. The Ties That Bind: Remitting Kinship to Cuba 58

Part II. Circulating Value

3. The "Mula Ring": Material Networks of Circulation through the Cuban World 87
4. The "e-Mula Ring": Digital Networks between Havana and the Cuban Diaspora 112

Part III. Returning Value

5. "Back to the Future": Nostalgia, Authenticity, and the Antiques Trade between Miami and Havana 143
6. *Patria en Muerte:* Making Death Matter 167
Conclusion: Constructing Cuban Culture from the Cracks of Society 188
Epilogue 208

Notes 211
Bibliography 219
Index 255

Figures

0.1. Map showing ethnographic fieldwork research sites   xiii

0.2. Map showing areas of significant Cuban migration in Greater Miami   15

2.1. Sign advertising immediate cell phone credit transfers from Hialeah (U.S.) to Cuba   64

2.2. Timeline plotting Milagros's family history of remittance-sending alongside political changes between the U.S. and Cuba   69

2.3. Kinship diagram showing remittance flows across 5 generations of Milagros and Lilia's family   72

2.4. Graffiti on a wall in Havana, saying "We are dividuals"   78

3.1. Map showing destinations across the Mula Ring, and the directional flow of items   93

3.2. A taxi/hostel service targeting Cubans in Guyana   101

3.3. Mulas about to start packing the goods in Guyana   103

3.4. Store targeting Cuban mulas in Colón, Panama   104

3.5. Cubans waiting to board a flight back home from Georgetown, Guyana, with their goods   105

3.6. Shop sign in Miami advertising merchandise made in Peru to be sold in Cuba   106

4.1. Diagram showing structure of distribution for *el paquete*   119

4.2. Handwritten "order form" for *el paquete*   120

4.3. Price list displayed in the window of a *paquetero*'s home in El Cerro, Havana   121

4.4. Social call via Instagram for help transporting hard drives to New York from Havana   126

viii · Figures

4.5. Merchandise with an *el paquete* design, for sale in a museum gift shop in New York 127

4.6. President Obama appearing on a Cuban television show 136

5.1. Havana phonebook from 1958, for sale in Miami 150

5.2. Cuban diaspora visiting the Nostalgia Fair in Miami 154

6.1. Dominican cigars made from "Cuban seeds" for sale in Key West, Florida 184

6.2. Shrine to St. Lazarus containing a Cuban cigar, in a tree in a parking lot in Miami 185

7.1. The launch of Little Havana's new flag in Miami 189

Acknowledgments

I owe a debt of gratitude to a long list of people for supporting me through the years of research and writing that have got me to this point.

First and foremost, my sincere thanks to Kevin Yelvington, the editor of this series, for his long-standing support of my work, and his help throughout the research and publication process. My deepest thanks go also to the Yelvington-Cruz family, for being a family away from home when I was in the field, and for all their continuing support and help. This would not have been possible without you. Thanks also to the excellent editorial team at University Press of Florida, to my peer reviewers, and to Stephanye Hunter for her expert guidance.

My thanks to Danny Miller for his unfettered support of this project from start to finish (and beyond!). Mette Louise Berg, Martin Holbraad, and Jorge Duany also all provided invaluable and detailed feedback on earlier drafts of this material, for which I am very grateful.

This research would not have been possible without generous funding from the Economic and Social Research Council, as well as additional financial aid from the Royal Anthropological Institute of Great Britain and Ireland's Emslie Horniman Prize and the Radcliffe-Brown Fund.

I am particularly grateful to the Cuban Research Institute at Florida International University for supporting me in my U.S. visa application and providing support throughout my fieldwork. Similarly, thanks go to the Cuban Heritage Collection at the University of Miami for providing access and occasional workspace, as well as for sheltering my research notes throughout Hurricane Irma!

I am tremendously grateful to my family and to my little community of anthropologist friends in London and beyond, who have all been a source of constant support for many years and provided much-needed intellectual challenge and emotional nurture along the way. There are too many to name here, but thanks in particular to Sandhya Fuchs, Tiziano Quarx · Acknowledgments

antotto, Sabine de Graaf, and Andrea Lathrop Ligueros for their input and encouragement throughout.

Special thanks go to Nestor Siré Mederos in Havana, who generously helped me in my research and provided some of the photos in this book, as well as to Michel Pardo García, Adrián García, Gustavo Arcos Fernández-Britto, Victor Fowler Calzada, Yaima Pardo Castillo, Zoe Gómez Alonso, and Glexis Novoa Vian, to name but a few, all of whom were instrumental to my fieldwork in Cuba. Alberto Sosa Cabanas and Eliecer Jiménez Almeida provided much-appreciated support and encouragement while I was in Miami, as did Corinna Moebius, Ralph de la Portilla, and Martin Tsang.

And lastly, but most importantly of all, my heartfelt gratitude goes to everyone who participated in this research. While I share the success of this work with all those named above, and more, any shortcomings are entirely my own.

Mil gracias por prestarme una tajada de sus vidas.

Chronology

1868–1878 — First Cuban war of independence from Spain begins; thousands of Cubans settle in the U.S.

1886 — Ybor City is founded near Tampa, Florida, and becomes a base for Cuba cigar factory workers

1898 — Cuba gains independence from Spain

1899–1902 — U.S. military occupation of Cuba, until Cuba is formally inaugurated as an independent republic

1958 — Cuban revolution begins

1959 — Batista flees Cuba; Fidel Castro becomes prime minister; first wave of Cuban migration to Miami begins

1960 — All U.S. businesses on the island are nationalized; a partial trade embargo begins; Operation Peter Pan begins

1961 — U.S. breaks diplomatic relations with Cuba; the Bay of Pigs invasion fails; Cuba is declared a socialist state

1962 — U.S. embargo of Cuba is extended to all trade; Cuban Missile Crisis takes place

1965 — Second wave of Cuban migration begins with the Camarioca boatlift and "Freedom Flights"

1966 — Cuban Adjustment Act is approved by U.S. Congress, allowing Cubans the right to apply for permanent citizenship

1977 — Limited diplomatic relations are established with the opening of interest sections in Washington and Havana

1980 — Third wave of Cuban migration takes place with the Mariel boatlift

xii · Chronology

1991 — Economic collapse of the Soviet Union, "Special Period" of economic hardship begins in Cuba

1992 — Cuban Democracy Act is passed by U.S. Congress to prohibit U.S. subsidiaries in third countries from trading with Cuba

1993 — Cuban government legalizes use of the U.S. dollar on the island alongside the Cuban peso

1994 — Balsero crisis begins as Cubans flee economic hardship on the island

1995 — "Wet foot / dry foot" policy begins in the U.S.

2004 — Bush administration announces new restrictions on travel and remittances to Cuba

2009 — Obama administration eases restrictions on family visits and remittances to Cuba

2011 — Obama administration allows U.S. citizens to travel to Cuba for cultural and educational exchanges

2013 — Cuban government eliminates the *tarjeta blanca* (exit permit) requiring a letter of invitation from abroad and allows Cubans to live abroad for up to two years; an undersea cable connects Cuba to Venezuela, enabling public access to the internet for Cubans for the first time

2015 — Thirty-five public Wi-Fi hot spots are opened across Cuba

2016 — Obama visits Cuba; commercial flights to Cuba are reinstated; Fidel Castro dies

2017 — Termination of "wet foot/ dry foot" policy; Trump administration extends restrictions; "acoustic attacks" reported in U.S. Embassy in Havana

2018 — Significant reduction in consular services at U.S. Embassy in Havana, effectively meaning Cubans must travel to a third country to apply for U.S. visas at the consulate there; 3G mobile internet data becomes available for Cubans on the island

2019 — Trump administration bans most commercial flights to Cuba

2020 — Cuban government removes 10 percent tax on U.S. dollars; U.S. government prohibits remittances to Cuba via some companies and extends travel ban to include chartered flights

Figure 0.1. Map showing ethnographic fieldwork research sites.

Introduction

I'm standing in the middle of a line that snakes its way along an uninspiring airport corridor toward Gate 84 in Miami International Airport. We are a motley crew, the others in the lineup and I. It's 5:30 in the morning, yet you could cut the air with a butter knife, such is the adrenaline shared by this group of several dozen wide-eyed, tight-lipped travelers.

Many seem remarkably overdressed given the temperate climate of Miami during hurricane season. A man fidgeting ahead of me is wearing several sombreros piled up one on another, and is sporting a hefty, padded winter jacket; a young man behind me is wearing an outfit entirely of iridescent gold fabric, such that I can see my own tired visage reflected back at me from his sunglasses down to his trainers. He quietly offers to sell me Cuban convertible dollars at a better rate than I can get in Havana.[1] A woman who seems to be thumbing her way through every contact in her cell phone has also opted for what seems an odd sartorial choice: her jacket is bedecked with buttons, as are her trousers, and underneath her low-cut top I can see she is wearing several different neon-colored bras.

A uniformed Cuban man works his way along the line, tersely asking to see passports, visas, and "Cuba Ready" stamps on our boarding passes. His hostile manner does little to relieve the building tension. The middle-aged woman near the front unconsciously raps out a rhythm on the metal gate with her acrylic nails. Others arrange and rearrange their carry-on luggage, trying to cram medicines, clothing, and all manner of snacks into their portable Pandora's boxes. From the corner of my eye, I glance over at one woman and her box of 24 Krispy Kreme doughnuts, which, in my naivety, I think rather a lot of food for a mere 45-minute early morning flight.

At the last possible moment, we are invited to board, and there is a rush toward the gate as people scrabble to get ahead and stake out as much of the limited overhead storage space on the plane as possible. I take my seat between an elderly Cuban woman, who is fiddling with her watch, and the young man dressed in gold, who is quickly scrolling through his social media for one last time before we take off. A hush descends over the plane once in the air; it is in fact such a short flight that we barely have the chance to unclip our seat belts before our pilot announces our descent into Havana. The elderly woman to my left is quietly crying now as she looks out of the window and wrings her hands.

We bump down onto the tarmac, and I realize that I, like those around me, have been holding my breath and am starting to feel dizzy. One man across the aisle claps; another looks like he might throw up. The woman to my left has gone quiet and closed her eyes, but leans back in her seat and takes in a deep breath. The young man on my right turns his phone on: it has no signal now, but he clutches it in his hand all the same, a ghost limb that he can still feel.

We pile out into the hot sun and start to walk across the tarmac toward the terminal, met by two large adverting billboards—one for cigarettes, and the other for socialism. We are funneled along humid corridors to a dimly lit hallway crammed full of people waiting to hand over their paperwork to a line of stern- (or perhaps bored-)looking Cuban officials, and then finally through into another hallway, where we collect our baggage and line up to have it screened by customs officials.

I join the back of this line, my burgundy European passport in my left hand and my backpack in my right, while the others clutch navy-blue American or Cuban passports and roll their plastic-wrapped spheres of luggage ahead of them. I am quickly waved through into the arrivals hall, but others are pulled aside and ordered to open up their luggage or pay a "tax" on the items they have. Through another set of double doors and I'm met with a wall of people waiting for relatives, customers, and business contacts. I feel a dozen eyes scanning me, as if expecting me to walk up to them and greet them as an old friend. The elderly woman from the plane has also walked through and has fallen, sobbing, into the arms of a young man who I presume must be her grandson. The woman with Krispy Kremes is met by a small horde of relatives, each of whom is given half a doughnut. Others are loading up their plastic parcels onto trucks or handing them over to what look like other relatives just outside the terminal entrance.

[Extract from field note diary, November 2017]

Introduction · 3

This book tells the story of the creation and creators of an emerging transnational network of circulation: a network that punctures the reified political boundaries that lie at the heart of one of the longest diplomatic conflicts of the past century. In so doing, it explores the permeability of what is arguably one of the most politicized and reified borders in the world: that between the U.S. and Cuba. Despite decades of diplomatic hostilities and economic sanctions, the border between Miami and Havana is in a state of constant flux, with ceaseless flows of both people and things moving in both directions. First and foremost, then, this book foregrounds the strategies and agencies of many thousands of people, who are usually considered to have been swept up by the Cold War and separated by the U.S. embargo of Cuba, but who in fact have developed ways and means of navigating these restrictions. Drawing on fifteen months of ethnographic research following the flows of people, material items, and digital content between Miami (U.S.) and Havana (Cuba), as well as to Panama, Guyana, and Mexico, I trace these circuits to understand how and why they constitute everyday life for millions of Cubans who, aside from political rhetoric, negotiate extraordinary circumstances on a daily basis to maintain their family connections, cultural identity, and ultimately, to live what they consider to be meaningful lives.

In their collectivity, these circuits of exchange—or the "Mula Ring" as I will later call them, mirroring Polish-British anthropologist Bronisław Malinowski's infamous formulation of the "Kula Ring" (1922)—reveal an informal network of transnational circulation that should be considered a dynamic and creative indigenous approach to combat political and economic isolationist courses taken by and imposed upon Cuba for decades. By tracing the informal material and digital flows that constitute Cuba's extensive transnational presence at the beginning of the twenty-first century, we also confront evolving dynamics of gender, relatedness, value, and personhood. In so doing, we glimpse a story that is largely unwritten, but whose telling has become all the more imperative in the light of political developments both in the U.S. and in Cuba that seek to reconsolidate long-standing discourses of conflict, separation, and opposition.

But this book is more than merely the story of a particular corner of the world, and the routes of passage that open and close between those countries. It is also the story of how, from the deep cracks that form in societies that have faced rupture and conflict over decades, new and dynamic cultural forms can emerge. Moreover, these emerging cultural forces can take shape where we least expect them: in the marginalized and often disenfranchised communities of migrants at the edge of mainstream society. In the face of the larger ideologies that so often dominate conversations such as these—democracy and dictatorship, capitalism and socialism, freedom and oppression—this book thus speaks to the spatial practices that animate such categories, and to the strategies regular people mobilize to navigate a world of extremes. Indeed, in many instances it is through an actor's capacity to creatively mobilize the interstitial spaces or cracks between analytical categories of person and thing, family versus employer, public and private, capitalist and socialist, and so forth, that this incipient world of possibility is most successfully navigated.

One of the overarching arguments put forward by this book, then, is that ruptures—or the "cracks" of social life—can be crucial to the emergence of new cultural forms. In so doing, the ethnographic material the book presents lies at the heart of what is so often called "creative destructionism" (Schumpeter 1992) or the "dual aspect of rupture" (Holbraad, Kapferer, and Sauma 2019, 1). When put together and considered as a growing informal network of circulation, the spaces and people presented throughout this book convey a sense that "jurisdictional outsides also become times of perpetual emergency within a spatiotemporal politics" (Kahn 2019a, 12).

Ultimately then, this book is an exploration of the pragmatics of worldmaking as enacted from the bottom up, by communities that are not typically considered to be powerful agents in the light of international diplomatic conflicts, but that, over decades, have built up their own worlds and infrastructures of possibility, the likes of which point to a more hopeful future than many accounts of these communities relay. This book is an attempt at encapsulating the encounters, geographies, and negotiations that point us in that direction.

Economic Entanglements between the U.S. and Cuba

While this book builds on multi-sited ethnographic fieldwork undertaken across five countries (see figure 0.1), the primary two fieldsites were in Cuba and the U.S., and the complex and entangled relationship between these two countries is essential background for framing the arguments I will make in due course. The U.S. and Cuba have a long-shared history, reaching as far back as the early eighteenth century when Spanish-occupied Cuba became a center of tobacco and sugar production and a considerable trade partner in the region. The British occupation of Havana in 1762 opened up trade with the British colonies in North America, while Spain opened Cuban ports to North American commerce officially in November 1776. During this period, it even seemed likely that Cuba would become part of the U.S.; in 1820 Thomas Jefferson thought Cuba "the most interesting addition which could ever be made to our system of States" and told Secretary of War John C. Calhoun that the United States "ought, at the first possible opportunity, to take Cuba." By 1877, Americans were purchasing 82 percent of Cuba's total exports (Pérez 1991, 69). North Americans were also increasingly taking up residence on the island that had become so key to the U.S.'s commercial success, as recognized by U.S. Secretary of State James G. Blaine in 1881:

> [T]hat rich island, the key to the Gulf of Mexico, and the field for our most extended trade in the Western Hemisphere, is, though in the hands of Spain, a part of the American commercial system. . . . If ever ceasing to be Spanish, Cuba must necessarily become American and not fall under any other European domination. (Foner 1972, xxviii)

In 1897, U.S. President William McKinley offered to buy Cuba for $300 million (M. Fernández 2001). Rejection of that offer, and an explosion that sank the American battleship USS *Maine* in Havana Harbor, led to the Spanish-American War, which in turn resulted in U.S. military rule of the island until 1902, when Cuba was finally granted formal independence.

The U.S. continued to play a powerful role in the economic realities of Cuba, however, and throughout the 1920s and '30s, U.S. companies owned 60 percent of the Cuban sugar industry and imported 95 percent of the total Cuban crop (Dye and Sicotte 2004). It has been suggested that the sugar boom of the early twentieth century contributed to Cuban per capita incomes that were roughly 80 percent of European levels in the 1920s, while other estimates suggest that per capita incomes were on a par with those in some southern U.S. states (Ward and Devereux 2012, 105). The U.S. presence on the island remained strong, and General Batista's second term of rule in Cuba (1952–1959) was initiated by a military coup that received military and economic support from the U.S. (H. Thomas 1987). Until 1959, Cuba was one of the wealthiest countries in Central and Latin America, ranking fifth (of twenty countries) in terms of per capita gross domestic product in 1955 (Eckstein 1986, 503). Cuba also likely had the second-largest level of investment from the U.S. in all Latin America (Mesa-Lago 1981, 8) at this point, and was a popular tourist destination for wealthy Americans.

Up until this point then, the U.S. and Cuba were closely connected economically, and there was a frequent circulation of people and commodities

6 · Circulating Culture

between the two countries. Diplomatic relations quickly deteriorated after the Cuban revolution of 1959, however, due to concerns regarding agrarian reforms and the nationalization of industries owned by U.S. citizens. As state intervention and takeovers of privately owned businesses continued, trade restrictions on Cuba increased. The U.S. stopped buying Cuban sugar and refused to supply its former trading partner with much-needed oil, with a devastating effect on the island's economy, forcing Cuba to turn to their newfound trading partner, the Soviet Union, for petroleum.

On January 3, 1961, the U.S. withdrew diplomatic recognition of the Cuban government and closed the embassy in Havana, and later that same year Cuba resisted an armed invasion by about 1,500 CIA-trained Cuban exiles at the Bay of Pigs. Tensions between the two nations reached its peak in 1962, after U.S. reconnaissance aircraft photographed the Soviet construction of intermediate-range missile sites, the discovery of which led to the Cuban Missile Crisis. The same year saw a further escalation of sanctions by the U.S., and by February 1962 the U.S. government had imposed a full embargo on all exports to Cuba, which remains in place to this day, albeit with some exceptions.[2]

The Cold War eventually ended with the collapse of the Soviet Union through the late 1980s and early 1990s, leaving Cuba without its major international sponsor. The ensuing years were marked by extreme economic difficulty and widespread hunger in Cuba, a time known euphemistically as the *Período especial en tiempos de paz*, or Special Period in Times of Peace.[3] U.S. law allowed private humanitarian aid to Cuba for part of this time. However, the long-standing U.S. embargo was reinforced in October 1992 by the Cuban Democracy Act, which prohibited foreign-based subsidiaries of U.S. companies from trading with Cuba, travel to Cuba by U.S. citizens, and the sending of family remittances to Cuba. Sanctions could also be applied to non-U.S. companies trading with Cuba. As a result, multinational companies effectively had to choose between Cuba and the U.S., the latter being a much larger market, and so the economic hardship experienced in Cuba was drawn out throughout the 1990s and into the early 2000s. Under the Bush administration (2001–2009), relations remained tense and further travel restrictions were applied, in part to gain much-needed support from the Cuban American community in Florida to secure reelection of the Republican Party.[4]

Travel, communications, and economic restrictions were gradually eased under the Obama administration (2009–2017), marking a thaw in relations between the two nations. Embassies were reestablished in Washington and

Havana in 2015; Obama visited Cuba in March 2016, and five months later the first direct commercial flight since the early 1960s traveled between the two countries.

On June 16, 2017, from the center of Republican Cuban Miami, President Donald Trump announced his intention to suspend what he called a "completely one-sided deal with Cuba" (Hirschfeld Davis 2017) with a policy imposing new restrictions on travel and economic exchange. New tensions due to alleged "acoustic attacks" on U.S. diplomats in Havana in 2017–2018 resulted in a partial closure of the embassy, affecting tourism and consular services. In October 2019 the U.S. government reversed its travel policies and banned flights from the U.S. to any part of Cuba other than the capital city. As of June 2020, all chartered flights also became subject to an annual cap. In November 2020, Western Union suspended money transfers between Cuba and the U.S, while in July 2021, President Joe Biden issued new sanctions on Cuba, leading to an increased level of tension between the two states.

It thus seems important to note explicitly the tumultuous recent political context (2016–2022) against which the research and writing of this book have taken place. When I embarked upon fieldwork in 2016 for the first time, President Barack Obama had done much to open the door once again to Cuba and had himself recently visited the island. While I was in the field, Fidel Castro died and Donald Trump assumed the presidency of the U.S. Trump then did much to reverse the changes that Obama had implemented, and in a sense, my fieldwork took place in a short window of opportunity for less-restricted travel between Cuba and the U.S. As I was leaving the field, this window was already closing, and by the time I was writing this book, the newly elected President Biden was issuing further restrictions.

Migratory Flows between the U.S. and Cuba

This book argues that Miami and Cuba have been so interconnected (perhaps all the more due to an ongoing rhetoric of rupture and separation) over the years that one simply could not exist without the other; indeed, they reinforce the very idea of one another. Each exists in the imagination of the other; Miami and Cuba are as two magnets, bound by a force of equal parts attraction and repulsion. The two are mutually informative and revelatory, and so any notion of Cuba, or a *cubanidad* (Cuban cultural identity), must surely be situated precisely in this back-and-forth.

This may seem unsurprising in the light of decades of anthropological scholarship discussing the unbounded and dynamic flows that constitute culture and sociality (Appadurai 1991; Kearney 1995; Marcus 1995). Yet in arguing this, I go against the grain of much that has been written about the Cuban diaspora, which has typically focused upon themes of loss and separation (Pérez Firmat 2012; Rieff 1993; Tweed 1997). Discussions around who should be included in or excluded from categories of Cuban, Cuban American, etc., abound, and can become quite heated. Indeed, much of the ethnographic material in this book will demonstrate how hotly contested these terms were among my own interlocutors, and how fraught the term *cubanidad* can be. Cuban American scholar Ruth Behar acknowledges an "undecidability" or difficulty in classifying what constitutes a Cuban in her own interweaving of ethnography and personal memoir:

> Cubans outside Cuba are perhaps immigrants, perhaps exiles, perhaps both, perhaps neither, and Cubans inside Cuba are in certain ways perhaps more exiled in their *insile* than the so-called exiles themselves. Diaspora embraces all these possibilities and others, including earlier periods of displacement in Cuban history. (1996, 144–145)

In this book I focus on the agency and creativity inherent in Behar's term here—"possibility"—which lies at the heart of these assertions of cultural identity. I argue that different cohorts of Cubans on either side of the Florida Straits mobilize the interstitial possibilities that emerge from a fractured set of cultural identities wherever possible as a means of navigating considerable geopolitical and socioeconomic change.

Before I move on to the more theoretical aspects of these arguments, however, it is important to briefly set out the internal borders that are erected and maintained within the communities this book will focus on. While the U.S. and Cuba have had a long and complex history of migration and trade, the relationship changed most dramatically in response to the social, economic, and political restructuring of Cuban society in the late 1950s and early 1960s. More than one-tenth of Cuba's present population migrated to the U.S. in response to the revolution, and those who migrated benefited from changes in American immigration policy during the Cold War that privileged those fleeing from communist regimes. Throughout the following decades, migration from Cuba to the U.S. occurred in waves, each bringing a distinct subsection of Cuban society to the rapidly expanding

Cuban enclave in southern Florida, and these internal borders are still cited to this day by many of the interlocutors presented in this book as a means of distinguishing and interpreting cubanidad.

The "Exiles"

The first migration after the revolution began on January 1, 1959, when the dictator Batista fled the island, and lasted until the Cuban Missile Crisis of October 1962. This initial wave brought a quarter of a million Cubans to the U.S., and the Cuban Refugee Program was established in 1961 to provide relief and help these migrants adapt to the U.S. labor market. By the time the program drew to a close in 1973, the federal government had invested more than $950 million in this group of migrants—in housing and medical care, education, and vocational training (García 2007, 77). This also coincided with Operation Peter Pan, which saw the evacuation of 14,000 unaccompanied Cuban children to the U.S. (primarily Miami) between 1960 and 1962. This initial wave of post-revolution migration predominantly consisted of the social and economic elite of Cuba—those who had the most to lose from Castro's revolution—and so this wave of migrants was largely drawn from Cuba's upper and middle classes, who in turn were overwhelmingly classified (both in Cuba and the U.S.) as white. They resettled in Miami, many fully expecting to be back in their Havana mansions within a year or two. As this became less and less likely, they formed what has been called an "ethnic enclave" in South Florida (Portes 1987), which in turn gained considerable economic and political power in the U.S. over the decades that followed. Most noticeably, this group developed a staunchly anti-Castroist politics centered in Miami (particularly in Little Havana and Coral Gables; see figure 0.2), and most were opposed to any return travel to (or even contact with) Cuba. Their politics and ideological views became hegemonic among the larger group that I refer to as the "Old Cubans" throughout this book.

The Freedom Flights

A second official migration of Cubans began on September 28, 1965, when Fidel Castro announced that those who wished to leave the island would be permitted to do so. Following a curtailed U.S. attempt to evacuate Cubans from the island by boat from the Port of Camarioca, a memorandum of understanding was signed between the two countries whereby the U.S. agreed to send chartered planes to Varadero (a coastal town 150 km east

10 · Circulating Culture

of Havana) twice each day to transport between 3,000 and 4,000 Cubans each month. In what came to be known as the Freedom Flights, priority was given to those who had immediate family already in the U.S. The pool of emigrants was carefully screened by the Cuban government, however, and those of military age or with technical skills beneficial to the revolution were prevented from leaving. The flights continued until 1973, by which time over three thousand flights had carried almost three hundred thousand refugees to the U.S. (Pedraza-Bailey 1985), most of whom rapidly incorporated themselves into the expanding Cuban community forming in Miami.

Until this point, the Cuban diaspora forming in southern Florida was largely unrepresentative of the wider population back on the island. In particular, Afro-Cubans either had less opportunity to leave Cuba or, for the most part, chose not to (Wirtz 2017). The 1953 census in Cuba reported that 27 percent of the population identified as Black or mixed-race—a number that in reality was likely higher than recorded due to the problematic categorization of race or ethnicity in censuses (see de la Fuente 1995). Yet in 1970, reportedly fewer than 3 percent of Cubans in the United States were Black (García 2007). This would change in the third wave of Cuban migration to the United States and would irrevocably alter the Cuban diaspora in Florida (Current 2008; Portes 1984; Skop 2001).

The *Marielitos*

In April 1980 Castro announced that all who desired to leave the island would be permitted to do so; thousands of Cuban exiles sailed in fishing boats and yachts to the port of Mariel to collect their relatives, and almost 125,000 Cubans arrived in the U.S. this way between April and October 1980 (García 2007, 79). However, the Castro government also used the episode as a means of ridding the island of "undesirables"—namely, criminals and homosexuals. Prisons were emptied, and 26,000 of the Cubans setting sail for the U.S. had penal records (García 2007, 79).

Demographically the Cubans of Mariel (or *marielitos*) were also distinct from the Cubans who had arrived in Miami during the 1960s (Eckstein and Barberia 2002). Studies of those detained in refugee camps upon arrival in Miami showed that the Mariel population was younger by about ten years (averaging thirty years of age), was nearly 70 percent male, and reflected a wider geographic distribution from the island itself (García 2007, 80). This group also contained a higher percentage of Black and mixed-race people (roughly 20 percent), and these individuals in particular had a very different reception into the Miami diaspora than those who had come before (Aja 2016). Such disparities have persisted within the Cuban enclave of South Florida. In 2003, non-white Cuban males in the U.S. were reported to be earning 15 percent less than their white counterparts (Zavodny 2003, 201).

Unlike the Cubans who had immigrated between 1959 and 1973, the Marielitos were also not considered legitimate refugees by the U.S. authorities. Many relied upon Cuban networks already in Greater Miami to get a roof over their heads and a job (Duany 1999). A minority of them turned to crime, resulting in a 1980s Miami renowned for cocaine cowboys (as memorialized in Al Pacino's depiction of a Mariel gangster in the film *Scarface*), and growing stigma and discrimination against Cuban and Latino immigrants in South Florida (Moghaddam et al. 1995), which in turn reinforced preexisting stereotypes of race and class (G. Fernández 2007).

For the Old Cubans who had settled in Miami in the preceding decades, this was also an abrupt reminder that the lost Cuba they had so pined for over the years was in some ways a figment of their collective imagination. In particular, the inherent racism and classism of many Cuban exiles already in Miami was brought to the fore (Fulger 2012; Woltman and Newbold 2009), alongside the uncomfortable realization that Cuba had continued to change in their absence. From the 1980s onward, these newer generations of Cuban migrants would increasingly settle in different parts of Greater Miami, most notably Hialeah and Miami Springs (see figure 0.2), which are generally considered more working-class and ethnically diverse neighborhoods to this day.

The *Balseros* and Post-Soviet Migrants

The next wave of Cuban migration continued to create friction between these distinct groups, or "diasporic generations" (Berg 2011), each of which had had its own social, economic, and political trajectory. The collapse of Cuba's primary economic partner, the Soviet Union, in 1989 was disastrous for the Cuban economy. The island plunged into inflation and hunger, provoking another wave of emigration. The logical destination for most who were able to leave was Miami, due both to proximity and a significant Cuban diaspora ready and waiting for them. Most had no option but to make the dangerous journey on makeshift rafts (*balsas*), earning them the nickname *balseros* (rafters). Many died at sea; others were allegedly even shot at by the Cuban Coastguard as they left. To pressure the Castro government into restricting illegal emigration, the U.S. government prohibited the sending of economic remittances to the island, and chartered air traffic from Miami to Cuba was indefinitely postponed.

Despite these reversals in policy, the balseros kept coming. During the last two weeks of August 1994, the U.S. Coast Guard picked up an average of 1,500 balseros each day (García 2007, 81). A revised immigration policy for Cubans—which came to be known as the wet foot, dry foot policy—was introduced in 1995 as an alteration to the Cuban Adjustment Act of 1966, and remained in effect until January 2017, six months after I arrived in the field. Any Cubans found in the waters between the U.S. and Cuba (i.e., with wet feet) would be returned to Cuba or sent to a third country, but those who made it to shore (i.e., had dry feet) would have the chance to remain in the U.S., and pursue residency one year after arrival. To this day, some Cubans still attempt the journey by raft, usually because they are unable to afford a flight to the U.S. or have been denied a visa, but since the termination of this policy in 2017, many arrivals have faced the same challenges and hostilities that any other migrants from elsewhere in Latin America and the Caribbean might encounter. From the 1990s onward, the Cubans migrating to South Florida have increasingly done so more due to economic need than an overt rejection of Cuban politics. These more recent arrivals have often been observed to take less staunchly Republican political positions upon arrival in Miami than their diasporic forebears (Girard, Grenier, and Gladwin 2012), and have been far more likely to make return visits to the island when possible and to send remittances to relatives left behind (Spiegel 2004).

The "New Cubans"

Thus far, these various diasporic generations have been well documented by scholars, but a new generation has also begun to take shape, distinct from those that went before. The reinstatement of diplomatic relations under the Obama administration (2009–2017) allowed for greater migration between the two countries again, and a new five-year visa (discontinued in 2018 just as I completed my fieldwork) meant many Cubans on the island had the option of traveling back and forth with unprecedented regularity throughout my period of fieldwork.

This meant that in the six years immediately before this research took place, migration had increased considerably alongside more open commerce, with a nouveau riche of *cuentapropistas* (self-employed Cubans

Introduction · 13

working in a limited emerging private sector) often making frequent business trips to Miami (as well as various other destinations; see chapter 3). These "New Cubans," whom I will introduce in greater detail in chapter 1, are the first generation to be living between the two countries so openly, and many of the interlocutors presented throughout this book traveled back and forth regularly, making the complexities of diplomatic relations, travel restrictions, and changing policy work to their advantage wherever possible. Meanwhile some Cuban exiles in Miami who had maintained Cuban nationality have been buying Cuban passports to visit the island again, and even starting up businesses and investments or considering repatriation in their retirement (Moreno 2018).

Being Cuban in Miami

Six decades after the first migratory wave arrived following the revolution, the Cuban diaspora in Greater Miami is around two million strong, and growing. As of 2019, over 30 percent of all Caribbean immigrants to the U.S. had migrated from Cuba (Lorenzi and Batalova 2022), making the Cuban diaspora in Greater Miami the largest Caribbean diaspora in the United States. This diaspora comprises an enormously complex assortment of social, economic, political, educational, religious, and ethnic backgrounds, and this, unsurprisingly, does not result in a homogeneous view of what it means to be Cuban. Indeed, this diaspora now incorporates Cubans who have just got off the boat or plane, Cubans who have lived in Miami for sixty years, and Cubans born in Miami who have never set foot on the island and perhaps even speak limited Spanish.

The constant confrontation between diasporic generations across the decades has led to a variety of interpretations of cubanidad, forming an ideologically charged battleground in Greater Miami. These debates in fact go back a long way, and Fernando Ortiz, the famous Cuban lawyer and anthropologist working in the first half of the twentieth century, wrote extensively on the subject. He defined cubanidad through a now much-cited metaphor, drawing on a type of Cuban stew called *ajiaco*. As anthropologist Stephan Palmié explains, the most characteristic feature of this stew (which is explicitly comprised of various ingredients of European, African, and Indigenous origin) is that it is never finished, but rather is in a constant state of cooking, "an incessant bubbling of heterogeneous substances" (2013, 98) that eventually all boil down into a thick sauce. Inside the *olla cubana* ("Cu-

14 · Circulating Culture

ban pot"), ingredients cannot be separated, and there is a constant process of ingredients decomposing as they cook and recomposing into something new. This is radically different from the more typical formulations of Caribbean and Latin American identity as "hybrid" or "creole," whereby "the more one attempts to pin down the diversity that 'creole' represents, the more one creates a static (as opposed to fluid), predictive (as opposed to contingent), and monolithic (as opposed to multi-layered) category" (Khan 2001, 271). Ortiz's metaphor, as developed further by Palmié, instead accentuates the absolute totalizing nature of Cuban identity as more than the sum of its parts, in which each constituent and inseparable ingredient is crucial to the recipe. Where other models of hybridity or creolization have often focused more on the separate "ingredients" going into the "pot," Ortiz and Palmié encourage us to look closer at what is new and emerging as a result.

It is perhaps all the more ironic, then, that so many generations of Cubans, both on the island and in Miami, have sought to determine what exactly should be included in the "recipe" for cubanidad, trying to separate constituent "ingredients" in the process. Lines have been drawn many times over, excluding others according to political position, religion, race, place of birth, language, and so on. Reinforcing a particular version of cubanidad became particularly important for some of the Old Cubans, or earlier exile generation, who left between the 1950s and 1970s, as they looked for ways to remember and celebrate the past, reinforce their feelings of nationalism, and assert a distinct identity in the U.S.

The earlier waves of Cuban migrants tended to settle in and around the Little Havana and Westchester neighborhoods of Miami, while the wealthiest settled mostly in Coral Gables (see figure 0.2). Yet Greater Miami has since become home to multiple Cuban cultures; its various neighborhoods have become palimpsests of generations of Cuban sociality, in some ways mirroring the changes taking place on the island itself. As each new wave arrived, they inscribed their own, "updated" cubanidad, fresh from Havana, or Cienfuegos, or Santiago, onto the diasporic landscape of Greater Miami, meeting resistance from the older vanguard who sought to preserve older forms of Cuban sociality according to their own preexisting notions of race and class (see chapter 5). At the point of my fieldwork, 58 percent of Cubans in the U.S. had entered before 2000, but 25 percent had entered in the 2000s, and 17 percent after 2010 (Grenier and Gladwin 2016, 2018). From the 1980s onward, New Cuban immigrants have increasingly tended to settle more to the north of the city, in the historically more blue-collar districts

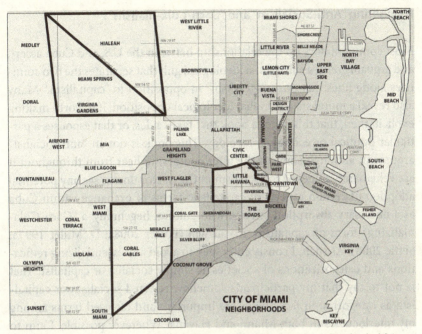

Figure 0.2. Map showing areas of significant Cuban migration (*outlined in bold*) in Greater Miami. Adapted from map courtesy of "By Comayagua99" at English Wikipedia, CC BY-SA 3.0, https://commons.wikimedia.org/w/index.php?curid=23038578.

of Hialeah and Miami Springs (see figure 0.2). These later generations, who grew up entirely under socialism in Cuba, are a new dynamic force in the performance of cubanidad within both Greater Miami and Cuba and are the main subject of ethnographic exploration in this book.

The multi-sited nature of the ethnographic research presented in this book, then, which takes notions of flow and flux (rather than bounded categories of belonging and identity by nation) as its starting point rather than its conclusion, explores the sheer dynamism of cultural identity in its creation, curation, negotiation, and mobilization. The case of Cubans living on either side of the Florida Straits is an excellent example of this precisely because of the amount of back-and-forth between these two sites (among others). Throughout all these decades of supposed isolation in Cuba, and of supposedly unidirectional migration, there has in fact been extensive contact, maintained over a long period of time, in both directions, the course of which will be plotted through ethnographic vignettes scattered throughout this book.

Navigating "Anti-Socialism" and "Coca-Cola-nialism"

Most commentators on the relationship between the U.S. and Cuba assert, and arguably reify, a substantial ideological gulf that separates the two countries along lines that posit "socialism" in opposition to "capitalism." Many also reveal a moral stance on that ideological opposition. It is worth making explicit, then, that this is not a book that takes sides, or that espouses a particular political or economic ideology. This book is not an "anti-socialist" argument, although some of the interlocutors we hear from throughout it are vehemently opposed to socialism in Cuba. Nor does it see any potential adoption of certain aspects of capitalistic forms of exchange within Cuba as a necessary absorption of American cultural hegemony, a "Coca-Cola-nializing" form of capitalism, if you will (Foster 2008a; D. Miller 1997a; Settle 2008). As such, I consistently seek to avoid any essentializing reifications and categorizations of societies as simply socialist or capitalist. That is not to say that my participants somehow rejected socialism or capitalism as categories: in fact, they were important and oft-used terms among my interlocutors in both Miami and Havana. Wherever possible, I aim to distinguish clearly between these terms as analytical categories (employed to advance my own theoretical arguments), and as emic categories showing how my interlocutors discussed what socialism or capitalism meant to them, which I endeavor to replicate faithfully.

Much writing on the relationship between Cuba and the U.S. has presumed a transition from one ideological position to the other, implying that Cuba may be "holding out" as socialist for now, but will eventually fold into capitalism like everywhere else (Halebsky and Kirk 1992; Hoffmann 2001; Otero and O'Bryan 2002). This notion of transition from socialism to capitalism has been problematized before, most notably by scholars of postsocialism in the 1990s in their appraisal of adjustments toward capitalism in much of Eastern Europe during that decade and since. The idea of a neat transition from Soviet socialism to market capitalism is severely flawed, not only because it often rests upon neoevolutionist premises (which presume a unidirectional socioeconomic shift aligned with the moral values of "progress" and "freedom"), but also because it overlooks the locally experienced ambiguities that accompany the navigation of shifting socioeconomic landscapes. An important contribution of anthropology across the former Soviet bloc was to highlight that transition is not just a unidirectional process initiated from above (Harboe Knudsen and Frederiksen 2015).[5] This book therefore joins a body of anthropological work acknowledging the myriad ways in which supposed top-down "transitions" at times of intense socio-economic rupture are countered, negotiated, and mobilized (to different ends) from below.

Indeed, much of the ethnographic material in this book problematizes the very categories of socialist and capitalist, let alone a seeming transition from one to the other. All the following chapters reveal how the actions of everyday people trying to "make the best" of things rarely align neatly with top-down formulations of what capitalism or socialism "should" look like. In fact, much of the ethnographic material in this book exposes the ethnocentricity of these categories, which draw on a Global North-informed model of textbook capitalism, value, and exchange.

When considering contemporary Cuba, thinking through the lens of neosocialisms and neocapitalisms is perhaps more apt, as Cubans are flexibly reworking preexisting socioeconomic paradigms to navigate increasing globalization and neoliberalization, in line with wider economic shifts affecting people across the globe, living within socialist and capitalist systems alike (Archibugi 2008; Comaroff and Comaroff 2001; Harvey 2007; C.-Y. Ho 2015). This sense of "new" (neo) gives us a better sense of the agency people mobilize in refashioning systems that no longer work for them, in a context of rupture and uncertainty that is at odds with the sense of order and stability that ideological categories of socialism or capitalism might suggest. This book instead points to how contemporary processes of globalization demonstrate that capitalism and socialism are continually reinvented by everyday people negotiating the ambiguities of contemporary life between places and social orders.

A further limitation of thinking through the term "transition" is that it suggests moving from one state to another, and thus, implicitly, an impending "arrival." This framework allows little room for maneuver when thinking of places, peoples, and cultures that characterize themselves as somehow in between. This book begins and ends with the scene in a waiting lounge in an airport, an image reminiscent of what Marc Augé calls a "non-place" (1995, 77), insofar as it resembles a zone of transit(ion), an in-between place lacking a specific localized identity. The image of airports as placeless and meaningless spaces may fit into the mental landscape of passengers with settled lives, but, as Laia Colomer points out, Augé's "non-place" excludes much of the experience of people for whom mobility is a key aspect of their lives (2020, 156).

This book invokes the airport lounge as an image precisely because it deals not with a direction of travel so much as with the impatience, boredom, frustration, even chaos, of waiting, "between-ness," of being neither fully here nor there. This book ethnographically explores a prolonged period of rupture and crisis, whether that be political, economic, emotional, or material, in the lives of people in Cuba and its diaspora, and the responses of everyday people in navigating and repairing these ruptures to create a meaningful identity for themselves. An acknowledgment of ambiguity can help us to navigate some of the extreme discourses that often dominate in the Cuban diaspora, and I therefore follow the lead of some of my New Cuban interlocutors in considering the ambiguities, tensions, and ruptures inherent in a notion of "transition" as horizons of opportunity calling for exploration. Moreover, I argue that these moments of "interstitial possibility" (as I call them) are highly generative. With this in mind, we can perhaps start to see Miami and Havana as co-constituting spaces, where the one informs the other, rather than polar opposites. The connections between the two are the constant flows of people and things acting as couriers of cultural exchange, which are the main subject of exploration in this book.

Out of the Ordinary

Historically, anthropologists traditionally documented cultures as though they were more or less coherent in themselves, with a set of mutually agreed traditions and customs that practitioners could trace back across a lengthy history, which in turn contributed to an overall sense of community. Many of the discipline-defining anthropological accounts from the twentieth century present us with culture in this form: established, coherent, following an internal logic that participants configure and reconfigure in various guises. This has been subsequently termed by Joel Robbins as anthropology's "continuity bias," which he identifies as often central to our conception of culture (2003, 221–222).

The Caribbean has also historically been considered somehow "exceptional" in this regard, setting it apart from the greater interest in inwardly coherent systems and traditions that was so much the focus of anthropological inquiry in Asia, Oceania, and Africa in the twentieth century (Bourdieu 1972; Evans-Pritchard 1940, 1976; Leach 1970; Mauss 1954). The origins of the modern-day Caribbean region are located in the (re)creation of the area as a nexus of transnational flows in the sixteenth century and onward, and in this light, the Caribbean becomes a prime example of modernity (broadly understood within discourses of globalization) constructed through colonialism, violence, transnationalism, and the concerns of capitalism (Mintz

1986; Olwig 1993). Viewed through this lens, the Caribbean appeared perhaps less "authentic" to early European anthropologists, insofar as it was a construction of European colonialism, and thus not "untouched."

Scholars working across the Caribbean have themselves commented on this out-of-the-ordinariness the Caribbean has historically evoked, characterizing the region as "hybrid," "fluid," perhaps even indirectly as inauthentic in a world that has often fetishized the perceived coincidence of "culture" and isolation from global economic flows. In an attempt to encapsulate this fluidity often seen as definitive of the region, anthropologists and social theorists working across the Caribbean and Latin America have adopted various metaphors and analogies over recent decades: creolization (Hall 2015; Trouillot 2002), hybridity (Puri 2004), *bricolage* (Benítez-Rojo 1996; Réjouis 2014), *décalage* (B. H. Edwards 2001), and *mestizaje* or *mestiçagem* (Hale 1996; Ribeiro 2000; Wade 2005), to name a few. As Michel-Rolph Trouillot reminds us,

This region where boundaries are notoriously fuzzy has long been the open frontier of cultural anthropology: neither center nor periphery, but a sort of no man's land where pioneers get lost, where some stop overnight on their way to greater opportunities, and where yet others manage to create their own "new" world amidst First-World indifference. (1992, 19)

In his work on Haiti, Trouillot (2020) has argued a focus upon such exceptionalism obscures the all-pervasiveness and "ordinariness" of inequalities and injustices experienced there every day by ordinary people living out their lives in contexts of ambiguity, flux, or even chaos. Likewise, Greg Beckett describes an "atmosphere of crisis" in Haiti, distinguishing between the more typical usage of "crisis" in a political sense of momentary rupture and the broader experiential state that pervades all aspects of everyday life in Haiti to the point where it becomes ordinary, even "unremarkable" (2020, 80). Henrik Vigh suggests that "[i]nstead of placing crisis in context . . . we need to see crisis as context—as a terrain of action and meaning" (2008, 5); following this line of thought, the Caribbean as a region becomes an ideal conveyance for theoretical revisions of "the culture concept" (Khan 2001, 272), refocusing discussions on fluidity and instability, rather than cohesion and continuity. Arguably the Cuban case does this twofold: not only does it sit within the Caribbean and Latin American imaginaries of postcolonial and postmodern flux outlined above, but it is also associated with the rise (and "fall") of Soviet state socialism, and the associated economic crises experienced there (Appel and Orenstein 2018). As such, it doubly embodies the prolonged precarity and crisis-as-context that can be generative of new cultural forms.

There is a long scholarly history of thinking about rupture as being limited in time and eventually giving way to stability, which has informed both popular and analytic understandings (Koselleck 2006; Roitman 2014; D. A. Thomas 2019), yet there is also ample evidence to suggest that "instability and uncertainty have been the norm in most social, cultural, and historical contexts" (Narotzky and Besnier 2014, S8). In such circumstances, people must contend with the unpredictability of their life projects, making crisis rather than continuity an integral part of their horizon of expectations. This book emphasizes that Cubans are not all passively being swept up in some temporally limited moment of liminality or crisis, but rather can respond creatively to ambiguity and mobility as celebrated aspects and even moments of opportunity in ordinary, everyday life, drawing on a long history of mobilizing hybridity and ambiguity. This book takes rupture not as its conclusion, but rather as a generative point of departure, in recognition that "ordinary" life in Cuba is here and there and in between, and always has been.

Flux, Flow, and Counterflow

This book is an ethnography of people who have been uprooted, either physically, economically, or emotionally, and who live their lives entangled between cultures and contexts, but who nevertheless not only aspire to live coherent and meaningful lives, but against considerable odds actively create possibilities in constricted spaces. Throughout my fieldwork, I consistently encountered Cubans and Cuban Americans whose experience of everyday life was one of upheaval, ambiguity, and constriction. Thus, when I write about the flows (or circulation) of people, things, and information throughout this book, I do not seek to portray a sense of easy back-and-forth or connectedness. Rather, this book traces the mundane moments of everyday life that motivate these flows, often across substantial impediments. Through the mother-daughter relationships described in chapter 2, or the extended kin-neighbor relationships of chapter 3, or the end of familial relationships through bereavement in chapter 6, we see how the flow of people and things back and forth between Miami and Havana is crucial in informing cultural forms of kinship, gender, identity, and even death, not because of the ease of flow but precisely because such flows are constricted in this ethnographic case.

The kind of flow this book follows is thus arguably more in line with Anna Tsing's (2011) notion of "productive friction," which focuses on transnationalism not as a set of structured or unstructured flows, but rather in terms of the tensions and creative possibilities that propel such flows in the first place. This book argues that it is this friction, or what I generally refer to as a state of flux, that encourages the development of incipient cultural logics and forms, more so than flow. In this way, this book is more an ethnography of counterflow, of the ambiguous, unequal, unstable, and tense interconnections in both directions between Miami and Havana across substantial geopolitical, socioeconomic, and rhetorical differences. "Counterflow" helps us to get at the sense of people carving their own paths, against the grain, against the provided and approved route, which to my mind better captures the sense of agency and struggle (Spanish: *luchar*) that my interlocutors so frequently described to me.

My focus upon flows and counter-flows seeks to establish how, through circulation, people and things can inhabit different "regimes of value" (Appadurai 1986, 15), and I argue that the possibilities this opens up can be generative in expanding culture beyond and between binaries of capitalist/socialist, local/global, or national/diasporic. This allows us to consider a social world of increasing connectivity through the global circulations of cultural and material capital, while also allowing for these circulations to move in both directions without assuming a neoevolutionist or unidirectional transition from Global South to Global North, socialist to capitalist. It is precisely this approach that this book seeks to establish, and for this reason the book privileges circulation and exchange (rather than production or consumption) as the key to understanding how multiple regimes of value are created and reinvented on the ground.

Moreover, I go further in arguing that this state of flux—or the inbetweenness that was quasi-permanent to many of my interlocuters—is a generative force, enabling new cultural logics to take hold and expand. The cultures I present here are emerging from socioeconomic and geopolitical rupture, but the interlocutors I present are not simply sticking the pieces back together as they repair the damage. They are creating something new, and it is the sheer unstructured possibility of this that seems so remarkable and is so often lost in wider discourses about Cuba and Cubans. A focus on the interstitial possibilities to be discovered amid the flux of emerging

22 · Circulating Culture

cultural forms in both Miami and Havana—as co-constituting spaces—also becomes an important lens through which the multiple and often competing narratives of cubanidad throughout this book can coexist and collide without essentializing any single "true" Cuban culture.

Ethnographic Fieldwork

I turn now to setting out a little of the background to this book, which has been many years in the making, yet which at best still can only offer a very partial view of the world I seek to describe. This book draws upon data gathered over fifteen months of ethnographic fieldwork (from June 2017 to October 2018) split between communities in both the United States and Cuba. Primary fieldsites were in Greater Miami and Havana, with some short research trips to visit other participants (usually related to community members in my primary sites) in Mexico, Spain, Guyana, Panama, New York, and some other regions of Cuba (see figure 0.1). Time (and money) did not permit what would doubtless have been similarly fruitful visits following participants to Haiti, Russia, Peru, and Ecuador, although in some cases digital media provided some degree of contact.[6] Participant observation began in Miami, where I spent time in Cuban businesses, restaurants, cafés, and shops dotted around Cuban neighborhoods of Miami and Hialeah, and then after a few months I started traveling to Havana to follow up with contacts' relatives and friends on the "other side." Given this book's focus upon circulation and movement, I thus inevitably had less time at each site: thus, the sections of the book dealing with Cuba are very Havana-centric in their focus. Time and resources did not allow for what would have been, undoubtedly, fruitful research in other areas of Cuba. This fieldwork also consequently strongly focuses upon urban areas and did not explore how the informal economies presented then move into rural areas. This will inevitably have ramifications for the picture I paint throughout this book of economic and cultural mobility, as well as access to goods and communications infrastructure in Cuba.

Given the immersive nature of ethnographic fieldwork, I quickly became a key point of contact between Cuban communities and found myself operating as one of the very loci of exchange I had hoped to observe. Toward the end of my fieldwork, I seemed to embody my own transnational space of exchange and circulation, as wherever I traveled became the place for participants or their relatives to send and receive items and messages. This research gradually escalated to incorporate other sites as my participants traveled through the networks of exchange I will describe throughout this book. Another primary fieldsite for the research was online, as this is a key space in which Cubans on the island and in the diaspora contact one another and the norms of cubanidad are negotiated. Research typically followed a methodology of "following the thing" (Marcus 1995) as a means of capturing the dynamism of both material and cultural flows among these interconnected sites, beginning in Miami and spiraling ever further outward. In another sense, my research also became the opposite of Marcus's proposal; often the things actually followed me (if I was delivering them), and so inevitably, one of the main things connecting fieldsites and participants was in fact my body. This perhaps should not be so surprising; it is increasingly true of anthropological fieldwork of migratory trajectories that we, ourselves, are the only clear tie linking together otherwise highly mobile communities. In a sense, the one characteristic that united all my participants is they all sought me out (rather than the other way around).

From the outset, I knew that working with communities that at times operate in gray areas of the law and that are not accustomed to (nor enthusiastic about) outside attention would be difficult. For this reason, I decided at an early stage to begin my research in Miami, where I hoped it would be easier to gain the trust of interlocutors, and from there gain introductions to their relatives on the island. I had not anticipated the levels of paranoia and mistrust I encountered, especially in Hialeah, where many of my participants were recently arrived migrants who were either undocumented or simply wished to keep their heads down and focus on establishing new lives for themselves. Upon arrival in Greater Miami, I began by simply showing up at Cuban businesses and loitering, offering help whenever I could, in the hope that this would eventually establish trust. It in fact had the opposite effect, and on several occasions, I was accused (rather to my surprise) of being a spy working undercover for the Cuban state (see also Driscoll and Schuster 2018). After about a month of trying this, and eventually finding myself in a rather hostile encounter, I conceded that the traditional ethnographic methods of observing and gradually building trust would not work for me. This was also in part because I was not working in a single, coherent community; Miami is a vast city, and one where most people spend an inordinate amount of time in their cars, commuting. They themselves often go long stretches of time without seeing one another, and communication is often through private social messaging platforms, rather than face-to-face. Simply hanging around in the hope of observing something in such a context is thus particularly challenging.

24 · Circulating Culture

As so often happens to anthropologists in the field, access came when I least expected it, and in guises I never could have anticipated. Most of the interlocutors whose voices feature in the book in fact found me—in many cases, online through social networking sites. Of course, I was also able to help many of these people, given the relative ease with which I (with a British passport) could carry things back and forth between Miami and Havana. My own participation in networks of material exchange over many months ultimately facilitated my entry into many of the Cuban families and more domestic scenarios I describe in this book. In particular, the extended family I describe in chapter 2 were all related by marriage to an American friend of mine. I began to carry items for them to Cuba on my visits, and also to help various other families to send items or messages to their relatives on the other side. Over the months, I gradually became incorporated into Cuban notions of extended family. I discuss this at length in chapters 2 and 3, as it was my own experience of accessing these family links that made me realize (quite accidentally) that material flows are the bedrock of Cuban kinship.

Most of the voices we hear from in this book are those of young Cubans, typically aged between about 20 and 35. Most were born in Cuba, and in the cases where they had moved to Miami, they had done so only two or three years before I arrived in Miami myself. About one-third had arrived after the termination of the wet foot, dry foot policy, and were undocumented and working without a permit, or waiting for paperwork to come through. The vast majority still held Cuban passports. A little over half of the participants in Miami had a university qualification or were in the process of undertaking further education. All the Cuban participants on the island had completed high school, and many had started at university, but most had dropped out, opting to make more money from tourism or as entrepreneurs (cuentapropistas).

The majority of my participants in Miami (as well as Panama and Guyana) were phenotypically white and considered themselves as such; this was not because I sought out such characteristics in my interlocutors, but rather something attributed to a broader demographic pattern in the diaspora in general (Yelvington 2001). In Havana my participants were more ethnically diverse, and more than half considered themselves Afro-Cuban. This I attribute to several factors: first, that the population in Cuba in general, and in the neighborhoods such as Central Havana where I was working, is more ethnically diverse and has a much larger Afro-Cuban population than the diaspora. Second, my research focused upon people operating on the periphery of society, insofar as they were often dealing in gray- or black-market trading or choosing to work within networks of trading and smuggling out of need to supplement their low state income. In chapter 3 I suggest that my research focus upon following material and digital transnational flows shaped my results to increasingly encounter Afro-Cuban participants in Havana, as due to inequalities in Cuba, this group is less likely to have remittance income from abroad, or the education and contacts to establish larger "legitimate" businesses on the island (de la Fuente 2016; Hansing 2018).

Finally, the data presented throughout this book is derived more from male interlocutors than female, although I have done my best to counter this bias, and in particular I focus upon the role of women in these networks of exchange in chapters 2 and 3. On the whole, though, most of my interlocutors were young men, which I attribute in part to the fact that I am a young female researcher, and, for whatever reason, they made themselves more available to me, and in part to the topic of research, as such networks are often dominated by young men (Congdon 2015; Williams 2009), as discussed in chapter 3 and 4. While it depends on the nature of goods being transported, many *mulas* ("mules," i.e., people transporting goods) are young men due to the gendered nature of what is considered hard physical work, and my own positionality as a female researcher will inevitably have limited my access to these networks to some degree (see also Evans 2017). I constantly had the (frustrating) sense that I was only able to scratch the surface.

I have anonymized all the participants in this research, and, in fact, three of the characters presented in this book are composite characters with pseudonyms, formed from ethnographic vignettes I gained from various people. Some might criticize this approach, arguing that I have changed important details such as gender, age, linguistic ability, and so on, but wherever possible I have not changed characteristics that seemed significant to the arguments I present here. I make clear through translations (in brackets) where quotes were originally in English or in Spanish; I followed interlocutors' leads in using the language they felt most comfortable in. One of the main reasons for using composite profiles is because I did not want to invade the lives of my interlocutors or intrude upon their privacy too much (Markham 2012; Samuels-Wortley 2021; Willis 2019). Moreover, there are many instances when I present people in morally dubious circumstances, either because they were knowingly breaking the law (and themselves considered that problematic), or, as was more typical, they were taking advan-

26 · Circulating Culture

tage of others who found themselves in vulnerable situations. There were countless instances of this in my research, and I have occasionally struggled to present all my participants in a favorable light, as they would perhaps wish to be presented. Several of my male participants were cheating on their spouses, in some cases with many different partners both in Cuba and the diaspora, and while it was relevant to my argument to include this fact, I also wanted to ensure no one could identify them from my writing. My aim, then, was to create characters that are true to the spirit and voices of the people I met, but that combine elements of different people's stories, such that my interlocutors (and their close acquaintances) would not necessarily recognize themselves in my writing.

This approach is common among anthropologists and social geographers, especially those working within communities that are subject to criminality, violence, exile, or trauma (Eltringham 2004; Jones and Rodgers 2019; Malkki 2007; Malkki 2012, 56–58). It is also an approach that has often been discussed and adopted by scholars working in Latin America and its diasporas as a way of balancing their wish to relay shared stories and experiences, and their vividness, without compromising the safety or privacy of their interlocutors or themselves (Bourgois 1990, 2003; Hecht 2006; Oglesby 1995; Rodgers 2019). In his work in the Dominican Republic, for example, Jon Wolseth explains that while "characters are sometimes composites . . . the tangibility and plausibility of street life has remained" in his ethnographic account (2013, 18). I hope that in my portrayal of some of these figures from my own research I have managed to strike an equitable balance among their stories, their voices, and my own (see also Ortner 2003).

There are two notable exceptions to the anonymity. First is the case of Nestor Siré, a Cuban artist who has worked in the world of *el paquete* ("the package," which is a network for the exchange of digital content in Cuba), and whom we encounter in chapter 4. Nestor became and remains a good friend, and a renowned international artist in his own right. He graciously permitted me to reproduce his work and some of his photos in this book and has been supportive of my research from the outset. I am keen to abide by his request and to attribute his work to his name. Second, Danys (one of the *paqueteros*, or "packagers," i.e., people who operate and sell content within the paquete network) wanted his name to be credited, I believe in the hope that it would help him to build his personal brand and might lead to further foreign media interviews (see chapter 4). At the time of our conversations, he had already publicly disclosed his identity in numerous international newspaper interviews, some of which are also cited in this book.

This brings me to another ethical quandary I encountered many times throughout my research, namely, my interlocutors' own motives for wanting to participate in my research, which at times was at odds with my own objectives. This is something that often seems neglected within anthropological discussion, yet it seemed very clear to me that ultimately, all the participants whom I present here are the people who chose to make themselves available to me, and in fact on most occasions sought me out, rather than the other way around. They did so for myriad complex reasons, and I frequently felt myself being pulled in different ideological directions. Some wanted me to write about the pain of the Cuban exiles and how cruel socialism is (see chapter 5); others wanted me to promote Cuba as a glorious tourist destination for digital detox. Some hoped to make money by advertising their own personal brand through my writing, which they saw as a potentially international platform for exposure, while others hoped I would be able to save them some money by transporting items to relatives on the "other side." In some cases, motivations only became clear late in the fieldwork, and I was besieged by requests when I announced I would be leaving for good. Wherever possible, I have met their requests (I certainly carried many items back and forth) and tried to ensure that their participation in my research was fruitful for all parties. If my research ever bordered upon exploitative, insofar as I subjected people to long periods of questioning about their private lives, I also consciously allowed many of my participants to exploit me in various ways, which I hope to some degree leveled the power balance.

A word should be said about the ethics of working with people involved in illegal activity. I never sought to spend time with people breaking the law, either in Cuba or in Miami, although I nonetheless frequently found myself in such circumstances. In most cases, I opted to leave when I felt legal, ethical, or moral lines were being crossed, and at times felt conflicted when my own sense of morality or ethics was at odds with that of my interlocutors. In most cases, the people I followed were operating within a legal gray zone, rather than overtly breaking the law. Francis Pine notes that in such instances, the anthropologist often ends up observing and "doing things which are often not in themselves illegal—they may involve stealing, or more rarely violent crime, or types of financial crime, but usually do not—but which are taking place/carried out below the radar of the state" (2015, 28). In my

28 · Circulating Culture

own ethnographic context, this was largely because the mulas I followed were involved primarily in importing domestic goods such as clothing and food, which is restricted by the Cuban government due to import charges but is not illegal activity. I never participated in any trade networks moving illegal goods, such as smuggling alcohol, drugs, narcotics, or people. The closest I observed to this was in the selling of counterfeited branded goods, which, given the lack of copyright in Cuba, most of my participants did not view as problematic, and did not expose them to particular risk of arrest. Similarly, the paqueteros I followed operated under legal licenses for audiovisual production, even if they did make additional profit on the side through advertising revenue (which is illegal in Cuba).

Structure of the Book

My intention was always that form would mirror substance in this enterprise of writing and thinking through ideas of flow and counterflow, rupture and repair, the betwixt and the between. The research itself, as I have described, felt messy, even chaotic in nature, and so for clarity's sake I have also tried to impose some kind of order upon the ethnographic and theoretical material I present. This book unfolds in three sections, each of which attempts to follow the back-and-forth that is so central to the arguments I present.

In part 1, we start out with two chapters exploring how these flows originate in the first place, and how value originates and is created within the social world the book then follows. Chapter 1 introduces the main fieldsite of the book and presents a "new" group of Cubans, who were raised under socialism in Cuba and have recently (since 2014) moved to South Florida to try to forge successful lives for themselves and their families. I critique this notion of "success" ethnographically, showing how different diasporic generations within Miami have competing notions of what having "made it" means. Using the case study of a pawnshop in Hialeah, I link this to material culture to understand how value is created within this community, in ways that can be at odds with more hegemonic or Marxian understandings of how value is created and exchanged. I instead outline the inventive ways that these New Cubans consume material things across differing socioeconomic models of ownership in order to create and perform personhood and success to an audience back on the island.

Chapter 2 then contextualizes the trajectories of such material flows within Cuban systems of kinship, arguing for diasporic remittances as a "substance" of relatedness within Cuban kin networks stretching across the Florida Straits. The chapter charts one family's story over several decades to understand how their notion of relatedness has in fact expanded and grown closer since the exile of the two key matriarchal figures and argues that material care is a key aspect of gendered family life in a Cuban context.

In the central section of the book (part 2), I turn to address the ways in which the value established in part 1 is in turn centered upon circulation, both physically, between places, and perhaps more ontologically, insofar as I describe shifts between our understandings of "person" and "thing" here as well. In chapter 3 I address how items that arrive in Cuba by various informal means constitute a larger informal network of material circulation, which I argue is the primary means by which most Cubans on the island directly or indirectly acquire material goods. I call these informal networks in their totality the "Mula Ring," drawing analogies here with Malinowski's infamous Kula Ring to reveal how mulas (mules) in the Caribbean are involved in expanding networks of circulation and exchange, the likes of which are also creating new social hierarchies and cultural vernaculars both in Cuba and overseas. I follow several mulas as they travel between Cuba and various destinations to acquire items, and I address how this emerging network in turn draws upon the gendered spheres of everyday life outlined in chapter 2 to reveal the agency of women, who arguably use traditional gendered spheres to their economic advantage. The chapter also draws parallels with Nancy Munn's work on Kula (1977, 1987), examining the way traders mobilize social networks to acquire and expand their own prestige, personhood, and wealth, thus using both local and transnational circulation networks to travel beyond their own social worlds both physically and symbolically.

Chapter 4 continues this line of argument, but turns to the digital, which in Cuba is particularly material in its everyday manifestation due to reliance upon material infrastructure to circumvent state restrictions on some aspects of digital access. In this chapter I chart the rise of Cuba's largest digital network of circulation—el paquete—and show how new hierarchies of power are emerging as a result on the island and in the diaspora. I also consider how, through digital media, Cubans envisage themselves as connected to larger social worlds, and introduce the concept of the "e-Mula Ring," whereby Cuban cultural products are circulated, and in fact exported from the island and imported into the diaspora as migrants seek out connections with their homeland. In parallel to the Mula Ring described in chapter 3, this digital public sphere offers some Cubans the opportunity to expand their prestige and personhood beyond the constrictions of their immediate surroundings.

The final section of the book, part 3, then addresses how value comes full circle as items make their return trip around these networks of circulation. Chapter 5 returns to the diaspora in Miami to examine the way value is attributed to the nostalgic and affective capacities of material items originating in Cuba. The chapter ethnographically explores several antiques shops, and traces some of these historic items to address the way that different groups of Cubans mobilize material goods in political ways, ultimately seeking to create and perform a heightened sense of a curated and often ideologically charged notion of Cuban identity. The chapter considers how hegemonic gazes onto Cuba and its cultural history are reproduced and marshaled according to sociopolitical projects, which map onto identity anxieties rooted in the ambiguity and upheaval of diasporic life in exile.

In chapter 6, I turn to the materiality of death to consider this central issue of Cuban identity when it matters most. I consider how the circulation of human remains and associated objects between Cuba and Miami relates to notions of what it means to be Cuban in life, and how the parallels between trajectories of circulation between people and things evoke different layers of meaning for my interlocutors. I also consider how earth, soil, and seeds gain an affective, almost spiritual significance when transported beyond Cuba, and the relative power of those able to navigate geopolitical uncertainties to transport these materials.

Finally, in the concluding chapter 7, I address the different ways in which anxieties about cultural identity are performed and curated through narrative devices, using theatrical and artistic showcases as my ethnographic examples. This chapter then draws upon the earlier chapters of the book to argue for the creative possibilities inherent in moments of political rupture, economic upheaval, and cultural flux, showing how it is precisely the constrictions placed upon the flows between Miami and Havana that have facilitated the emergence of incipient cultural logics, enacted through inventive strategies adopted by people on both sides of the Florida Straits. Countering characterizations of Cuba and its Miami diaspora as isolated communities hermetically sealed off from one another by the U.S Embargo, I instead emphasize a reading of Miami and Havana as co-constituting spaces, to highlight the interstitial possibilities that are opened when we frame communities in this way.

I

Creating Value

1

Creating Value

1

"Fake It to Make It"

Conspiciously Consuming Fantasy
in Hialeah and Havana

Miami is a city both physically and figuratively made up of crossroads, of incongruous points of meeting, of frictive encounters. It is a city where the geographic and allegorical North stretches its tentacles southward to incorporate cultural, economic, and social semblances of the Global South, thus bridging chasms between Latin American elites and impoverished undocumented migrants, conservative U.S. foreign policy machinations and the inherent domestic social injustices prevalent in a location that positions itself as "south of the South."[1] Miami's position bridging the so-called Global North and South is undoubtedly in large part due to its unique position in Latin America, both economically and culturally; Miami represents a place where Latino/a and Caribbean identities can be articulated outside of the boundaries of nationalism, as a plural, performative, and ambiguous manifestation of a host of "Latinities" (F. Rivera 2019; Yúdice 2005). Urban geographer Jan Nijman characterizes the city as a place of transience, with an "urban culture [that] invokes the metaphor of the city as a hotel: people check in, use the facilities, and check out again" (2011, 135). For much the same reason, I open and close this book with vignettes from the Miami airport, a similarly evocative symbol of transience and crossroads.

For many of its inhabitants, whether adopted or "native," Miami embodies a site of both refuge and creation, a frontier space[2] between old and new worlds manufactured through comings and goings. In her landmark text theorizing border culture as *mestizaje* (or cultural mixing), Gloria Anzaldúa describes the U.S. border with Mexico as "*una herida abierta* [an open wound] where the Third World grates against the first and bleeds"

34 · Part I. Creating Value

(1987, 3); Miami is a site of similar wounds. Miami, and especially Cuban Miami, for all its outward prosperity and jauntiness, is "a city in pain, a place where the dead are never far from people's minds, and in which the past and the present are constantly being elided" (Rieff 1993, 22).

Miami is therefore evidence of the ways in which people make their lives under these conditions; it is a place not just of pasts and presents but also visibly oriented toward creating futures, and in this regard arguably embodies what might be called the "dual aspect of rupture" (Holbraad, Kapferer, and Sauma 2019, 2), whereby new social forms can emerge from the rifts and damage experienced in the past. Miami represents a potential switch-point in the lives of many of the interlocutors presented throughout this book, both as a place that requires breaking with their existing conditions of life "before," and as a place that propels them forward into something new; as a city it thus embodies both the negative breakage and positive dynamic impulses of rupture.

In this chapter, I introduce Greater Miami as a city long conceived of as a liminal and even magical place, assuming its position as switch-point or crossroads between the negative aspects of rupture (such as the pain and struggle associated with exile and migration) and a more dynamic impulse toward the emergence, reconstitution, and renewal of new cultures and communities taking form. It is against this backdrop of rupture and renewal that new Cuban migrants are forging alternative cultural logics of value and identity to redefine what it means to be both "successful" and "Cuban."

Bienvenido a "Big Havana"

Unlike the postcard images of bejeweled beach-side districts lined by Art Deco hotels, the inner-city district of Hialeah lacks Miami's famed luster. This working-class neighborhood is packed with some 44,000 retail, wholesale, and warehousing businesses, of which about 80 percent is Cuban-owned. Compared to the rest of Greater Miami, Hialeah has more non-English speakers, more persons per household, and is more densely settled than averages for the wider city, state, and, indeed, nation. Hialeahans are typically less educated, earn less, and have lower rates of homeownership than their neighbors in nearby districts, too.[3] Hialeah is made up of 96.4 percent Hispanic or Latino residents, with more than 74 percent born overseas, making it the city[4] with the highest number of immigrants per capita in the whole of the U.S. In this regard, it perhaps embodies better than any other Greater Miami district a Cuban "ethnic enclave" (Scarpaci 2015; Stepick 1994a), one of those neighborhoods Gustavo Pérez Firmat describes where a resident "could be delivered by a Cuban obstetrician, buried by a Cuban undertaker, and in between birth and death lead a perfectly satisfactory life without needing extramural contacts" (1995, 55).

Hialeah is a blue-collar city right in the center of Greater Miami, and far from the tropical tourist trail of Miami Beach or Little Havana to the south. It resembles a grid of broad avenues of gridlocked traffic lined with strip malls, bordered by residential streets of tightly packed one-story bungalows with concrete parking strips in front, surrounded by chain-link fences. Often these houses boast large Cuban and American flags or have extravagant water fountains or Greco-Roman-style pillars lining the entranceway. Iconic elements of cubanidad (Cuban identity) pervade everyday life in Hialeah, with corner stores selling *pastelitos* (pastries) of cheese and guava, *bodegas* (grocery stores) selling *yuca* (cassava) and *malanga* (similar to yam), and sunburnt old men sitting on upside-down plastic buckets at each intersection, selling sunflowers, *puros* (cigars), chewing gum, and *charada china* (Cuban lottery) tickets. *Botánicas* (religious stores)[5] sell the statues of the Virgen de la Caridad that take pride of place on many front lawns,[6] coffee *ventanitas* (windows) mete out tiny cups of sugary espresso to customers, and remittance stores advertise quick transfers of cash, phone credit, and goods to Cuba by somewhat vague means.

More so than any other part of Greater Miami, this neighborhood is outwardly geared toward Cuba—residents often affectionately call it "North Havana"—and most businesses evidence the constant material and digital interactions between kin on either side of the Florida Straits in some form or another. Pharmacies quietly deal out medicines without prescription ("*Pa' Cuba, verdad?*" / "It's for Cuba, right?"), minimarkets offer bulk deals on sachets of seasoning (also destined for Cuba), and factories and stores such as ¡Ñooo! que barato (Damn, that's cheap!) even manufacture Cuban school uniforms destined for the island's classrooms. The store's owner is proud of the growth in this neighborhood, fueled by growth in the local Cuban-born population of 21 percent between 2010 and 2017: "[F]orget about Little Havana," he says, "now we have Big Havana. It's called Hialeah" (Wile 2019). Every strip mall has a familiar run of stores: a video rental, a grocery store, one or two hair salons, a coffee window, wholesale clothing, a pharmacy, and a pawnshop.

The "New Cubans"

The use of the label "Cuban" as an identity marker is a particularly polemic one in Miami. The wider Cuban community fractures and divides itself along seemingly infinite fissures, with people positioning themselves along indices of Cuban versus American, capitalist versus socialist, "free" versus communist, and so forth, making the label often one of exclusion more than of inclusion. Moreover, the experiences of these various sub-groups have been in some regards so disparate as to warrant a need to further demarcate discrete groups, diasporic "cohorts" or "generations" (Duany 1999; Eckstein and Berg 2015; Grenier and Stepick 1992; Stepick, Grenier, Castro, and Dunn 2003). Broadly speaking, scholars have typically separated Cuban Americans into four waves of migration; the "Exiles" who fled the revolution (1959–1970s), the Marielitos who fled due to political repression in the 1980s, the balseros who fled economic hardship in the 1990s on rafts, and then, more recently, what Susan Eckstein (2009) calls the "New Cubans," who have moved to Miami since the early 2000s seeking economic opportunity. In contrast to the earliest waves of Cuban migration, these New Cubans grew up predominantly during a time of considerable economic hardship and scarcity on the island (the Special Period of the 1990s) and had no prior experience of luxury or material wealth. For many, their primary motivation in leaving their homeland was not predicated solely on an inherent ideological or political stance, but more on a desire to materially improve their and their family's living standards. In this regard, they are starkly different from the earlier groups of Cubans that migrated to Miami, whom I loosely group together as Old Cubans in this book.

The New Cubans have predominantly settled in Hialeah, where knowledge of English is rarely needed in day-to-day life, and where a community of more recently migrated Cubans awaits them with employment opportunities and connections. This also explains the visible abundance of businesses in Hialeah that cater to those sending support back to the island. As Eckstein has shown, the New Cubans, with no organized political agenda of their own, have in fact done more to transform Cuba under Castro than any of the richer and more politically powerful earlier Cuban arrivals in previous migratory waves. These New Cubans have "unwittingly planted seeds of socialist transformation from the U.S. side of the Straits, a by-product, in the aggregate, of their transnationalized family commitments" (Eckstein 2009, 4), by sending regular remittances and maintaining regular contact with friends and family back on the island. In a 2014 survey, 93.8 percent of

Cubans who reported sending money back to the island were aged between 20 and 49 (Scarpaci 2014, 261), revealing how New Cubans are emotionally, materially, and financially maintaining stronger links to household challenges there. It is these financial and material flows that are having profound impacts upon the lived experience of everyday Cubans on the island, and that Eckstein argues have done more to instigate economic and political change on the island than any ideological movements promoted by earlier diasporic cohorts.

These New Cubans, who are typically younger and arrived in the U.S. alongside an easing of travel restrictions instigated under the Obama administration (2009–2017), also represent an emerging group of immigrants who differ considerably from the "successful" earlier waves of émigrés documented in earlier studies (Stepick and Stepick 2002). This difference is most notably displayed through their openness to returning to Cuba and their commitment to making sacrifices to provide for relatives left behind. Newer arrivals from the 1990s onward have remained so enmeshed in life back home that they plan trips to coincide with birthdays, holidays, and other family festivities, which sets them apart from most Cubans who migrated in earlier cohorts who, for the most part, refused to return on ideological grounds, even when the opportunity did present itself. In the years under President George W. Bush, when Washington only permitted visits to Cuba for family emergencies, the claimed emergencies peaked during holiday season. The option to make more regular return trips during President Obama's tenure allowed recent Cuban arrivals to share in the celebration of family events, which, in turn, have reinforced and renewed kinship solidarity in new transnationalized forms.

The pressure to maintain a material presence in the lives of those left behind on the island is felt by many of these New Cubans, who mobilize considerable networks and resources to provide material care and thereby maintain and indeed create kinship links (as set out in chapter 2). In this regard, this cohort of New Cubans arguably bears a closer resemblance to other diasporic communities—presented in wider remittance literatures that highlight impoverished migrants' sacrifices in supporting relatives from overseas (Levitt 2001; Lindley 2009)—than to the older exile generation of Cubans, who have enjoyed relatively (materially) comfortable and successful lives in Miami when compared to wider norms within migrant groups from the Caribbean and Latin America (due in part to considerable financial and political support from the U.S. federal government). Any ethnographic analysis of Hialeah could hardly ignore the visible struggle and

38 · Part I. Creating Value

sacrifice undertaken by many New Cubans to be able to afford such care, which is visibly etched into each of Hialeah's many strip malls in the form of pawnshops, discount dollar stores, and loan sharks standing on corners, but, as we will see in the next section, financial struggle and social success need not be opposing concepts for the New Cubans, who do not necessarily subscribe to the normalizing (and classist) representations of "good taste" seen elsewhere in Greater Miami.

Pawning Saint Lazarus

You can find a pawnshop, or a *casa de empeños*, in pretty much every one of the strip malls in Hialeah. These little stores with big metal shutters and large "CA$H" signs offer small, secured loans against more or less any object that is considered to have resale value as collateral; if the client has not returned within 30 days to recoup their belongings, the store can then sell them. Such pawnshops provide a vital service in places like Hialeah to large segments of the population that either cannot qualify for loans or credit card advances from banks due to a lack of qualifying assets or have no American credit history.

For many of Hialeah's more recent arrivals from Cuba, who are used to a cash-driven economy and may never have dealt with banks before, pawnshops are an obvious way to levy cash in times of need. Moreover, in Cuba, where such practices are illegal and therefore happen behind closed doors, loans among relatives and friends are a risky but quiet norm. In Havana, I knew several men who had dealings with illegal pawnbrokers, or *prestamistas*, in order to be able to afford things that might help attract a suitable spouse. Cuba's most popular post-revolution band, Los Van Van, even allude to this in their song "Hasta las cuántas":

No creas que estoy siendo muy pesimista,	Don't think I'm being very pessimistic,
hace tiempo que estoy en manos de un prestamista,	I've been in the hands of a pawn broker for a while,
que quiere cobrarme la dicha de amarte	who wants to charge me for the joy of loving you

"The whole system comes down to trust" ("*Todo se basa en un círculo de confianza*"), my friends would tell me, and these moral systems and modes of material care extend into Miami's Cuban diaspora as well (Cordero, Gallardoy, and Sacasa 2017; see also chapter 3 on *confianza*). Thus, for many of Hialeah's residents, a regulated pawnshop with physical premises and written terms and conditions in fact represents a more stable and secure arrangement. The state of Florida has long had one of the highest numbers of pawnshops in the U.S., and in the 1990s such stores were visited by as many as one in ten adults state-wide (Caskey 1991; Oeltjen 1996). These numbers have likely increased in Miami since the recession and consequent austerity experienced in the city since 2008.

The "Real Deal" pawnshop in the heart of Hialeah is one of the more visible examples of this trade in the neighborhood, in large part due to the 30-foot-high rotating neon dollar sign drawing in customers from the nearby highway. Entrance is only granted upon ringing a buzzer to pass through two separate bullet-proof doors, before one emerges into a small chamber with counters on three sides flaunting glitzy hordes of gold chains, amulets, guns, chandeliers, and figurines, along with an assortment of antique baseball bats, golf clubs, cigarette lighters, and even the keys to a luxury yacht placed alongside some gold teeth. The owner, Tommy, and his Colombian wife Angela remain behind another bullet-proof glass screen, and speak to customers through a two-way microphone system, next to a large red button labeled "EMERGENCY." I could not help but agree with Tommy as he joked, "You know, I'm surprised I don't get more people like you in here, actually . . . where better to go to learn about Cubans than the place where they part with all their valuables?!"

Over 27 years of business, Tommy has seen pretty much everything and everyone come through his high-security doors, and his client demographic mirrors that of Hialeah more broadly: mostly Cubans, recently arrived, with a few Salvadorans, Nicaraguans, and Venezuelans passing through as well. "We always operate on a totally need-to-know basis," Tommy told me on my first visit, but as I started to spend increasing amounts of time in the store, I noticed how many customers would relate their whole life stories to him as they gingerly handed over their father's gold watch or their great-great-grandmother's broach. Moreover, I realized these pawnshops provided unique opportunities to understand Cuban systems of value, as customer after customer would argue over the sentimental or monetary value of an item being pawned to pay for a much-loved relative's education or health care.

One middle-aged woman, for example, argued with Tommy for at least twenty minutes upon discovering that her father's wedding ring—one of the few possessions he had been able to bring with him from Cuba—was not, in fact, worth all that much in dollars, and would not fund her husband's upcoming gallbladder surgery or her son's college fees. Holding back tears, she handed over the ring, and took her check, quietly noting that "it would be a shame to let family sentiment from the past hold back our future." The young man waiting in line behind her, who had come in to pawn an iPad to free up some cash to pay for a health care worker to visit his elderly mother back in Havana, nodded sympathetically. "We used to get a lot more of that, you know, people coming in with old family mementoes and antiques from Cuba, hoping to make money from them," Tommy told me later, "but nowadays I think most of them sell it online or something. We mostly only deal in hard value, jewelry, and gold." Tommy and his wife had even had customers come in with photos of valuable items still in Cuba, wanting an appraisal before deciding whether it would be worth trying to get the objects out and over to Hialeah to pawn. "The problem is it's hard to tell from a picture, and a lot of people bring in stuff which isn't actually the real deal."

On a visit a few weeks later, I was standing chatting to Angela about the recent hurricane when a car pulled up outside, and a very elderly man got out unsteadily, only to sit on the pavement for several minutes, fiddling with something in his hands. Angela rolled her eyes at me and said, "this one's definitely going to be a Cuban," and we waited as the man got up and struggled to ring the security buzzer. Upon entering the store, he seemed uneasy, and made out that he was "just browsing," vaguely looking through cases of blingy jewelry. Eventually, having worked his way along one entire side of the shop, he approached Angela, and said he had a very important religious medallion he wished to know the value of. He produced from his fist a gold medallion of the much-venerated Saint Lazarus. "It's been in my family for years, and we held onto it all the way through the Special Period, diamonds and all" he stated proudly. He mumbled something about his grandson getting married and wanting to buy a house and passed it through the metal grill to Angela. As I caught a closer glimpse of it, I saw the figure's eyes had been painted over in what looked like sparkly nail polish. The man explained that he had not wanted Saint Lazarus (patron saint of the downtrodden and destitute) to see that he was being pawned, and so had covered his eyes before entering the store. After inspecting the medallion for several minutes, Angela had to inform the man that his much-treasured religious heirloom was, in fact, not made of real gold and diamonds, and as such had little monetary value, even if it was of great familial significance: a heart-rending assertion of the clash between *priceless* and *price-less*. Ashen faced, the old man left the store, and sat in his car for a long time before eventually driving away.

As Niko Besnier and Ping-Ann Addo note in their ethnographic research in a pawnshop in Tonga, in such spaces the required expertise in assessing the quality of valuables quickly shifts from being an assessment of people's sociocultural capital to being an assessment of the monetary value of objects (2008, 41), and the two can stand at odds with one another. In a Marxian understanding of value, it "can only come into concrete existence in the form of exchange value" (Turner 2008, 50)—in other words, when an item is exchanged for money. Pawnshops are thus interesting ethnographic sites of tension between different formations of value, or what Daniel Miller calls "the incommensurable polarity between value as price, and value as priceless" (2008, 1122); for they are places where material objects, with all of the emotional trajectories they might embody, must be reduced solely to their exchange value. In this case, Angela was the arbiter of what could here be defined as valuable; the man's family story of surviving the Special Period was rendered value-less and could not be leveraged to help his family build a future now. "In my job, people always try to make things sentimental, but you just can't be that way and make it in this industry," Angela noted to me afterward, highlighting her position as intermediary between these two formulations of value.

In Besnier and Addo's Tongan case, clients experience shame at patronizing a pawnshop, as such actions signal that one is not only materially poor, but also poorly integrated into a local system of social relations whereby the kinship system "should" provide for everyone's financial needs (2008, 44). Here, we see the opposite. The old man clearly felt shame that he was attempting to pawn a religious item, but at the same time was also proud that this item denoted his social connectedness. The value of the medallion was closer to Nancy Munn's definition of value as situated in that which is considered essential to communal viability (1987, 3). The Saint Lazarus medallion represented the material trajectory of his family, through the Special Period in Havana, through migration to Hialeah—and, moreover, it was to be pawned precisely to provide continuing care for kin. As such, this medallion was an important demonstration of kin connectedness, in terms of both its own trajectory and what it could be levied for; it was a relic of his relatedness as much as it was a religious token.

Had the medallion been made of gold, like the various others lining a cabinet in the corner of the room, it would likely have been quite valuable, according to the pawnshop owners. "Cubans absolutely love gold," Tommy told me once. "They come in here and their eyes just light up! It's a very traditional display of wealth in Cuba, so if you want people back there to

42 · Part I. Creating Value

think you've made it in Hialeah, you want to be wearing gold chains." Many of Tommy and Angela's customers in fact used the store as more of a rental resource than a pawnshop, knowing that so long as they did not leave items for more than 30 days at a time, those items could not be sold without their permission. "Every day we get people coming in to buy gold jewelry because they're going to Cuba tomorrow and they want to look successful, then the second they're back, they return it and use the cash on bills or rent or whatever." The jewelry actually stays in the shop most of the time, and customers use the store almost as the opposite of a pawnshop, renting back their items when it suits them.

Crucially, then, gold is convertible in its value, unlike cash, which is difficult to move back and forth between Miami and Havana due to Cuban and American government restrictions. Money becomes less of a "universal yardstick against which to measure and evaluate the universe of objects, relations, services, and persons," as Marx, Weber, or Simmel might have argued (Maurer 2006, 16; Simmel 1990),[7] due to the challenges in circulating it across this particular geopolitical border. Gold, however, can be circulated and exchanged with less impediment across both socioeconomic systems, and becomes a better conduit or translator of value. Gold can act as currency or as a monetary alternative (Carruthers and Babb 1996), or, when worked into an artefact (such as jewelry), can wield a distinct form of social power (Schoenberger 2011). "One of the most interesting things about gold jewelry as a form of inalienable wealth is the articulation between it being both a repository of social memory and identity and of economic value . . . gold jewelry is, as often as not, in the pawnshop, part of an ongoing cycle of indebtedness and reclamation," Mark Johnson argues in relation to gold jewelry and value among members of the Filipino diaspora (1997, 228). In the case of Hialeah's New Cubans, gold arguably occupies a middle ground between alienable and inalienable possessions (Weiner 1992) and is all the more valuable precisely for its capacity to switch between regimes of value (Appadurai 1986). On the one hand, it is more freely transferred than cash in this particular geopolitical context, yet it also conveys a family's history, and thus is a marker of cultural authenticity. This material is worth more than money precisely because it has an ability to move or flow between places, unlike most people and things in this context. It can also speak to different systems of value across different socioeconomic contexts, and thus can be leveraged as a symbol and receptacle of value in more flexible ways.

For Yani and her boyfriend Reinaldo, who had only arrived in Hialeah three years before, it was a struggle to keep up with their rent and the growing financial remittance needs of their relatives back on the island, and so owning expensive jewelry and handbags was a distant fantasy. They were paying $1000 a month to a Cuban man (who had arrived fifteen years prior to them) to live in what was essentially his garden shed, albeit a large one with basic facilities, which was certainly not the image of diasporic glamour they had heard about back in Havana. But with some friends they had pooled together to purchase some golden jewelry, which remained in the Real Deal pawnshop most of the year and could be borrowed back in advance of making a return trip home. Upon arrival in Havana, they would be able to play the part of the successful returnee, who had made it in the big city. "There's a lot of pressure to show that the sacrifice of leaving everyone behind is worth it, and it makes people happy at home to know we're doing well" Yani explained, "and besides, it's not so weird for us anyway. In Cuba you don't always own your own things, do you?!" On that occasion Yani had been in the shop to get her cheap metal charm dipped in gold to appear solid in advance of an upcoming return trip home. A few weeks later, she posted a selfie of herself and her boyfriend in front of a Lamborghini (which had been rented for one hour) on social media with the hashtag #onlyinHialeah and tagged her relatives to make sure they saw. For Yani, the unavoidable need to send remittances to her relatives on a regular basis, along with managing her own rent and bills, meant owning luxurious items was impossible, yet thanks to her inventive use of pawnshops and mobilization of material and digital social networks spanning Hialeah and Havana, she was able to at least participate in these symbols of success, and feel like she was "moving up" (*avanzando*) in the world.

Conspicuous Consumption

At first glance, it might seem surprising that New Cubans such as Yani and Reinaldo, who had grown up at the height of 1980s and '90s socialism in Havana, might go to such lengths to conspicuously perform material consumption. Central to the revolutionary vision that swept across Cuba in 1959 was the idea that a combination of education and economic arrangements based on moral incentives would help to forge an *hombre nuevo* ("new man"). Discourses of choice, leisure, material desire, and so forth became associated with capitalism and were thus excluded as bourgeois indulgence (Holbraad 2014a, 2014b). Such contrasts remain reference points on the island to this day, yet various ethnographers from the 1990s onward have also reported increasing dollarization and thus raised stakes in what

44 · Part I. Creating Value

"enough" might constitute (Padrón Hernández 2012; Pertierra 2011; Porter 2008). A growing fondness for "compulsive window-shopping" to browse new arrays of (largely unobtainable) consumer goods in Havana has been interpreted as a "quantity fetish" (Holbraad 2017, 85), whereby Havana residents partake in the "fantasy of commensuration" that the shopping malls (*las chopin*) promote. Indeed, consumer culture is visibly present in Havana (Cearns 2019), and consuming citizens are closely tuned into prices, brands, and monetary values on both sides of the Florida Straits (Brotherton 2008; Gordy 2006; Morales and Scarpaci 2012; Ryer 2017).

When taking Cuba's intimate history with nearby Miami into account, this is not so surprising. French, Spanish, and North American tastes were established on the island long before state socialism arrived. Louis Pérez Jr. argues this process began with the end of Spanish rule in 1898, when

> products designed for the US market projected into the Cuban market new concepts of gender relations, sexual modalities, and standards of beauty not simply as cultural types but as commodity related, accessible as an act of consumption . . . US products were appropriated to facilitate social integration and self-definition. (1999, 306)

By the 1930s, a dazzling display of consumer goods had brought "the appearance of abundance within reach" (Pérez 1999, 306), and by the eve of revolution, North American goods—from cars to refrigerators to telephones to furniture to fashion items—were certainly widely incorporated into daily usage and the national imagination (Speck 2005).

Meanwhile, for more than a century Miami has been promoted as the "epicenter of conspicuous consumption" (McClure 2008) and was in large part designed to fulfill this fantasy as a tourist retreat where wealthy Cubans and Americans alike could enjoy sun, sand, and sea at ease. In the 1950s, both Miami and Havana were "place-based fables of abundance," with casinos, nightclubs, and bars where alternative values and pleasures could be realized (Bush 1999, 155). Cuba therefore came to state socialism from a different commodity history and aesthetic sensibility compared to many of the other socialist societies of the twentieth century. The revolution was in many ways a reaction to considerable excess and abundance (which evidently was not a domain open to everyone), yet the fables of such luxury and material success have remained, and are even memorialized, in sites like Havana's famous Hotel Nacional, once a stomping ground for the likes of Al Capone and Winston Churchill.

After the revolution, the term *yuma* emerged to denote the U.S. and, by extension, the capitalist consumption practices so associated not only with North America but also with Europe and capitalism at large. As Paul Ryer (2017, 2018) has charted, this referent came to be an adjective during the Special Period of the 1990s, denoting anything good or desirable (*"Que cosa más yuma!"* or "Wow that's so *yuma!"* is still a phrase one occasionally hears in Havana today). For many Cubans enduring the hardships of material scarcity in the 1990s and since, *la Yuma* has represented an idealized land of "milk, honey and capitalism," akin to the phenomenon Alexei Yurchak (2005) calls the "Imaginary West" in the Soviet Union under socialism. Parallels also abound with discourses of "the normal" in late socialist and early postsocialist Europe (Rausing 2002; Veenis 2012), which was rooted in tastes, desires, and an idealization of Western life. In so doing, (post)socialist consumers referred to "things that were clearly extraordinary in their local context, but were imagined to be part of average lifestyles in Western Europe or the United States" (Fehérváry 2013, 27). In contemporary Cuba, many of the material items seen while one is window shopping, or advertised and circulated through informal networks of exchange (see chapters 3 and 4), are firmly fixed in the imagined cosmopolitan, capitalist, *yuma* world represented by Miami, and underpinned by more than a century of cultural and material interchange between the two places, alongside a historically shared and co-constitutive fantasy of abundance.

For Paul Ryer (2017), the high status of *yuma* imported goods in Cuba (and, it would follow, their consequent abundance in Hialeah) is akin to what Daniel Miller calls a "meta-symbol" in his consideration of appropriations of Coca-Cola in Trinidad (1997a, 170). In other words, the values accorded to global brands or global systems of value are largely perspectival; in the case of Cuba, Ryer maintains such *yuma* goods are not symbols of resistance to socialism, as might too easily be presumed, but rather are displays of social connectedness to kin overseas and therefore privileged remittee status (see chapter 2).

While this is indeed a more ethnographically informed reading of the symbolism of material goods and conspicuous consumption in both Hialeah and Havana, I would also argue that it maps onto oft-fetishized binaries of local versus global. What is valued at a local level (in this case, the high status accorded to conspicuous consumption, material abundance, and "bling") is constructed through an imagined global (the imagined prosperity of kin overseas), and vice versa: many Cubans in the diaspora construct

46 · Part I. Creating Value

their cubanidad materially drawing on items from the island itself (as explored in chapters 5 and 6). The local and global become co-constitutive, insofar as each responds to its imagined other. The mutual history of Miami-Havana is deeply rooted in the representation and performance of desired future states, willed into being through the possession and mobilization of material symbols, which in turn are taken to be indicative of present success and progress toward achieving and realizing this imagined future. Thus, to fully appreciate the extent to which Miami and Havana materially co-create one another, we must ethnographically interrogate what *success* actually means and looks like to consuming citizens on either side of the Florida Straits.

Myths of Success and Return

Many sociological accounts of the "Cuban enclave" in South Florida have highlighted how "successful" Cuban immigrants have been (Grenier and Stepick 1992; Portes and Stepick 1993; Stepick 1994a; Stepick Grenier, Castro, and Dunn 2003), especially when compared to Haitians, Bahamians, Nicaraguans, and so forth, who have not realized such prosperity in Miami. It is worth ethnographically scrutinizing such projections of success, however, as while Cubans have integrated themselves into the labor market to a considerable degree, and earlier waves of migrants were afforded considerable support by the U.S. federal government, only 20 percent of Cubans by the late 1980s were exhibiting the "profile of success" ascribed to them in earlier research (2014, 120). Indeed, by the markers of success (taken broadly as median household income, car and home ownership, employment, and education status) applied by most scholars, Hialeah's New Cubans do not appear anything like as successful as their diasporic forebears. Despite so much discussion of Cuban success, few scholars seem to have interrogated what Cuban migrants themselves might deem symbolic of "making it" in Miami, relying instead on top-down, classist, and normalizing definitions that are ideologically inflected and render the myriad and potentially positive experiences of migrant life somewhat hollow.[8]

For most Americans, pawnshops have overwhelming associations with poverty and need, and embody the opposite of the success encapsulated by an American Dream premised on an equation between material ownership and "freedom." To be sure, it is no coincidence that pawnshops proliferate in low-income neighborhoods and draw in a clientele with less access to the larger banking, educational, and health care institutions of the country. For many of the New Cubans frequenting such stores in Hialeah, however, the possibility of pawning items, and thereby the freedom to navigate among regimes of symbolic, sentimental, and monetary value according to need, is the very mark of success. In Cuba, looking "like a rich, successful, and modern person is . . . almost as importantly valued as being one" (Rausenberger 2018, 827). Being a successful Cuban is not just about having fashionable items, but also a mode of bodily performance representing a modern, urban, "civilized," and wealthy lifestyle in dialogue with global material referents of success, which in turn is contingent on social connectedness and social capital, and thus the outward projection of self is fundamental to processes of self-creation.

These conceptualizations of personhood through performative consumption are numerous in Cuban society: Heidi Härkönen, for example, details how coming-of-age *quinceañera*[9] parties are "to show off; the more I have the more I value" (2011b, 14), and a family will sell its most valuable assets to put on a good party for a daughter. In Havana, money has become firmly linked to attractiveness and the possibilities of creating relationships (Cabezas 2009; Härkönen 2015, 2018; Stout 2014a, 2015), and thus, in a sense, the performance of success or money becomes an affective strategy. The ability to give the impression of success becomes just as important as actual material possession. This strategy is arguably reflected by the very business model of a pawnshop: this is a site where one can redeem high-status objects when needed in order to display them socially, and then convert this value into monetary capital when needed. The social display is always temporal, and the flexibility inherent to this model fits perfectly with Cuban conceptions of materially performing success.

Indeed, for Yani and Reinaldo in Hialeah, the access to and impression of ownership were arguably more important than ownership itself, and they considered themselves to have successfully navigated the transition from Havana to Hialeah insofar as they were making ends meet in Miami while also showing their kin back home that they had "made it." To be able to maintain access to familial objects of sentimental value and items carrying social cachet, but also exchange them for monetary value when needed, was the ultimate marker of opportunity and freedom. "In a sense," Yani joked to me once over *cafecito* (Cuban coffee), "that American saying 'Fake it 'til you make it' is kind of wrong, isn't it? For us faking it *is* making it!" she laughed. Such approaches mirror well-established Cuban practices of "invention" (*invención*), whereby the social skill required to materially "resolve" (*resolver*) challenges is a fundamental element of being a successful Cuban in the eyes of others (Del Real and Pertierra 2008).

For many decades, Cuban migration was understood as a one-way process: "[O]nce Cubans come to Miami, very few return" (Stepick 1994a, 130). New Cubans like Yani evidence the way migration is becoming a more circular process, implying not only leaving home but also realizing the "mythical return" (Kasbarian 2009) multiple times, which has long been discussed amid other diasporas, but which for so long was not a readily available or ideologically palatable option for most Cubans. Given the distinct politics and socioeconomic status of many of these New Cubans compared to earlier waves of immigrants to Miami, interlocutors like Yani are also now more open to making migration a more circular process. They are often the sole family member to have emigrated, while earlier waves of Cuban migrants would often move as a family unit. Thus, these New Cubans now also carry an increased responsibility, or even duty, to maintain material links with relatives back on the island. The key role of the narrative of "successful return" revolves around migrants' ability to move back to or visit their place of origin with sufficient earnings to create a comfortable life for themselves and others (Byron 2005; Horst 2011b; Olwig 2012).

This act of return is a highly material one, hinging upon the movement of goods, objects, and people across borders and spaces, and the most visible of objects (such as clothing, gold jewelry, home furnishings, and so forth) become particularly important in performing such a return. As Richard Wilk aptly remarks, just as "people use objects to invent tradition, they also use them to invent the future" (1995, 98), and in this case they use conspicuous consumption to perform imagined futures in the present (see also chapter 5). Superficially, this might appear as emulation, but here it is not so much a question of copying as of producing modes of selfhood; the image of success is tantamount to success itself. The very items that might be read as statements of emulation in one context can be reconsidered as emblems of local categories of success in another.

"When I go back, I'm a king"

Oscar is in his late thirties, and has lived in Hialeah for twelve years, but travels back to Havana several times a year to check on his business interests there. From his family house in a well-to-do neighborhood of Havana he runs a tourism company, arranging "authentic" visits for high-paying

American clients who want to meet "real" Cuban artists, musicians, and the like. His mother remains in Havana to attend to their guests, and Oscar handles the business side of things in the U.S. He also ensures his mother and their employees have all the supplies they need, and often undertakes trips back and forth to carry material items and hard cash. When he is unable to carry items himself, he sends them with friends or with *mulas* ("mules," or people who carry items across national borders; see chapter 3), in return for a small cut of the profit. Back in Havana his family is doing well, and has in fact just purchased their next-door neighbor's house for a bargain price: the neighbor had been caught embezzling money and fled to Miami, and so was willing to strike a good bargain in return for being paid for the property in dollars on "the other side" in Miami.[10] And so Oscar's business is soon set to expand, and he plans to put in a bar/art gallery space next door to increase his revenue.

As I sit with him on the veranda of his Hialeah apartment, he reclines in his chair, smoking a cigarette and stretching out contentedly. "For me, it's perfect being able to split my life fifty-fifty between the two places," he tells me. In Hialeah he was living on limited means and had in fact gone a few months with no work. The recent "acoustic attack" and subsequent reduction of U.S. embassy services in Havana (2017–2018) was causing consternation, and business had slowed somewhat. "But here I also feel free, you know? I can go to gay bars and come home with a different guy every night and that's fine, 'cause I live on my own. I don't have people breathing down my neck and meddling in my business all the time." But likewise, Oscar's access to material items of cultural cachet in Miami meant that his life had significantly improved over in Havana as well. "Over there I'm the boss now. The guys I grew up with on the same street as me are the guys I pay to come 'round and fix things, and if they speak to me in a way I don't like, I can send them packing," he told me. "All the people in the area who own restaurants and stuff know who I am, and they give me discounts because I take tourists there. In Havana, when I go back, I'm like a king! It doesn't matter who my family were before; now it's all about who has money and things, and then you can make stuff happen."

A couple of months later, I went to visit Oscar and his mother in their house in Havana, where they were preparing to host a group of wealthy American tourists for an evening of cigars, rum, and jazz. Oscar had got an old childhood friend to come and serve as barman, and this friend had also brought along his girlfriend to wait on tables. Shortly before the guests arrived, the girl showed up at the back door, her hair carefully tied back and sporting eye-wateringly high stiletto heels and fishnet stockings. "Oh, for God's sake!" Oscar muttered to me as he caught sight of her, "no one here has any idea about dress sense. . . ." He marched over to her and told her to remove the garments, which, to his mind, made her look "like a whore, not high-class like the people coming here this evening." She disappeared into a back room and reemerged twenty minutes later, by which time the guests had started arriving. Oscar later told me she had been "grateful" for the explanation: "she has no reference point for these things, so it's helpful when someone like me can explain how to look high-class." When I quizzed him about it more the following day, he clarified that "she obviously got those things from someone who'd smuggled them in from Hialeah. Taste here is defined by excess, not restraint. So, lots of color, lots of sex, lots of bling. But that's not what those wealthy Americans wanted to see, it's not classy."

Fast-forward another few months, and I found myself in an expensive cocktail bar in the affluent neighborhood of South Miami Beach, seated opposite Oscar and a young Venezuelan guy he had recently met online. Oscar was dressed up in tight ripped jeans, slip-on suede shoes, and several thick gold chains hanging against a tight white shirt. While we waited for our drinks, he and his friend began bickering, which gradually increased in volume until most of the bar had little choice but to listen in. From the next table over, I heard a haughty older Cuban American woman, dressed in expensive designer brands more akin to highly "cultured" values in an American tradition, complain to her companion "these new Cubans. They really are everywhere!"

#onlyinHialeah

The need to visibly perform material success-through-excess both in Cuba and among New Cubans in Hialeah also, unsurprisingly, assumes the role of visibly demarcating Cubans by socioeconomic class and diasporic generation. Gold has long been particularly esteemed in Cuban culture— indeed, across Latin America—as a constant symbol of wealth and social prestige. Much of the origin myth of the "discovery" of Latin America revolves around this precious metal; the small lumps of gold that Columbus took back from the island of Hispaniola (now the Dominican Republic and Haiti) in 1493 were enough to convince the Spanish monarchs to fund a second, more organized expedition, and by 1510 Spain was transporting African and Indigenous people across the entire continent to labor in

"Fake It to Make It": Conspicuously Consuming Fantasy in Hialeah and Havana · 51

mines. A year later, King Ferdinand was said to have instructed his armies to "get gold, humanely, if possible, but at all costs, get gold," setting in place the fabled search for the legendary city of gold, El Dorado.

To this day, across much of the Spanish-speaking world, gold remains a solid, dependable valuable, which can be drawn upon in times of need; a period of austerity across much of Europe and Latin America has consequently seen an increase in pawnshops advertising for gold specifically (Barragan 2014; Bernstein 2000). Many Cubans (of all ages) wear as much gold as they can, from necklaces and bracelets to watches, earrings, and even golden teeth, as a "symbolic medium of wealth . . . aimed at displaying an image of successful identity" (Rausenberger 2018, 834). Gold has long been valued also for its multiple affordances to be held as an economic reserve that may be redeemed when needed, as a repository of family or cultural heritage, and, of course, as an item to be displayed performatively (Moors 1998, 208). Moreover, at the outset of the Special Period, a whole generation of Cubans was encouraged to hand over family relics made of gold to the government (in exchange for symbolic currency that could be spent on much-needed goods in a government-run chain of stores), making it even harder to come by in Cuban families on the island today (Rosenblum 2013, 101).

The strong influence of Cuban rap, hip-hop, and reggaetón music has also become an important nexus for promoting what might be called a "bling culture" in Cuba (Gámez Torres 2012; Whynacht 2009), which of course also draws on visual tropes from across the world, most especially from the neighboring United States. Product placement in music videos, disseminated with greater reach through new digital circulation networks (see chapter 4), and combined with increasing flows of tourists and return migrants from Miami, have driven brand promotion as well as tastes for symbols of conspicuous wealth, often including blingy jewelry and clothing. This sits comfortably within Cuban frameworks of material care, wherein it is deemed important to look after one's own clothes and present oneself with care. I have often seen Cuban men in Havana carry a cushion (or newspaper) through the streets with them, to enable them to sit down in white trousers without dirtying them. Much of this clothing is procured initially in Hialeah, which in turn orients its business needs toward the tastes and desires of the island.

A particular style, articulated somewhere in a fantasized space of success between Hialeah and Havana, has thus emerged since around 2010,

52 · Part I. Creating Value

known across wider Miami as "Hialeah chic," which to older migratory cohorts in Greater Miami is largely associated with vulgar, gaudy displays of "blingtastic" wealth. The need to outperform one's friends through symbols of socioeconomic status (in particular, gold, but also branded consumer goods and cars) is so visible in Hialeah as to warrant frequent discussion in the media (Moreno 2017) and across social platforms, resulting in the popular hashtag #onlyinHialeah. Established Cuban American comedians and celebrities have played on such stereotypes, drawing humor from tensions between the middle-class earlier waves of Cuban migrants and their disdain for the "poor" or "vulgar" taste of more recent migrants, who have been raised with different aesthetic and cultural referents regarding taste and class.

A popular social media channel called "cubalseros" (combining Cuba with the word "balseros," typically portrayed as low-class Cuban refugees who came to the U.S. for economic rather than ideological reasons) celebrates and scorns images of New Cubans in Hialeah, for example, ridiculing their "vulgarity." It's safe to say, then, that the desire to outperform one another through potlatch-esque tournaments of conspicuous consumption (both online and off-line) does not stem from New Cubans' need to somehow fit into the preexisting Cuban social landscape in Greater Miami. Although conspicuous material consumption in Cuba can be traced back through many centuries of close connection with the U.S., the competitive and performative aspects of the practices outlined in this chapter have their origins in the decades of economic scarcity and hardship experienced on the island from the 1990s, which in turn fused notions of material care with social success and kinship embeddedness.

There have been various social theories of material excess, most of which explain the performativity of expenditure in functional terms: for Veblen (1899), it marks a display of status; for Simmel (1957), the differentiation of socioeconomic class; for Baudrillard (1981) and Bourdieu (1984), it is the communication of a social identity; while for Douglas and Isherwood, excess is a means to regulate sociality (1979). Drawing on Sidney Mintz's (1986) work looking at the transition of sugar from luxury to staple commodity, Samuel Martínez takes a less-utilitarian line, making a case for excess as "sensation," whereby for those living on the edge of poverty, nonutilitarian expenditure of money can signify setting aside "humiliation, mistreatment, and indifference to their most basic needs from wider society" (2007; 2009, 220).

This keen interest in performing material success has various parallels with people belonging to other historical waves of migration to the United States, for whom "a peculiar faith in the principle of a rising standard of living" has been considered a crucial aspect of Americanization, with the adaptation of immigrants to the "perspective of abundance" constituting an "essential part" of adapting to American life (Heinze 1990, 3, 21–26; Kammen 2012; Potter 2009). For many of my newly arrived Cuban interlocutors, there was certainly an element of exploring ways to enjoy the tropes of a new life, making their many sacrifices feel more worthwhile. Crucially, though, the outward performativity of this excess, directed firmly back toward Cuba, also reveals these New Cubans to be embedded in a dense network of transnational kin ties, which in turn relate to notions of being a "good" Cuban, as will be explored in chapter 2.

For many of these New Cubans, such success is visibly performed in Hialeah precisely to be broadcast back to Havana, even at times to the denigration and scorn of wider society in Miami, which commends distinct cultural logics of taste and distinction, drawing on different socioeconomic notions of class and material culture. For Bourdieu (1984), the concept of taste is more fixed and localized, an "ahistorical structuralism" that fails to account for the historical changes produced in culture through class struggle (Gartman 1991, 421). In understanding these esthetics of distinction or success exhibited by the New Cubans, we must ground our interpretations in the struggles of a generation that is attempting to span differing cultural constructions of socioeconomic class in both Cuba and the U.S., and also maintain the priority for most New Cubans, which remains imagining, performing, and therefore embodying (quite literally) the successful returnee.

This performativity of being is something that will be a recurring theme throughout this book, and to which I will return in the concluding chapter. For those Cubans who have left the island in the last decade or so, for whom symbolic referents of socioeconomic class may not necessarily map onto hegemonic notions of "gaudiness" or "vulgarity" held by previous migratory cohorts, the localized interpretation of such consumptive practices reveals a group of people suspended between two social worlds, trying to personify success to a dual audience across transnational contexts in order to realize a glittering future for themselves and their families. These New Cubans are living in one social world, but playing to the rules of another, navigating a more complex set of taste practices across a transnational setting than Bourdieu's original formulation allows for.

The Magic City

Perhaps also, in a sense, the fantastical presentations and reinventions of self we have seen in this chapter embody Miami to its core. Since its foundation, Miami has constructed itself as a landscape where dreams come true—a real fairyland or site of transgression (Capó 2017). It is no coincidence that Walt Disney chose to construct his theme park in Florida, which was conceived of as a destination to which to flee from hard and cold realities from as early as the nineteenth century. From its very beginnings, then, this metropolis, built out of swamp and mangroves, has possessed an "air of unreality, a playground divorced from its natural habitat by the deeds of Yankee developers. For a while it seemed that no fantasy, no matter how farfetched, could not be enacted here" (Portes and Stepick 1993, xi). This fantasy has continued to this day, with celebrity sightings, round-the-clock entertainment, and discourses of instant wealth underscoring Miami as a destination for those escaping the hard realities of winter for a fun-loving, fast-paced, fashionable lifestyle bathed in sunshine.

Its reputation as the "magic city" has taken on financial connotations, too, and for many Latin American investors it has acquired the reputation of "a hyperreal vision of urban paradise" (F. Rivera 2019, 63), compounded by its status as investment and cruise-ship capital of the broader region. Leisure and wealth are two sides of the same coin in a city obsessed with money and its conspicuous mobilization. A myth seems to have emerged around the fabled Miami, then, where precarity can be converted into excess, poverty into luxury, making it a potential frontier between precarious pasts and successful futures.

Anna Tsing has conceived of "frontier culture" as "a conjuring act because it creates the wild and spreading regionality of its imagination. It conjures a self-conscious translocalism, committed to the obliteration of local places" (2011, 68). Yet Miami, and in particular Hialeah with its abundance of conspicuous consumption, seems not so much an obliteration of local places as a constant reinvention of them through lenses of the imagined global. Hialeahans respond to economic and aesthetic shifts in Havana just as much as Havana syncs itself with the imagined West of *la Yuma*. For Arjun Appadurai, the imagination "has now acquired a singular new power in social life" (1996, 52). In the case of Miami and Havana, this has long been the case: for decades each has lived in the shadow of the fantasy of the other, and for many New Cubans arriving in Hialeah confronted with precarious reality rather than a fairyland, a crucial part of "making it" in Miami is to mirror this fantasy of success to others, both in Hialeah and Havana.

Conclusion

In Nancy Munn's work on Kula exchange on the island of Gawa, she describes how individuals strive to rise through "levels of value" to extend their influence in what she terms "intersubjective spacetime" (1987). In this formulation of how value is created and expanded through material exchange, Munn stresses that value emerges in "creative action," or what we might loosely call "labor" within a much-expanded sense of a Marxian paradigm of value creation (Foster 2008b, 17). This is the process by which a person's invisible potency is transformed into realized, perceptible form. In the Melanesian case, this value manifests in the form of "fame"; one's rise through levels of value demands social recognition, not only political prestige or economic wealth. Munn's line of thinking challenges the oft-fetishized dichotomy between gift and commodity; rather than choosing between the market value of objects and the importance of social relations, we see both as refractions of the same thing. As Appadurai notes, then, the Kula as a material network of relation constitutes a "complex system for the intercalibration of the biographies of persons and things." He continues,

> [A]s in the Kula, so in such tournaments of value generally, strategic skill is culturally measured by the success with which actors attempt diversions or subversions of culturally conventionalized paths for the flow of things. (1986, 21–22)

When we think about value chains as socially embedded within networks of perspectives, we also encourage a form of labor politics "that takes shape as a politics of knowledge" (Foster 2008a, 20). In other words, through the exchange and consumption of things (which have their own biographies and social meanings), people produce and circulate value, but also produce *themselves* as valuable, in whatever guise that takes at a local level. For many New Cubans in Hialeah, the acquisition of the visible tropes of success (akin, perhaps, to how Munn uses "fame" as socially visible value) in fact causes scorn in their immediate surroundings and is interpreted by previous cohorts of (more middle-class, phenotypically white) Old Cubans as "vulgar." An ethnographic interrogation of these consumptive practices through transnational circulation, however, reveals similar motivations to

56 · Part I. Creating Value

those Munn describes as central to Kula exchange circuits. While I do not suggest that t-shirts or jewelry are directly comparable to Kula armshells and necklaces—they certainly do not belong to such an elaborate hierarchy as set out in the Kula Ring—I do argue that these material goods, and the symbolism they project by moving back and forth across New Cubans' kinship transnational networks, express what Munn calls the "fame of Gawa" through an emerging Cuban cultural idiom.

New Cuban migrants arriving in Hialeah seek to perform material success according to the idiom developed under socialism of an imagined capitalist "West" known as *la Yuma*. Such fables have at their core a long-shared history of material exchange between Cuba and Miami, which has endured through decades of economic embargo, alongside intense promotion of Miami as a magic city of dreams. The acquisition (even if only temporarily) of such items becomes part of a strategy to construct a new "normal" for oneself (Jansen 2015; Rausing 2002), as well as a way of constructing oneself as successful and a person of value. Moreover, the ability to perform and even embody such symbols of material success maps directly onto key Cuban approaches to the expansion of the social self in the world (Härkönen 2015, 2018).

Cuban notions of "inventiveness" as a tool for successfully navigating the challenges of life become central to interpreting current tastes for conspicuous consumption both in Havana and Hialeah, as well as differing models of ownership, while belying a strong sense of individual agency mobilized toward making things happen for oneself. Meanwhile, Miami has long assumed the role of a liminal or even magical fantasyland, and as such the city is also a frontier among past, present and future, where futures can come true if you make them. Material success in New Cuban terms becomes defined in terms of access to both people and things—and particularly people or things that have the ability to move back and forth between Miami and Havana, physically or symbolically—more than in terms of ownership, as in the traditional American dream of "making it." This is also a key arena in which the foundations of desire for material goods in Cuba take shape within cultural logics of value performed within diasporic communities outside of the island, the ramifications of which will be explored in chapters 3, 4, and 5. For new arrivals from Havana, then, the conspicuous performance of material success, which through an etic Old Cuban lens might be read as somehow "fake," is at an emic level in fact tantamount to making it in Miami for New Cubans, who, by sheer force of will, convert an imagined future into the material present. Moreover, material care establishes itself as a key premise of Cuban systems of kinship, and thus the overtly visible performance of material care evidently fits into a growing diaspora's preoccupations with maintaining close links to relatives back home, as we will see in the next chapter.

2

The Ties That Bind

Remitting Kinship to Cuba

After a couple of months of regularly going back and forth to Cuba from Miami International Airport, one of the security guards had started to recognize me, or rather, to recognize the increasingly long and apparently random list of items I had in my carry-on luggage each time I passed through. "What've you got in there this time?" he would quip. "Anything I'm supposed to confiscate? Any more sex toys and drugs?" he'd ask with a wry wink. André was very used to seeing mulas in all shapes and sizes carrying weird and wonderful objects through to the departure gates, Cuba-bound, but most were tense about going back to Cuba and anxious to deliver their goods, and certainly not open to some casual chatter and light flirtation. He himself, as a Cuban migrant who had come to Miami in the '90s, was all too familiar with the scarcities on the island fueling this flow of goods, and jokes provided the perfect vehicle for expressing his ambivalence about such things without getting "too political" (Yeh 2017). Meanwhile I, with my privileged British-citizen status, felt more at ease traveling to Cuba than most Americans or Cuban Americans typically did, accompanied as always by a large quantity of material goods that I was to deliver to an ever-growing list of friends and their relatives on the other side.

On the previous occasion when I had bumped into André, I had been carrying some supplies to a friend's cousin (who owned a brothel in Havana and had requested "business supplies"), as well as various medications to acquaintances with an array of maladies, and some gifts anticipating the birth of my new "nephew." My friend Clara, who was shortly to give birth to her second child, had been receiving items from relatives in Hialeah courtesy of my research trips for several months by that point, and I had found myself absorbed into this growing family dynamic. After a few deliveries, I was invited in to stay for dinner, and noticed Clara had started jokingly referring to me as her "big sister." "You shouldn't joke about such things," chided her mother from across a plate heavy with rice and plantains, before insisting I serve myself with another bowlful. "You build your family [*se construye la familia*], and 'la Yeni' [Jenny] is more present here than half of that bunch over in Miami."

Eduardo Viveiros de Castro writes of the "mysterious effectiveness of relationality" (2009, 243), or how it is that people experience transpersonal ways of being, insofar as they live each other's lives, and die each other's deaths. Marshall Sahlins follows suit with his conceptualization of "mutuality of being" to cover a variety of local formulations of what denotes kinship, whether by procreation, social construction, or a combination of the two (2011a, 2011b). Advocates for a "new kinship" have most typically concentrated upon this "mutuality" as constituted through substantive "flows" (Carsten 1995b, 2011; Strathern 1988; R. Wagner 1977) or "vectors" (Hutchinson 2000). A focus upon "substance" as key to relatedness has effected a shift of attention toward bodily flows and transfers, highlighting fluidity, transferability, and transformability in analyses linking kinship, gender, and the body. Anthropologists have expanded our frameworks of what constitutes kinship to incorporate a variety of substances—blood, semen, milk, bone, genes, flesh, soul, food, and so on—as central to understanding relatedness as a fundamentally culturally constituted process that often cites transfer or flow of a substance as an idiom of relatedness.

In this chapter I employ these analytical frameworks of "substantive flow" from "new" kinship studies to focus upon the material flows of transnational social remittances, arguing that these material flows are equally crucial to the cultural construction of relatedness, personhood, and identity. Daniel Miller's work on the everyday act of shopping and material consumption points to how flows of material things create and maintain kinship, as relationships of all kinds are grounded in and continually recreated through material relations and the consumption of goods (1987, 2001). Material culture becomes a valuable lens onto kinship as it often belies normative attitudes toward how a relationship "should" be within a particular cultural framework, compared with how it actually is; it is through the act of consuming and giving material items to others that we perform and realize our relatedness to them.

In this chapter, then, I too conceptualize relatedness or kinship through a lens of substantive flow, but rather than tracing substances that are socially constructed as "biological" (such as blood, etc.), I instead focus upon material items more typically conceived of as inert (such as money and material remittances), and follow Viviana Zelizer's (1994, 2005) example in linking these items to realms of affect and emotion. In so doing, I seek to connect what I see as complementary approaches within social anthropology (Carsten 2004; Strathern 1992), material culture (Mauss 1954; 1997b; Munn 1987; Weiner 1992), remittance studies (Burman 2006; Levitt 1998; Levitt and Lamba-Nieves 2011), and diaspora studies (Bernal 2014; Brah 2005; Brinkerhoff 2009; Clifford 1994) to show how the transnational flow of material items between the Cuban diaspora and their relatives (broadly conceptualized) on the island is key to the creation and maintenance of notions of relatedness and Cuban identity both at home and abroad. Moreover, an examination of ties of relatedness through this lens of social-material remittances provides us with new ways of envisaging kinship and personhood across national borders, and the way these are constructed and affirmed through the circulation of material goods in a geopolitical context where things must often move in the stead of people.

A Brief History of Cuban American "Substantive Flows"

Despite the U.S. embargo of Cuba since 1962, people, ideas, practices, and money have continually traveled (albeit at times irregularly) between Havana and Miami. To many of my interlocutors this seemed obvious, yet most scholarly accounts do not clock this. Susan Eckstein maintains, for example, that between 1959 and 1989 "most Cuban émigrés and island Cubans reinforced the socially constructed wall across the Straits that their respective governments had put in place," and that they did so because they ascribed to the values on which the wall was premised, namely, "disassociation with compatriots who opposed their stance on the revolution" (2014, 289). Furthermore, social dynamics on both sides of the Florida Straits discouraged cross-border ties, meaning such transfers were often covert, and not easily documented.

Although we have very limited accurate data on remittances to Cuba, it is certainly probable that in comparison with other Latin American populations in Miami, the Cuban diaspora remitted less back home in the decades immediately after the revolution. The imposition of economic and diplomatic sanctions against Cuba (otherwise known simply as the embargo) by the United States in 1962 made it extremely challenging for Cuban exiles who had arrived in Miami to maintain contact with relatives left behind on the island. Moreover, most Cuban exiles were unwilling to send material or financial support to a place where they judged an enemy regime would seize and appropriate the efforts of their labor. Hostilities were in turn mirrored by the Cuban state; in Castro's first years of rule, the government tightened control over the populace's use of dollars, the possession of which subsequently was made illegal in the late 1970s. Moreover, during much of the Soviet era the Cuban state stigmatized those who fled in opposition to the revolution and penalized those who remained and maintained diasporic ties by denying them Communist Party membership, which carried further socioeconomic repercussions.

Nonetheless, dating as far back as the 1960s, even the most cursory look at the Cuban exile press reveals just how common shipments to Cuba were at the time. In the most anti-Castro publications imaginable, one finds advertisements for individual agents, pharmacies, full-fledged companies, and mom-and-pop operations pledging to help Cubans send canned foods, vitamins, even complete *Noche Buena* (Christmas Eve) dinners to their relatives (Bustamante 2021). A small number of exiles clearly did continue to maintain some form of contact with relatives on the island, even though sending items was an enormous logistical and emotional challenge (not to mention an illegal one), which involved sending parcels via a third country such as Mexico, Canada, or Spain, at great expense. Such transfers generally had to happen discreetly, partly due to the embargo, and partly due to societal pressures within Cuban Miami. In some cases, family back on the island was more important than political stance, and many went to great ends to find ways of supporting kin from a distance while disguising the fact from others in Cuban Miami.

In 1980, 125,000 Cubans were permitted to flee Cuba in the Mariel boatlift and settled predominantly in Miami. This third wave of migrants was generally more inclined to maintain contact with relatives back on the island and participate materially in their lives (Eckstein 2006, 156). Their ability to do so varied throughout the following decade, depending on volatile U.S. policies toward remittances and travel to the island. This trend continued in the 1990s, and the economic collapse of Cuba after the fall of the Soviet Union further induced many Cubans in Miami to find ways of sending material and financial aid to their relatives back on the island. While U.S policies still greatly restricted this, a change in the Cuban government's response to diasporic support facilitated increased flows between the two places; where they had portrayed émigrés as *gusanos* (worms) before, they now began to reframe the diaspora as a "Cuban community abroad."

Despite U.S. government attempts to limit remittance flows only to "immediate kin" (a definition which, as will be discussed later, is problematic in a Cuban kinship cosmology), remittances continued to rise throughout the 1990s, as Cubans both on the island and in Miami took the initiative in accelerating contact and material flows connecting the two communities. In an effort to catch up with a booming black market fueled by scarcities and informal use of two currencies, the Cuban government consequently legalized possession of dollars in 1993, and by the end of the decade the state had even become a transnational hard-currency transfer agent (Eckstein 2010, 1050), with state-owned remittance businesses facilitating cross-border income-sharing and profiting in the process. By the early 2000s the state was receiving over $100 million in wire service charges of up to 30 percent of the transfer amount (Barberia 2004, 382; Eckstein 2010, 1050). It was during this period that the Cuban government also permitted pre-1971 émigrés to return to visit for the first time on U.S. passports (this is still the case, although these émigrés must also apply for an HE-11 visa). Remittances to Cuba increased steadily between 1990 and 2020, most notably during the Obama administration (2009–2017), with estimated figures rising from $2.6 billion to $5.7 billion between 2010 and 2015 alone, placing Cuba as the number-one recipient of remittances in all of Latin America and the Caribbean during this period (World Development Indicators Database).

Meanwhile, attitudes toward receiving material goods in Cuba from diasporic relatives have also changed considerably since the 1990s. While Cubans might once have been socially shunned for possessing counterrevolutionary symbols of American-style consumerism, the materialistic lifestyle commonly associated with the United States has become increasingly valued in Cuban culture on the island, and imported goods are coveted, particularly by younger generations. By the early 2000s, one out of every ten Cuban Americans had traveled back to Cuba at least once, and this number rose to one in every three in South Florida (Duany 2007, 167). Meanwhile, Cubans on the island were spending 75–80 percent of their remittances at government-owned dollar stores,[1] thus meaning most diaspora dollars flowed to the state sector ("Report on Cuba" 2004). It was still difficult to send these remittances from Miami however, due to increased restrictions under President George W. Bush's administration, and so the diaspora sought alternative mechanisms which offered more flexibility. The use of mulas has emerged as a crucial means of creating and maintaining contact with relatives on the island (see also chapter 3); in 2005, 18 percent of senders were using informal travels to transport money, and this figure had risen to 44 percent by 2008 (Orozco 2009, 4). At the time of my fieldwork, Cubans in Miami were on average sending $200 a month back to the island, on top of an average $3,500 they carried with them on their annual trips to the island (Morales 2017).

It was only in 2009 under the Obama administration that restrictions were removed from remittance-sending processes, allowing the number of small businesses both in the U.S. and Cuba that operated in this arena to expand exponentially. Jorge Duany documents forty-seven companies based in the U.S specializing in the delivery of material goods to Cuba in 2004 (2007, 167), with more than 50,000 parcels being sent monthly from the United States to Cuba in 2002 (Barberia 2004, 397). In 2018, I counted eighty-six within two square miles in Hialeah alone. Several of the courier service providers I spoke to said they expected to earn more than $100,000 that year, and it is worth noting only the smallest operators seemed willing to talk to me.

At the time of my fieldwork, at least 50 percent of remittances sent to Cuba were thought to be transported by mulas (Hansing and Orozco 2014), although this is of course difficult to measure; others have put the figure of covert transfers at as high as 75 percent (Eckstein 2003, 15). Alongside employing mulas, many Cuban Americans were also sending money to island kin through "mini-banks" that circumvented both U.S. and Cuban regulations, whereby they deposited money with a Cuban American in Miami, and their relatives withdrew the amount from the banker's relatives on the other side almost immediately. Such transfers are often facilitated by services that allow the diaspora to top up their relatives' phone credit in Cuba remotely (see figure 2.1). Cuban Americans are 20 percent more likely to remit through informal channels than people remitting to other countries studied by the Pew Hispanic Center (Spiegel 2004, 87), largely because of ongoing limitations imposed by government bodies. In September 2019, the U.S. Treasury announced new restrictions limiting remittances to $1,000 per quarter to a "single close relative," and Western Union ceased transfers between the U.S and Cuba in November 2020; thus, while this research took place during a brief yet key moment of opening between the U.S and Cuba, we might reasonably presume informal channels of transfer will continue to increase in prevalence as policies and restrictions continue to shift.

What has become clear is how crucial the material flows of remittances have become to the economy and everyday well-being of regular Cubans on the island. Indeed, they have become the main source of income—either directly or through provision of materials for work (Statista 2019)—reaching

Figure 2.1. Sign advertising immediate cell-phone credit transfers from Hialeah (U.S.) to Cuba. Photo by author, May 2018.

as many as 70 percent of Cubans (Morales 2018). By 2017, cash remittances sent from across the whole world to Cuba (i.e., not including material items such as food, clothing, toiletries, medicines, restaurant and hotel supplies, etc.) totaled almost $3.5 billion, with a further estimated $3 billion in remitted goods; when combined, these flows are likely worth more than any of Cuba's export goods, including nickel, sugar, and tobacco (Morales 2018). The diaspora is the main provider of start-up capital for Cuba's rapidly expanding private sector and of the material resources required to start a business. As Katrin Hansing describes, "a casual visit to Miami's international airport attests to the strength of these transnational entrepreneurial ties, where long lines of Cubans regularly check in huge amounts of goods, ranging from pizza ovens to gym equipment, bound for the island" (2015; see also chapter 3).

Peggy Levitt and Deepak Lamba-Nieves describe social remittances' capacity to "scale up and scale out" (2011, 3), whereby remittances not only affect local-level organizational culture and practice, but also exert influence at regional and national levels, including the domains of economics, politics, education, racial equality, health, and religion. The vast expansion in remittance flows since the ease on restrictions under the Obama administration has without doubt had considerable impact on all levels of Cuban society. Earnings have come to hinge more on whom you know abroad than on hard work or education; it is commonplace to earn more as a waiter in a bar funded by diasporic money than as a doctor or lawyer. Remittances have also unquestionably fueled an informal black market (see chapters 3–6), contributing to a broader undermining of state moral authority. Moreover, these remittance flows have arguably eroded revolutionary precepts (Eckstein 2010, 1053) insofar as they have fostered a rising individualism and acquisitiveness in opposition to earlier emphases on collectivity and non-materialistic values (Holbraad 2014b, 2017). Finally, the majority of diasporic Cubans who remit to relatives on the island are white, and thus a large inequality is opening yet further along ethnic lines on the island, whereby Afro-Cubans have less access to the material goods and money so necessary to assert oneself in Cuba's emerging private sector (Blue 2007; de la Fuente 2016; Eckstein 2003; Hansing 2018; Hansing and Hoffmann 2020; Hansing and Orozco 2014).

The everyday human stories that in fact underpin these flows are, however, often obscured or overlooked in the larger economic debates that typically focus on quantifying monetary flows in and out of Cuba. Remitting, after all, is not just a transfer of material items, but a mechanism of familial and cultural reaffirmation. Remitting is a form of kin work, maintaining affective relationships over time and distance (Zontini 2004). Scholars working on remittance flows in the Pacific region have suggested a different metaphor—that of a network—to encapsulate the way such flows are "fluid and dynamic and [do] not recognize preconstituted boundaries such as the nation or the household . . . [but rather] the flows and practices that govern them" (Marsters, Lewis, and Friesen 2006, 43). In this light we can see the Cuban family as unbounded and constituted in part by the flows of people, identities, and remittances, as well as the practices involved in enacting this kin work. Moreover, building on ideas about personhood from the Pacific region, persons can frequently construct themselves as the plural composite sites of the relationships that produce them; a singular person can be imagined as a social microcosm insofar as they channel and reproduce the relationships of those around them, which, in the Cuban case, is enacted through material circulation.

"La cosa está de madre"

Milagros was born to a low-income family in Western Cuba in 1943, one of six children her father had by two different women. Aged fifteen, she met and fell in love with Alberto, who, out of "respect" for Milagros's virginity until they married, had also impregnated a local servant girl, Elisa. With the arrival of the Cuban revolution in 1959, Alberto left for the United States, leaving behind his wife Milagros (who, it turned out, was pregnant with their daughter Lilia), as well as Elisa and her daughter Eva, with the promise that he would send for Milagros and their daughter as soon as he could. Several years went by with no sign of Alberto, and so, on September 21, 1966, Milagros managed to get herself and her five-year-old daughter Lilia onto one of the "Freedom Flights" couriering Cubans to Miami exile, leaving behind her whole world, not out of political aversion to the situation on the island so much as a deep-set desire to find the father of her child, and leave behind the daily reminder of his infidelity.

Upon arrival, the by now twenty-one-year-old Milagros set about trying to locate Alberto, which, given her inability to speak English, proved difficult. She presented the immigration authorities with the last letter she had received from him—which had a return address marked from California—and not long after, she and her young daughter found themselves with one-way tickets bound there. If Miami had been difficult to navigate, California would prove even more so, but she was fortunate to soon make the acquaintance of a Cuban man there—Nuño—who offered to help her find her husband. Nuño drove her to the front door of the address Milagros had last been given, and together, she and little Lilia went and rang the doorbell. A blonde woman with a newborn baby in her arms answered the door; Alberto had evidently remarried (despite not having divorced Milagros), and now had a third child.

Eventually Milagros married Nuño, who had in fact been in love with her the whole time, and who himself had left behind a wife and child (Juana and Guillermo) in Cuba when he fled the country. As their family grew with the arrival of two more children (Ines and Esteban), they worked all hours to scrape by, and Milagros managed to get a job as a seamstress at which she would stitch clothing on an industrial sewing machine rented from a local factory while her children slept, only to wake them and begin her full-time day job as mother of three in the morning. Lilia grew up as a full-time interpreter, helping her mother navigate an anglophone world. The family eventually moved back to Miami and scrimped and saved to provide both

The Ties That Bind: Remitting Kinship to Cuba · 67

for themselves and any other people in the local Cuban community who needed help as they arrived to new lives. Unlike most of the exile Cuban community in Miami, Milagros had not left the island for ideological reasons so much as a desire to reunite with family, and so, unusually for the time, she started trying to find ways of sending items back to loved ones on the island from as early as 1966. "It was so hard to get in touch with them, it was so expensive to call and even when you got through, the line would break up or something. At first, I sent medicines and chewing gum they could sell, disguised as vitamins." By 1969, Milagros had found a relative in Spain who was able to forward parcels on to her mother back in Cuba, and so whenever they could save up enough to procure items, they would be dispatched to Spain. In 1977 Nuño and Milagros lost years' worth of hard-earned savings—over $8,000—to people smugglers who claimed they could get Milagros's mother Lourdes and her husband Arturo out of Cuba through Mexico. While the setback was a considerable blow, they immediately set about trying to save again to find another way, and the pair eventually succeeded in getting to the U.S. via Costa Rica, several years later, thanks to Milagros and Nuño's financial help.

At that point, the Cuban government would not allow post-1970 exiles to return with a U.S. passport (a policy that continues to this day), and so most exiles felt unable to return to the island for fear that on entering with their Cuban passports, they could be imprisoned there. By 1978, Milagros's concern for her relatives on the island had grown so acute that she decided to send her second child—Ines, who was born on American soil and by this point was nine years old—to Cuba on her own to deliver packages to relatives who would meet her there. She carried with her packages for Milagros's parents, and her siblings and their children, as well as for Nuño's family, and also Elisa and Eva (Alberto's abandoned family). The following year, Milagros was able to return to the island to visit for the first time since her departure 17 years earlier: "Everything was different, but everything was also kind of the same. They were all still there, my family [*familia*], and distance doesn't change that."

Such notions of familia bonds clearly do not rest on culturally constructed notions of biological relatedness or blood alone, as a year later, Milagros and Nuño took in Alberto's brother and his wife, Manolo and Rosalia, after they fled Cuba in the Mariel boatlift. Lilia, who by that point was a teenager and studying for exams, spent six months sleeping on the sofa so that they could all fit into the small Miami home, and by 1990 Lilia, too, had started to send remittances to Cuba, to an extended family she for the most part had never met or even spoken to. Milagros still sends packages to Karel, the "*mulatico*" village boy, who is the son of her half-sister's neighbor, and who, as a darker-skinned Cuban, receives no remittances from relatives abroad otherwise.[2] When I asked her why she went to such trouble to provide materially for a boy who did not seem to be related to her, she simply replied, "He's family [*Es familia*]. And if he wasn't before, he is now."

Throughout the 2000s and 2010s, Milagros began to visit the island with increasing frequency, carrying packages and money to an extended chain of relatives, and their relatives, and their relatives' friends or neighbors, as well as usually delivering parcels from her daughter Lilia on behalf of her growing nuclear family as well. At other times, Lilia would find contacts at work who were visiting the island who could take her mother's parcels for free; indeed, I myself became entwined in these familial flows when I offered to carry parcels from Milagros and Lilia to Iris and her son Dayron, who are both distant descendants of Milagros's mother's third cousin, Melania.

With improvements in communication technologies, it has become easier for Milagros and her daughter Lilia to keep in touch with relatives, but also for relatives to make specific requests of them, some of which are challenging to procure. On one of my visits, Lilia was searching the internet for user guides and mechanical parts to fix a long-obsolete model of printer, which presumably a relative on the island had obtained through a black market and could not use. A few years before, a particularly bizarre request had come through from Milagros's half-sister for a "*peluquín*" or "little toupee." Lilia and Milagros were perplexed as to what that could mean, until they received a letter explaining the sister was no longer having sexual relations with her husband, something which she blamed on the fact a skin condition had rendered her "bald . . . down there." This half-sister was confident that in the consumerist world of Miami, where virtually any product could be obtained, a solution to her problem would surely exist. Unsure what to buy her, but having heard on the grapevine that this half-sister was now rather overweight, they instead went to a local arts and crafts store, and bought a roll of black fake fur, which they cut into an approximate triangle and sent, along with some hypo-allergenic glue, in Nuño's carry-on satchel the next time they visited. Other items in his bag included a *consolador* (sex toy) and batteries, which the half-sister would rent out with the spare room she rented by the hour for additional income. When stopped at airport security and asked why he (a sixty-something-year-old man) had these items in his bag, Nuño merely replied, "*Pa' Cuba!*" (For Cuba!)—a response that

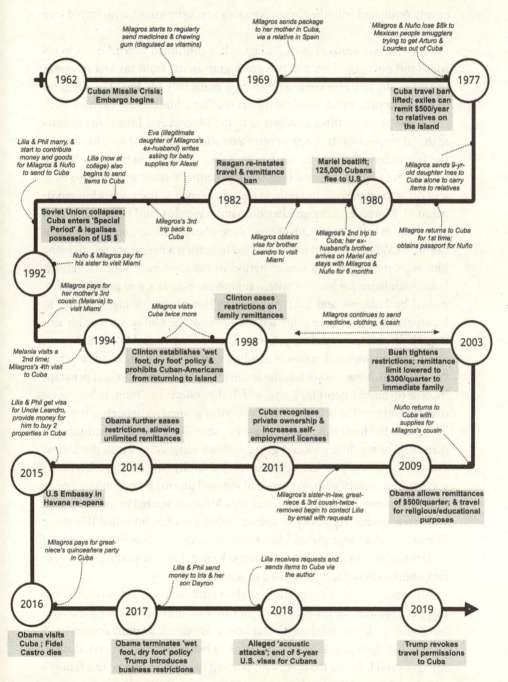

Figure 2.2. Timeline plotting Milagros's family history of remittance-sending alongside political changes between the U.S. and Cuba.

70 · Part I. Creating Value

clearly resonated with the Cuban American security guard, who waved him through.

Since Nuño's death in 2018, Milagros has continued to send items to his sons (and now grandson and two great-grandsons) from his first marriage in Cuba. She has also continued to care materially for Eva (the daughter resulting from her first husband Alberto's affair while engaged to her), Eva's son Alexei, and his three children as well. Milagros and Lilia alone assume material responsibility for the entire extended network of familia, despite the fact other members of the family have also since migrated to Miami (as shown in figure 2.3) and thus could potentially remit as well. Two have sent occasional parcels, but only to close kin (such as their own children or parents). Moreover, Lilia and her husband have also paid the costs to procure visas to bring some Cuban family members to Miami on a visit. Uncle Leandro (Milagros's brother) succeeded in getting a five-year visa, allowing him regular visits over a longer period of time; on each visit, he returns laden with items for his own wife, daughter, son-in-law, and grandson, furnished by Milagros and Lilia, but is unwilling to use his luggage limit to transport items for more extended members of the family, such as his siblings, half-siblings, and their progeny. Thus, Milagros and Lilia still rely on various other informal means of sending items to those who cannot get visas. All in all, Milagros spends the majority of her annual (limited pension) income on buying items for Cuba, which she collects in a room in her house over several months before sending everything when an opportunity arises. To be able to afford this, she maximizes use of food stamps and limits her own costs as much as possible, going without some comforts in the United States to be able to provide for her extended family back in Cuba. Leandro's visa expired in 2019 with no chance of renewal due to changes in U.S. policy under President Donald Trump, and thus Milagros started to travel to Cuba with even greater regularity to deliver items. Lilia has inherited this sense of material duty, and she and her husband have sent tens of thousands of dollars to Cuba to allow distant relatives to purchase property, while Lilia's two siblings do not feel compelled to send anything.

Milagros and Lilia's conceptions of their familia, or kin networks, are best mapped through the flows of material care that they have sent for decades (see figure 2.3). Viewed through this lens, this extended family centers itself around Milagros and Lilia (as successor to her mother's matriarchal role). Milagros and Lilia are the hinges supporting the doors between this family's social worlds, and if relatedness is created through material care, we can see that Milagros and Lilia are related to a sizable family in Cuba by virtue of how many people across five generations have received remittances from them (shown in figure 2.3). It is important to note here that Milagros and Lilia are not typical, even within a context of material generosity in Cuban culture, but in fact represent an extreme case from which I argue we can learn much about Cubans' normative ideas of gendered material care, here performed to their fullest extent. Milagros's notions of familia, as she conceptualizes it, when mapped out reveal a kinship chart that includes more formal notions of consanguinity, but also includes various extended networks of kin through material flows of care. When I once asked Lilia about how she viewed her own mother's enormous material network, which she was also clearly inheriting, her response, accompanied by a roll of the eyes, was "*Está de madre, eso,*" a phrase which roughly translates as a "deeply frustrating situation," but which literally translates as "It's a mother thing."

Caribbean Kinship

The role of Caribbean women as workers, mothers, and key players in the construction and maintenance of social relationships that cross national boundaries has been demonstrated by various scholars, alongside the degree to which Caribbean family units "are constantly being reshaped by the changing needs of global capitalism" (González 1996; Olwig 1993; Safa 1995; Skaine 2004, 50). Caribbean family structures have often been described as matrifocal, or relaying patterns of relationships within (and in this case without) households on a matrilateral basis. Across the Caribbean, kinship ideologies typically value the mother-child bond above all others, and this is considered the longest-enduring relationship (Clarke 1999; R.T. Smith 1996, 44). The dual roles performed by Caribbean women as both workers and mothers (or sisters, aunts, grandmothers) renders problematic the traditional Western distinction between the public world of work and the private domain of the home (P. Anderson 1986; C. A. Smith 2005), for many Caribbean women effectively manage a double workload in both emotional and financial spheres of life. This is frequently achieved through extended notions of relatedness and networks of care, including female kin but also friends and neighbors; some scholars designate such systems as so-called fictive kin (Chatters, Taylor, and Jayakody 1994; Ebaugh and Curry 2000), an inappropriate expression since there is nothing fictional about the relationship, or people's experience of it.

The existence of Caribbean transnational families has gender implications because the web of connections is constructed primarily by women

72 · Part I. Creating Value

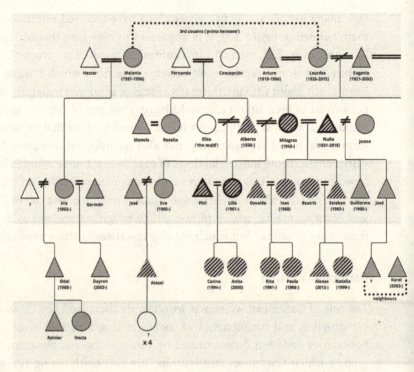

Figure 2.3. Kinship diagram showing recipients of remittances (*gray*) and senders of remittances (*outlined in black*) across five generations of Milagros and Lilia's family, split across Havana and Miami.

(Sutton 1992, 246). Women are the "protagonists in the drama of globalizing Caribbean kinship, which requires the active maintenance of circuits of exchange of goods, services, communication, travel, and personnel" (C.G.T. Ho 1999, 45). The Caribbean has long been considered a nexus of extensive webs of large kin-based networks. Since the region in its current geopolitical formation was created through capitalist concerns of slavery several centuries ago, colonial notions of kinship have also inserted themselves into local systems of relatedness; distinctions between "civilized" and "natural" sexual relations, for example, or "legitimate" and "illegitimate" births have mapped onto hierarchical class-based structures that have often in turn been closely mapped by social scientists (Momsen 1993; P. J. Wilson 1969, 1995). Yet while "blood" (substance) and law (code) are typically referred to as the definition of kinship in the region, lived practice also demonstrates a greater flexibility and inclusiveness in creating and maintaining kin networks. Indeed, in Cuba many couples in established relationships may often

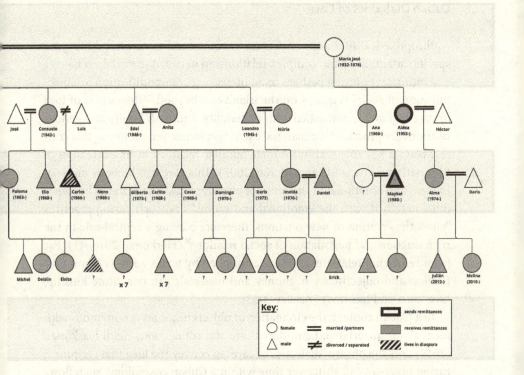

refer to their partner as husband or wife, whether or not they are formally married (Kummels 2014).

Much has been written by anthropologists to provide context for popular assumptions about the "looseness" of family relations, about sexual "promiscuity" and about the perceived "inadequacies" of childrearing across the region broadly speaking (R. T. Smith 1988, 37), and many ethnographic accounts of kinship in the Caribbean region have belied normative stances toward what family is. What is generally acknowledged throughout the literature is that family ties are both strong and extensive (Härkönen 2014), and, indeed, that it might be better to refer to "interlocking sets of parents and children" instead of somehow "distorted" nuclear families (R. T. Smith 1996, 56). One way to reenvisage Caribbean relatedness and personhood, then, is to focus not on "households"—which is unhelpful in an increasingly transnational context and privileges coresidence at the expense of the circulation between households so typical in Cuba—but rather to focus upon Sahlins' notion of "mutuality of being," set out earlier, which in this context is realized through material care.

Cuban Dialectics of Care

Anthropological literature on Cuban sexuality and personhood has paid specific attention to the complex relationship between material exchanges and intimacy, pointing perhaps to an increasing commodification or objectification of social relations on the island and beyond.[3] The notion of love or care (*cuidar*) is enmeshed with materiality, and both family and gender relations are practiced via material exchange; moreover, money in this context plays a key role within intimate familiar relations in its expression of transnational love and care (McKay 2007). This care can be both material in form and emotional in the sense of nurture; thus, "the material becomes intimately tied with the emotional and moral," and such caring practices "allow the creation of new relations, therefore playing a central role in the reproduction and negotiation of social relations" (Härkönen 2014, 41). Far from rendering relations abstract, as implied by terms such as commodification and objectification, money and materials can constitute kinship, love, care, and intimacy (Zelizer 2005).

In a Cuban context, the circulation of objects becomes synonymous with ideas about material and emotional care and connection. Heidi Härkönen (2014) uses the phrase "dialectics of care" to convey the idea that reciprocal caring practices can shift over time within a Cuban cosmology; such flows can change direction, slow down, or speed up at given moments, but this material (including the corporeal) is the idiom through which affect finds expression. This is as true of steady flows of goods and communication between Havana and more rural parts of Cuba as it is true of Cubans on the island and their kin overseas. Moreover, reciprocity need not be symmetrical in such transfers of care, and this notion is incorporated into Härkönen's "dialectical" ebbs and flows.

Maintaining such care takes time, intention, skill, financial resource and, above all, emotional energy. As Micaela di Leonardo points out,

> [W]e tend to think of human social and kin networks as the epiphenomena of production and reproduction: the social traces created by our material lives. . . . But the creation and maintenance of kin and quasi-kin networks in advanced industrial societies is work; and, moreover, it is largely women's work. (1987, 442)

Thus, women such as Milagros do not cease to be caregivers upon relocating abroad—these roles within networks of relation travel with them, and, as we see with Lilia, are also bequeathed to the next female carer. Gendered kin work includes the conception, maintenance, and ritual celebration of cross-household kin ties (through visits, letters, calls, remittances, etc.) for not only one's own familia but also one's familia's familia. Hence, Milagros assumes caring responsibilities for her extended kin, as well as those of both her past husbands, and their extended relatives, at home and abroad. In Milagros's case, her sense of embeddedness in such flows of relatedness is such that no obstacle, whether institutional, political, or informal, prevents her from participation in her family.

This, it should be noted, is exceptional, even within the wider framework of Cuban conceptualizations of extended family (in no other instance did I see someone remitting to an ex-spouse's children by another woman). Nonetheless, Cuban conceptualizations of relatedness are extensive, and sending remittances to kin outside of the nuclear family is in no way uncommon. Indeed, paradoxically, the restrictions of the particular U.S.-Cuban context seem rather to provide added reason to sustain, deepen, and expand Milagros's transnational ties through remittance giving and material care. If remittances hinge on transnational social capital formation, they rest on cross-border bonding, trust, and care; thus, "Cuban Americans and Cubans alike [must] defy state regulations and community pressures" to maintain their relatedness (Eckstein 2006, 150). This in turn resonates with other cases of diasporic remittances, where it is frequently the case that people migrate and create a diaspora precisely to look after their family.[4] Diasporic Old Cubans might be viewed as unusual within remittance literature in sometimes heeding political factors above familial concerns, yet in this case, we see that Cubans are perhaps not so "exceptional" (Whitehead and Hoffman 2016) after all. Moreover, we are perhaps starting to see Hialeah's New Cubans as more in line with other diasporas elsewhere that have been created precisely to care for those left behind.

"Estoy hasta la madre"

A concept of relatedness through the prism of mutuality of being "emanates a warm, fuzzy glow rather than a cold shiver" (Carsten 2013, 246), yet kinship can carry with it ambivalent or negative qualities, not merely happy experiences of connectedness and inclusion (Das 1995; Lambek 2011; Peletz 2000). Conflict "will always be part of caring" (Fisher and Tronto 1990, 56). Jeanette Edwards and Marilyn Strathern (2000) detect a pervasive sentimentalization of kinship in the academy, which prioritizes Euro-American conceptualizations of it, at the expense of the differentiation, hierarchy, exclusion, and burden that can also be synonymous with family. Kinship's ambivalence can be a double-edged sword, signaling both relatedness and obligation. The potential burden of kin comes to the fore more in literature dealing with remittances, where a sense of survivor's guilt and it being one's "turn to give" is prevalent (Duany 2010; Paerregaard 2014; Taylor, Wangaruro, and Papadopoulos 2012).

While Milagros never complained about her material ties to her family, from an outsider's viewpoint, such obligations certainly seemed burdensome. Milagros went through considerable difficulties and sacrifices to furnish her family with the material care necessary to create, participate in, and perpetuate her "transnational family" (Åkesson 2011; Madianou 2017; Madianou and Miller 2012; Povrzanovic Frykman 2016). When I asked Milagros and Lilia why they went to such efforts to materially care for kin whom they hardly ever saw, their answers both also involved the word *pena*, which can be translated as pain, (co-)suffering, empathy, or shame (as in the phrase "*No tengas pena,*" "Don't feel sorry for"), respectively. Both Milagros and Lilia "felt sorry for" (*tenían pena por*) those relatives who had been "left behind," which was not felt so keenly by those family members who had subsequently been born in the U.S. (like Lilia's younger siblings, who had never embraced any responsibility for supporting family back on the island, or Lilia's teenaged daughters, who felt less of a strong connection to an island they had never visited). Shame and perhaps guilt were also clearly central emotions, and the avoidance of shame through material care might be viewed as a way of living up to culturally embedded expectations of personhood, generosity, and feminine or familial care.

Over dinner one night, I asked Lilia's younger adolescent daughter if she would be likely to sacrifice things for herself to continue sending items to these relatives on the island in the future. "Probably not, to be honest, although I know I should help them," she replied, darting a guilty look across the table at her mother. "I send old things I don't use anymore, but I'm not sure I'd go to the same trouble my mom and grandmother do to get hold of everything." Nonetheless, this sense of material care for extended family and community is an ethos that Lilia in turn has certainly impressed upon her two daughters; throughout my stay with the family, she would regularly send her daughter off in the car to deliver a "care package" of Cuban food and other helpful items to nearby friends, and even her husband Phil's colleagues. Her daughters were clearly already well-schooled in an emic, polysemous, and pervasive Cuban notion of *pena* as a double-edged sword of love and responsibility.

In this regard, Loretta Baldassar's (2015) argument for guilt as a "positive" motivating force in maintaining and sustaining relationships over time and distance is a resonant one. To feel guilty, while not a pleasant affective state, is to express appropriate levels of care, and can thus be considered confirmation or affirmation of one's status as a "good" relative, properly embedded in material ties of care across national borders. This is not to dismiss conceptualizations of guilt as a damaging emotion, but rather to acknowledge guilt also as a "potentially positive and constructive social response" (Baldassar 2015, 89), which in the case of Milagros and Lilia is arguably a productive aspect of the maintenance of family, community, and their own positionalities as caring individuals within this network. This assumes a gendered quality as well when we consider that a sense of obligation to care is defined by the shared cultural understandings embedded within kinship relations; such affective labor applies itself differently to different members of the family, contingent upon their own (often gendered) position as caregiver and/or caretaker (Burrell 2008, 2017). On one occasion, as she ran out of the door to dash to a shop before it closed to acquire another requested item for a relative she had never met, Lilia sighed, "*Estoy hasta la madre con todo esto!*" ("I've had it up to here with all this!"), as she absorbed dealing yet further with the request on behalf of her own mother. This turn of phrase—which literally translates into English as "I'm up to the mother with all this"—is coincidental in its reference to motherhood, yet apt insofar as it again underlines both Milagros's and Lilia's emotional labor in fulfilling their roles, and thus their own expectations of themselves, as "good," caring Cuban mothers.

"Somos dividuos?"

French anthropologist Roger Bastide conceptualized a person as "divisible" in the sense that aspects of the self are variously distributed among others, as are others in oneself (1973, 38). Marilyn Strathern's (1988) formulation of the "dividual" also conceives of a personhood distinct from the Western understanding of a bounded individual. These ideas chime with Sahlins' "mutuality of being" (2011a) insofar as they point not to a personhood that is bordered, but rather to a cosmology where relatives are perceived as intrinsic to oneself and one's understanding of oneself. As Richard Werbner (2011) argues, "dividuality" of self means that the making of personhood is permeated by others' emotions as well as by shared substances. He provides the example of food as a material instance of nourishment and care; the

Figure 2.4. Graffiti on a wall in Havana, saying "We are dividuals." Photo by author, March 2018.

examples of other material remittances I have presented in this chapter are, I argue, equally compelling as examples of such "substances" of care, in this case serving as binding ties across borders and generations.

This is clearly not to argue that Milagros and Lilia were somehow divided or fractured people; indeed, they were, realistically, the glue holding this dispersed family together. It is rather to suggest that their positionalities as Cuban women in the diaspora to a large extent informed their own conceptions of themselves, and their life purposes. This kin work or affective labor was something Lilia had learned from a lifetime of watching her mother, and that she in turn was passing down to her own daughters as she taught them about how to create and maintain extensive relationships through material care. The Spanish word *compromiso* or "obligation," which is a word they used regularly, evokes this notion of united and shared endeavor through its etymological roots in Latin *com* ("with") and *-promittere* ("to send forth"). It is this extension of the self into the lives of others, materially, that also guarantees a response from cared-for ones, becoming the very locus of kinship in so doing.

Such notions of "mutuality of being" or "dividualism" resonate with others' discussions of Cuban kinship, and its typical focus upon love not through individualistic frameworks, but rather as a force that is not altogether autonomous. In this light, "the Cuban notion of personhood both recognizes considerable degrees of individualist agency and simultaneously highlights relationality as a fundamental aspect of existence" (Härkönen 2014, 43). Others in the family certainly expressed their connection to relatives in the same idiom—Uncle Leandro, for example, made his trips to take items back for his immediate kin, and various other Miami-based members would send occasional items to their parents or children on the island to "remain present." But the matriarchal caregiver role—the hinges on which the doorways between Miami and Cuba rested—lay firmly with Milagros and Lilia, which in turn bestowed upon them their status as loving and loved Cuban family members.

Later in my time with the family, some tensions arose as Milagros strayed (at least in the eyes of a few family members) from her role's script. A year or two after the death of her second husband, Nuño, Milagros began a romantic relationship with an American man who lived around the corner. The family had concerns at first that this man might be trying to take advantage of her, given the pair's obvious difficulty in communicating between Spanish and English and the fact he was twenty years younger than she was. One repercussion of her decision to potentially extend her family yet further (and in a potentially problematic direction) was that Milagros's son cut off contact with her, and prohibited her from seeing her grandson, whom she had helped to raise. Milagros was devastated at the loss of this connection and begged her son to let her see her grandson. But she also held steadfast in her choice: "Now that I'm old, this is my time, isn't it? I have the right to be happy, too," she insisted to me. In this regard, Milagros was arguably asserting herself in a more individual sense, potentially at the expense of her family, and some of her close kin perceived this as a betrayal. Milagros, however, saw it as her just reward. "I've spent my whole life caring for others, it's who I am, but they forget that when it's me wanting some of that back." Perhaps unsurprisingly, the family member who seemed most willing to see both sides of the conflict was Lilia, who, despite concerns for Milagros's well-being, also understood her mother's desire to receive care from someone else. Once again, the double-edged sword of the Cuban "mother load" caused tensions, as Milagros's capacity to continue to fulfill her respected role as prime caregiver conflicted with her choice to disrupt the status quo by making decisions for her own happiness.

80 · Part I. Creating Value

Conclusion: Politics, Rupture, and Proxies of Personhood

Anthropological analyses have often privileged kinship as an essential idiom through which social relations and order are manifested, and analyses have often focused more on mapping formal obligations between people rather than discussions of sentiment. Yet the Cuban revolution and subsequent cold war between Miami and Cuba have been portrayed as one of the longest-standing "family feuds" (Campa 2000, 7) in modern history. Remitting, or sending material care, therefore reconnects Cuban émigrés not only with a sense of family, but also with a larger lost family; remitting becomes a form of citizenship. Indeed, while citizenship is observed manifesting through the act of consumption, it is arguably even more evident in the circulation of material goods (Mitra 2013; Ong 1999; Porter 2008). Nina Glick Schiller and Georges Eugene Fouron (2001, 4, 61) have found that for many Haitians, patterns of obligation and family comprise a claim to political membership in a community that stretches beyond the territorial borders of a homeland. For Milagros and Lilia, sending remittances is a way of maintaining connection with a lost homeland, and a sense of themselves as Cuban.

John Borneman's work on kinship categories in East and West Berlin shortly after the fall of the Berlin Wall showed how,

> [b]ecause the two states publicly contested each other's membership categories, Berliners were quite aware of the arbitrary, political nature of belonging and therefore active in manipulating the official classification. (1992, 19–20)

Milagros's family history of sending material care to relatives in Cuba over the decades might in this light also be interpreted as an act of political resistance, insofar as they had to proactively assert kinship relations and perform them materially in defiance of policies designed to exclude or rupture such relations. President George H. W. Bush's policies in the early 1990s, for example, only permitted the sending of remittances to "immediate kin," as defined by American notions of nuclear family and relatedness, yet as others have demonstrated before, families often exist outside of "the politics of recognition" (Birenbaum-Carmeli 2009; Hansen 2005; Hansen and Garey 1998; Rytter 2010; Weston 2005). Similarly, up until the 1990s, the Cuban state's own definition of exiled Cubans as somehow non-Cuban also raised barriers that Milagros's family had to work around. We arguably see two potential ideologies of "fictive" kinship working at odds with one another here: Milagros's struggles to remit to her extended relations on the island, and the obstacles enforced by two states working within paternalistic idioms of biological and fictive kinship (Helmreich 1992; C. Lee 2013; M. Sahlins and Graeber 2017) to define the boundaries of state hegemony.

Evidently, the conversion and transformability of types of material substance demonstrate the permeability and porousness of geopolitical boundaries as well as of those ostensibly among objects, persons, and types of relation. Sharon Elaine Hutchinson's (2000) work among the Nuer, building upon Edward Evans-Pritchard's (1990) classic monograph on Nuer kinship structures, highlights the way blood and other bodily substances as well as other materials, such as food, soil, cattle, paper, money, and guns simultaneously invoke and rupture bonds of relatedness through social circulatory networks. In advocating a more "vectorial" approach to the study of relatedness, Hutchinson cuts across Evans-Pritchard's earlier preoccupations with showing kinship structures to be about unity and order, showing how Nuer systems of relatedness are "constituted through the flow of multiple substances," and how such practices of relatedness "are continually being reworked as people struggle—often under extremely difficult and bewildering circumstances—to live valid and meaningful human lives" (2000, 57).

Thus, local statements and practices of relatedness can be infinitely more dynamic, creative, or, indeed, destructive than analyses predicated upon straightforward divisions between biological/social, nation states, or people/objects might imply. The transnational objects sent by Cubans as remittances and material envoys of kinship formation are important because of their tangibility—they can be touched and held in a way distant family members cannot be—and in so doing stand in the physical place of longed-for people and locations. They matter because they stand for an absence of being in their very materiality, and because they represent affective labor and a commitment to continuing relations despite obstacles. Moreover, they are substantive; they enable people to do and be things that otherwise would not be possible.

In this regard, these objects echo some of Marcel Mauss's (1954) notions of the "spirit of the gift," not because they demand reciprocity in a timely manner, but rather because they embody that which is missing; they act as an envoy or proxy for what is lost and send forth a person-like agency. In so doing, objects of material care traverse emotional proximity and geographical distance (Baldassar 2008; Baldassar, Baldock, and Wilding 2007). I, as a visiting researcher who transported material items of care between relatives on numerous occasions, also came to embody this presence of transnational kin and country by proxy. In his work on shopping, Daniel Miller insists that

> we have to appreciate the degree to which objects are an integral part of the process by which relationships are formed and maintained. This means dissolving our usual dualist perspectives in which object and subjects are defined in opposition to each other. (2001, 51)

Rather than focusing upon these remittances as commodities being exchanged through ties of obligation and reciprocity, their affective agency reminds us that "understanding the object nature of persons is the other side of the coin to understanding the subject nature of things" (Miller 2001, 51). Igor Rubinov suggests the uncertainty created by mobility has "long demanded the intermingling of both objects and people" (2014, 193). The rupture invoked by such mobility makes migrants *bricoleurs* (Lévi-Strauss 1966), insofar as they must labor to create and re-create their sense of self and relatedness through whatever means and idiom available to them in a context of disorder and disunity.

The so-called death of kinship studies after the 1970s (Faubion 1996) was in part because "social stability was no longer the central issue in anthropology, [a]nd in one way or another, the study of kinship—whether in evolutionary, functionalist, or structuralist guise—had been bound up with explanations of social stability" (Carsten 2000, 3). In this chapter I have argued that kinship—when considered through a lens of material culture and transnational remittances—can in fact be seen as a force produced from moments of rupture and disorder, not social stability. Moreover, Cuban families have maintained and created family ties through material flows for generations (Pascual 2020), and this can be a valuable way of mapping relatedness across generations and transnational borders (see figure 2.3).

Relatedness is in fact "under construction" through everyday acts (Bodernhorn 2000) and is simultaneously productive and destructive. Cuban anthropologist Fernando Ortiz (1947) proposed a concept of "transculturation" as key for comprehending Cuba, emphasizing the flow (across geographic borders) of cultural practices from different sources and the emergence of a new hybrid culture. As Stephan Palmié (2013, 95) points out, Ortiz's use of *transculturation* was also an attempt to counter what he saw as an essentially ethnocentric aspect of the (mostly North American) term *acculturation*, which described a transition from one culture to another, rather than a focus upon hybridity and fluidity. In the ethnographic case presented in this chapter, the political definitions of kin and of country have arguably served to further strengthen the bonds of *familia* manifested through material flows, revealing, as Daniel Miller notes, that "what makes a relationship meaningful, as opposed to merely having meaning, is almost always a process of objectification" (2001, 3). This is the way in which, at a family level, Cubans realize the cultural logics of material value we explored in chapter 1, with Cuban mothers and daughters proving themselves to be central agents in such processes. In the following chapters, we will now turn to look at the impact of such flows and emerging systems of value at a societal level, and the way in which such networks of exchange extend beyond the family, or even the nation, to operate transnationally across much of the wider region.

II

Circulating Value

3

The "Mula Ring"

Material Networks of Circulation through the Cuban World

Up until this juncture, I have detailed the individual exchanges and origins of the material flows that I argue are central to the creation of value in this social world. Having established in the previous chapters how, in the Cuban world, material items accrue and assert value through fluid and creative mobilizations of ownership and exchange (chapter 1) and alternative conceptions of relatedness (chapter 2), this chapter will now outline the logistics of the material flows that those case studies presented, and consider the extent to which these flows are emerging into wider, transnational structures of circulation and personhood.

I argue that this value peaks in the act of circulation: it becomes indicative of the expansion of self beyond the individual (or even the family unit) by sending forth objects *out there*, in a way that people, in this context, can rarely do. In this chapter, I move beyond the individual to show how these exchanges multiply, and in their aggregate are tantamount to an emerging network of increasing socioeconomic impact, both in Cuba and beyond. I briefly trace the historical and political contexts of material consumption and circulation in Cuba before drawing upon fifteen months of ethnographic research in Havana (Cuba), Miami and Tampa (U.S.), Mexico, Panama, and Guyana to explore how Cubans in fact mobilize vast transnational networks to enable their systems of material circulation in the present day.

These transnational networks, which I call the "Mula Ring" ("mule" ring) in a loose pun with one of the best-known studies in the discipline of anthropology—Malinowski's "Kula Ring" of the Trobriand Islands (see below)—are tantamount to an economy unto themselves, an economy which, I argue, is redefining what it means to be Cuban in the light of decades of economic and social rupture both on and off the island. I show how this informal economy builds upon preexisting gendered spheres of circulation and exchange, as well as emerging modalities of power and value, the effects of which can be felt far from the island itself, as we saw in chapter 1. Indeed, this informal economy, which arises from a historical material scarcity under socialism, is leading to the reification of new class structures, the likes of which the revolution had initially set out to dismantle.

While many economists have focused upon the informal economy in Cuba as a system of stealing and circulating internal supplies (Henken 2005; Portes 1983; Ritter 2017; M. A. Rivera 1998), or upon Cuba's opening to world markets through formal international contracts (Feinberg 2017; LeoGrande 2017), less attention has been paid to the agency and power of regular Cubans in mobilizing these exchange networks. Here, I instead pursue what Cuban American sociologist Alejandro Portes deems the "most promising" aspect of informal economies, namely, "the opportunity to understand how peripheral economies operate as single and unified systems" (1983, 157)—in this case not only as economic systems but also as evolving gendered systems of power, kinship, and morality.

That being said, I hesitate to use the term "system" here for fear of reifying a collection of informal practices and assimilating them into a single, overarching model. Kula exchanges, for example, are carried out in a context of what is broadly recognized as an iconic, culturally constituted system, with clear protocols and strategies for the achievement of fame, representing a metacultural phenomenon with a long-recognized lineage. Any attempt to describe the incipient Mula Ring in such a coherent and systematized manner, meanwhile, inevitably ends up rather messier and more chaotic (something which may be of little surprise to scholars of Cuba, its diaspora, and associated geopolitics of the region over recent decades).

And so perhaps the ring of material flow that I outline in this chapter is better considered a bricolage (Knepper 2006; Lévi-Strauss 1966, 16–17) of informal practices, which is now happening on such a large scale as to begin to echo the structures and systems we might associate with Kula and other transnational networks of material circulation. In Lévi-Strauss's original formulation of bricolage, he distinguishes the *ingénieur* (engineer), who creates infrastructures through a potentially infinite selection of tools, from a *bricoleur*, who, constrained by working with whatever is to hand, must improvise and display arguably more ingenuity in constructing themselves within the world. In this light, I seek to emphasize the hybridity, fluidity, and mutability of these emerging networks, in line with other observations made of (post)modernity and cultural change in contexts of rupture across the Caribbean and Latin America (Khan 2001; Ortiz 1947; Palmié 2006; Puri 2004; Trouillot 2002).

Considered in this light, Cuban conceptions of material circulation begin to challenge outsider views of Cuba as an isolated nation, while also demonstrating the value of anthropological consideration of notions of flow and circulation of material things through transnational contexts in flux. Moreover, I describe an incipient network or structure that is both shaping and shaped by emerging expressions of Cuban identity, and that is cementing itself as an increasingly hegemonic formulation of cubanidad in light of long-standing socioeconomic rupture. For the purposes of demonstrating the social effects of the Mula Ring as currently experienced in Cuba, in this central chapter I limit myself primarily to discussing items imported to the island and some strategies and structures employed to facilitate this; the experiences and participation of the diaspora and the items exported from the island I address throughout the other chapters of this book.

Consumption and Circulation in Socialist Cuba

After the economic hardship suffered in Cuba through the 1990s, the Cuban state turned toward what it euphemistically called "reform socialism" (González-Corzo and Justo 2017), allowing a restricted degree of private enterprise to operate in Cuba for the first time in almost four decades. This trend has since continued; between 2009 and 2019 the number of self-employed Cubans rose from 2.8 percent (Desilver 2015) to 13 percent ("Los 'Cuentapropistas' Representan el 13% de los Trabajadores Cubanos" 2019).

It broadly remains illegal, however, for Cubans to (re)sell something not made by them or their immediate family unit, unless their business falls within the remit of a set number of licenses.[1] In reality, such restrictions have long been difficult to maintain, and a strong informal market has of course flourished in Cuba for decades (Cabezas 2004; Centeno and Portes 2006; Pérez-López 1995; Rosendahl 2001). This informal market is difficult to quantify, and several key studies of the informal sector across Latin America and the Caribbean have simply left the case of Cuba unconsidered (Peters 2017; Vuletin 2008). It also frequently interacts with formal or official markets, to the extent that illegality or informality is a widely recognized but often overlooked fact of everyday life in Cuba. In this regard, the Cuban case mirrors the extensive literature on informal trade and networks of circulation from studies of (post)socialism in Eastern Europe.[2] Indeed, the local vernaculars for speaking about these informal practices even bear striking

90 · Part II. Circulating Value

resemblance in some cases.[3] Since the crash of its closest economic ally, the Soviet Union, in 1991, Cuba's production ratings have dwindled. In 2013, 95 percent of all manufactured goods were imported (Desilver 2015), primarily from Venezuela (37 percent), whose economy has also subsequently crashed. Thus, with very little officially coming in, and limited materials for production on the island itself, many Cubans choose to covertly (re)sell items from abroad or that they have made from materials acquired abroad (Ritter 2005).

A Marxian focus upon production as key to understanding the social(ized) meaning of material things (Henderson 2013; Turner 2008) is therefore arguably less helpful to ethnographers in the context of contemporary Cuba, where there is little production of material items to be observed, and where value is derived from material objects more through their circulation and recirculation. Several anthropologists have already turned to the consumption of material culture in Cuba, including the various forms of sociality that develop as by-products of consumption, such as waiting in long queues, swapping information on which shop holds stock, and the growing importance of brand culture (Pertierra 2011; Porter 2008; Ryer 2017; Scarpaci 2014). Yet the circulation of material items through informal networks in and out of Cuba has largely only been examined by economists, who for the most part have neglected the emerging social paradigms that create and are in turn reinforced by these processes (M. A. Rivera 1998), or by sociologists focusing more specifically on remittance giving, which constitutes only one aspect of this larger material network of circulation I describe (Eckstein 2003, 2010).

And so in the particular case of Cuba I find James Carrier's argument, that circulation "pervades production in a way that production does not pervade circulation" (1995, viii), particularly resonant, as these social relations of circulation within Cuba and beyond are central to mapping how Cubans are negotiating decades of economic change and social rupture, as well as shifts in "regimes of value" (Appadurai 1986) both at home and in the diaspora, within a historical context of material scarcity. Just as some scholars have considered informality "a useful conceptual tool in moving beyond a 'varieties of capitalism' approach to transitional societies" (Morris and Polese 2014, 7), I argue a focus upon informal networks of circulation allows us to see more clearly how varying hues of both capitalisms and socialisms are conceived of and enacted in their own ways. As will be presented later in the chapter, many Cubans are successfully operating in more "capitalist" markets of buying and selling while also adhering to other norms of circulation and redistribution that might be more equated with "socialism"—thus any claim that Cuba is simply "becoming capitalist" misses the nuances of how Cubans are negotiating different systems in parallel, adapting and adopting various practices at once, and in combination, all while navigating the fluid boundaries among legality and illegality and various moral "systems" (Gámez Torres 2012; Holbraad 2017; M. Wilson 2014; Wirtz 2004) that arise from Cuba's very particular socioeconomic and political setting. My interest in value here is consequently more as an ethnographically emic concept, as opposed to an attempt to discover some foundational source for the production of value.

The Kula Ring

In his foundational ethnographic account *Argonauts of the Western Pacific,* Bronisław Malinowski (1922) describes a network of exchange—the "Kula Ring"—spanning eighteen island communities across the Massim archipelago in Papua New Guinea. Participants would travel at times hundreds of miles by canoe to exchange Kula valuables (necklaces and armbands), which Malinowski established were clearly linked to political authority and systems of hierarchy. In his reanalysis of Malinowski's data, Marcel Mauss further demonstrates how every aspect of social life in the Trobriand Islands is touched by these economic exchanges:

> [I]t is indeed as if all these tribes, these maritime expeditions, these valuables and objects for use, these foods and festivals, these services of all kinds, ritual and sexual, these men and women, were bound into a circle, following a regular motion around it, both in time and in space. (1954, 90)

Mauss continues, "Numerous things are solicited, requested, and exchanged, and all manner of relationships are formed in addition to the Kula" (1954, 90). Valuables acquire specific biographies as they move from place to place and hand to hand, just as the men who exchange them gain and lose reputation as they acquire, hold, and part with these valuables.

Perhaps of even greater significance to the ethnographic cases I will present later in this chapter, however, is Nancy Munn's (1987) work on Gawa (another island forming part of what Malinowski describes as the "Kula Ring"), in which she observes that the source of value within the island depends precisely upon exchange with that which lies outside of the island. The islanders view exchange as a key mode of value creation; items produced internally are made precisely to contribute to an engagement with the wider world for the purpose of securing and circulating valuables.

92 · Part II. Circulating Value

This is then returned in the form of "fame," Munn argues, explaining why people feel the need to become "argonauts" by venturing beyond their island to exchange items in the first place. Munn stresses that value emerges in creative action; it is the process by which a person's latent potency is transformed into realized, perceptible form, demanding social recognition from wider society. In short, the circulation of these items beyond the local is an opportunity for an individual to achieve local prestige by journeying (or sending something of themselves) beyond the local. It serves as a way for Gawans to become part of a much bigger cultural sphere within which they can gain a reputation and compete for "levels of value," rising up a structured hierarchy of social status. In her analysis, Munn therefore provides us with a general theory for how value is created, exchanged, and in fact increased through circulation, which—in the local context of Gawa—is ultimately realized as "spatiotemporal extension," or "fame" beyond one's immediate social sphere. I will now argue this general theory of value through circulation is also crucial to understanding emerging hierarchies of social status in a very different socioeconomic and geopolitical context: that of Cuba.

The Mula Ring

Cuba is popularly portrayed in the media as economically and politically isolated from the twentieth- and twenty-first century trend of globalization in the wider world, yet during my fieldwork following interlocutors among Cuba, the U.S., Guyana, Mexico, and Panama, it became clear that the island is part of informal networks of circulation spanning at least twelve countries. The *mulas,* or "mules," whom I traveled alongside were undertaking at times treacherous journeys of many thousands of miles to acquire and bring back material items to be exchanged on the island. Other items were meanwhile taken from Cuba to various other destinations, resulting in a network where certain items regularly traveled in one direction, while others moved in the opposite direction (see figure 3.1). These mulas' journeys suggest certain parallels with the famous "argonauts" of the Kula Ring (Malinowski 1922), whose adventures in obtaining Kula valuables are undertaken along specific trajectories and in specific directions to increase value back home, in the form of local prestige, or "fame" (Munn 1987).

Specific destinations provided specific items, and there was a large economy devoted to the acquisition and circulation of these items, which in turn drew heavily upon local and transnational kinship structures. The

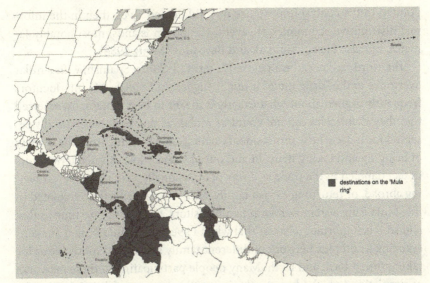

Figure 3.1. Map showing destinations across the Mula Ring, and the directional flow of items.

network relied upon strong kinship ties with diasporic Cuban communities that could either access material items themselves or could aid mulas in obtaining visas to travel (see chapters 1 and 2). Key loci for the network outside of Cuba were therefore Miami, Tampa, and New York (continental U.S.A), Russia, Mexico, and Puerto Rico, all of which have substantial Cuban populations. Guyana was also a key destination as one of the few places Cubans could travel to with no visa restrictions. Similarly, Latin American countries (Colombia, Venezuela, Peru, Ecuador, Panama) were crucial due to proximity and fewer travel restrictions for anyone holding a Spanish passport (which, in turn, is generally easier to acquire for Cubans of Spanish descent than for others). Meanwhile, Haiti and Martinique also featured prominently for their (relative) ease of access and low prices.

While this is by no means a coherent system like the Kula Ring that Malinowski describes, it is arguably a nascent one, as Cubans respond to the economic and social ruptures of recent decades by seeking new avenues to expand their material, economic, and social horizons. This is not an entirely new set of practices: the whole region has been caught up in informal and transnational material circulation for centuries due to the turmoil and ruptures brought about by colonialism (Benítez-Rojo 1996, 48–55; Cromwell 2018; Mulich 2020). Work by anthropologist Sidney Mintz in the 1950s

94 · Part II. Circulating Value

pointed to the central importance of "middlemen" even then in the informal distributive economies of several Caribbean islands, most notably Jamaica, but also Haiti, Trinidad, and Barbados (Mintz 1956).

The word *mula* can be a pejorative term in Cuban Spanish, with similar overtones to the "drug mule" it might suggest in English. My interlocutors frequently argued about what exactly it meant to be a mula; most asserted that they themselves did not count as mulas, as this term was typically reserved for those whose professional earnings mostly came from the activity of bringing and taking items in and out of Cuba. Most of my interlocutors in fact dabbled in the trade as a way of occasionally making money, traveling abroad, or returning to visit family. Many of the items that circulated in this Mula Ring also moved with family visitors, friends, or one-time mulas, and so it is important to stress that when I speak of a Mula Ring, I am generalizing a complex network of different family stories and motivations for taking things back and forth. Many people participating in these networks of circulation (which I here synthesize as all being part of the Mula Ring for the sake of perspicuity) would not necessarily refer to themselves as mulas, even if they were earning income from the act of carrying items for others. I should add, the felicitous pun between "mula" and "moolah" (i.e., "money" in American English), while perhaps apt, is coincidental.[4]

My argument here is that this sort of informal trading activity, which has long been common practice across the region, has expanded and solidified, centering around Cuba, into something we could start to see as an incipient network of value creation and circulation. The emergence of this network in the form that I encountered during fieldwork is a direct response to various socioeconomic and cultural ruptures that have torn at Cuban society in recent decades—from the revolution ending in 1959 through to more recent restrictions imposed by U.S. foreign policy under Donald Trump. Indeed, it is this Mula Ring network that enables the material consumption so notable in Cuba in the dearth of domestic production, for perhaps the most strikingly visible paradox on the streets of Havana is that, despite a decades-old embargo and an almost complete dearth of domestic production, Havana is full of *stuff*. Policemen hover on street corners looking at Chinese phones, hairdressers sell hair extensions made from real Russian hair, children play in school uniforms sewn in Hialeah (Florida), waitresses produce beers from fridges imported from Panama. In many other places such details might seem unremarkable, yet in Cuba, the acquisition of such items is evidence of significant social and economic capital, both of which are likely to stem from access to the "outside world" (*afuera*).

Most importantly, this network is indicative of power flows originating on the island itself, not solely in the diaspora. Remittance flows have often created new hierarchies, rendering the recipient country highly dependent on its diaspora (Duany 2007; Eckstein 2010; Morales 2017; Olwig 1993), and while this is certainly true in familial contexts in Cuba and its diaspora (as we saw in the previous chapter), the Mula Ring originates in Cuba itself, and Cubans on the island exert considerable agency in mobilizing networks both on and off the island to source (*conseguir*) items. Just as Nancy Munn argues that Kula exchange as a superstructure rests upon local processes and networks of production and exchange, often based on relations of kinship (1977), so here in the Mula Ring do internal networks feed external transnational networks. Indeed, this network not only imports vast quantities of items into Cuba, but also exports material items to the diaspora abroad, especially in Miami. Vials of Cuban soil (to be scattered with burial; see chapter 6), Cuban-grown herbs, beads, and horsehair (for Santería religious purposes),[5] as well as foodstuffs, rum, tobacco, and antique furniture (see chapter 5) are all among the items much-prized in the diaspora for their inherent "Cubanness," constituting an emerging objectified identity that is both imported and exported.

The importance of this informal network to Cubans both on and off the island cannot be overstated. It is the primary (indeed often the only) source of material things, from kitchen pots and pans to clothing, from cell phones and laptops to refrigerators, from family heirlooms and antiques (chapter 5) to religious and ceremonial beads, and from soil for burial practices to cremated human remains (see chapter 6). By the time I had arrived, it had also become a formidable force within an unregulated space in an emerging entrepreneurial aspect of the Cuban economy. The items circulated through this network are of such a high volume and so difficult to acquire through any other means that on the streets of Cuba, material goods brought in by mulas are omnipresent, in all strata and classes of society.[6] Indeed, various other aspects of Cuba's formal economy rely upon the very presence of this network; hotels and restaurants rely upon mulas to obtain bed linen and meal ingredients, manicurists source acrylic nails, bars and cafés and pharmacies need lightbulbs and opening hour signs, galleries and museums require canvases and frames.

This network in the form in which I encountered it was the by-product of a fortuitous combination of events: a relaxation in travel restrictions between the U.S. and Cuba under President Obama (2016), a small relaxation in some economic restrictions in Cuba after the death of Fidel Castro (November 2016), an increase in tourism to Cuba and therefore a greater availability of flights, a growing new generation of young Cuban diasporans who maintain ties to the island, and the rise of (limited) private enterprise on the island. Furthermore, the economic collapse of long-term trade partner Venezuela (2012–present; see Alvarez 2016; John 2019) led to the Cuban government eliminating the *tarjeta blanca* (the exit permit required whenever a Cuban wanted to travel abroad) in 2012, enabling Cubans to mobilize networks farther afield. Much of this circulation would not have been possible to such an extent prior to this change in Cuban law.

The acquisition of items from abroad in and of itself is nothing particularly new, however. Cuban consumers, whether under socialism or capitalism, have long "incorporated foreign goods as essentially 'local' components of everyday life, and are thoroughly used to inclusion in global circuits of cross-cultural production and consumption" (Pertierra 2011, 29). Indeed, a "huge repertoire of strategies for obtaining consumer goods and services" has consistently characterized socialist societies (Verdery 1996, 27), and in the case of Cuba, while illegal, these have long been normalized to the extent that even many state officials participate themselves, or accept "remuneration" at key points of exit and entry (Díaz-Briquets and Pérez-López 2002, 2006; Sweig and Bustamante 2013). Moreover, the whole region around the Caribbean Sea and Latin America was largely constructed in its modern nation-state guise through capitalist logics centered around the circulation of peoples and things as goods of exchange (Cromwell 2018; Kahn 2019b; Mintz 1986; Mintz and Price 1976; Olwig 1993), the likes of which did not altogether cease after the revolution and the imposition of the U.S. embargo. The aspect that has developed since around 2010 is the sheer scale and regularity of this emerging network, which cements both older social forms of exchange from the Special Period and new emerging hierarchies of prestige and social status.

This nascent system combines the norms of reciprocity and solidarity—observed in Cuba throughout the socialist period and the considerable hardship of the 1990s Special Period (Pertierra 2008; Rosendahl 1997)—with the formation of a growing elite who exert a new economic, and therefore political (in the sense of local prestige, rather than state-level engagement), authority. Older forms of sociality remain crucial to both the circulation of material items and the sharing of information regarding the availability and arrival of new material items. Perhaps the most common form of reciprocity, in which everyone takes part, is the giving, receiving, and repaying of information, as "the key to procuring anything in the informal or 'second' economies that tend to emerge under socialism is to establish some kind of private relationship with the seller." With the absence of an efficient legal framework to ensure that the right goods are sold at the right price, "people rely on knowing each other personally, or knowing people in common, to minimize the risk involved in informal sales and exchanges" (Pertierra 2011, 133).[7] This exchange of information not only creates relationships, but also accelerates them by establishing *confianza* (a trusting relationship). As with a gift requiring timely reciprocity, these tip-offs create a debt, which, no sooner repaid, is returned, comparable to systems of favor and exchange in much of the (post)socialist world (Henig and Makovicky 2017).

Modes of circulation through the Mula Ring also provide a mirror to local kinship structures in Cuba and beyond. As noted in chapter 2, kinship terms in Cuban Spanish do not mark only sanguine relation; it is common to describe a friend as *mi hermano-amigo* ("my brother-friend"), for example, and the two might be considered of equal importance.[8] Such kinship ties are crucial to accessing this new emerging economy as a participant. To become a mula, one must at the very least have confianza with someone who is hiring. This confianza is often spoken of in terms of relatedness, whether "imagined" or "real," and as such maps onto these kinship networks cemented through older Cuban sociality, as reported in other diasporic networks (Hearn 2016).

The mobilization of kinship ties in this network becomes particularly important because such exchange networks lie on the periphery of legal and moral frameworks in Cuba and are otherwise entirely unregulated. As with familial clans within the mafia or other gangs operating at the peripheries of state control, there is a strong reliance on the "unbreakable" ties of kinship as a bond of trust, minimizing risk in a world at the edge of government (Blok 2001; Hoshino 1973; Waltorp and Jensen 2019). Fulfilling one's material duties of provision to close relations has long been an important expression of kinship in Cuba, and the failure to do so can cause significant rupture.[9] While I never observed a violation of confianza in the Mula Ring first-hand, it was certainly more than a manner of speaking, and I was often warned that rupture of confianza or acting in its absence could have severe repercussions. As in other parts of the Caribbean, confianza invokes an irreversible kinship, unlike mere ties of friendship, which can be more easily broken (P. J. Wilson 1995, 141).

Having described networks of Kula exchange in Melanesia and of exchange through mulas across the Cuban world at some length, let me now

98 · Part II. Circulating Value

turn to my central argument, which is that as an analogy the Kula Ring can help us view Cuba in turn as an island best considered in terms of its circulation with other places that surround it, whereby Cubans gain access to and co-create emerging systems of expanding and hierarchical value through material circulation. The parallels of course have their limitations, and as many Melanesianists would be quick to point out, Kula valuables are highly symbolic items that move between people through ceremonial exchange. Evidently this is not applicable at all to the Cuban context I have outlined here—which focuses far more on the circulation of commodities through a context of scarce production—but, at least in my view, neither does it need to be a like-for-like fit to provide a valuable framework to think with.

Kula exchange has analogously contributed to discussions about commodities before: Alfred Gell (1992) has shown how men elsewhere in New Guinea barter over commodities based upon the boundaries between groups and seek adventure in a spirit analogous to Kula exchange, for example. Gell's analysis also sought to dissolve the reified boundary between gift and commodity that for so long dominated discussions of exchange in the Melanesia region. Robert Foster has continued in this vein with his parallels between globalization through commodity circulation and Kula "paths," asserting the valence of the analogy "because of the centrality it gives to the concept of value" (2008b, 12). Rather than observing a traditional Maussian view (which would distinguish the Kula Ring's social networks of gift-exchange from the mula circulation of commodities), then, I instead focus on how objects can circulate through different social "regimes of value" (Appadurai 1986, 15; Kopytoff 1986). The networks of kinship-based commodity circulation so typical of the (post)socialist world arguably do much to blend such distinctions anyway (Ledeneva 2017; Polese 2008). In the Mula Ring, social embeddedness in kinship systems of confianza is central for commodity exchange and circulation to be viable—it is the foundation for barter and negotiation—and this circulation in turn becomes a vehicle for the expansion of social status, economic wealth, and personhood for all parties involved.

Ultimately, the critique leveled at Malinowski's Kula Ring—that there is "no transcendent view from nowhere" that allows participants to name the totality of exchanges (B. Lee and LiPuma 2002, 201; Malinowski 1922, 83)—is equally true here of what I call "the Mula Ring." This is not a coherent system viewed by its participants as such, but rather a complex bricolage of practices that coincide to such a degree as to point to general emerging directions of flow. As a lens onto strategies of creating personhood at a local level while expanding social worlds through transnational circulation networks of material items, however, the comparison between Kula and Mula here is, I argue, a fruitful one. For very different historical reasons, both relate to islands that generate external circuits of flow, which then become central to the creation and expansion of value internally, and which are mechanisms creating new possibilities for individual achievement, associated with reputation but also adventure, as well as wider cultural and social engagements. Both result in an expansion into the world that matters greatly to those involved, as new possibilities arise for the creation and expansion of value. It is in this way that both the Kula and Mula Rings as analytical lenses can challenge the discourses of nations and people as isolated in time and space that scholars of Cuba have long rejected (Damián J Fernández 2005; Herrera 2007a; Krull 2014). The result is what Nancy Munn terms "intersubjective spacetime," or "self-other" relationships formed across distance that signify an increase in value at a local level (1987, 9–12). In a similar way, long-distance social networks of circulation in the Cuban context also create and expand value on the island, as experienced at a local level, and which allows communities on the island to assert their own internal viability within a larger transnational context.

A Return Ticket to McDonald's

At this point, it seems pertinent to discuss at greater length what this actually looks like to the many thousands of mulas working their way back and forth across the Mula Ring. Yohan is in his early thirties and works at a hotel just east of Havana. He prides himself on his appearance and takes meticulous care of his chin stubble ("It has to be the right length"), his phone ("You have to have the right apps") and, most importantly, his clothing (on this day in particular he was sporting an orange T-Shirt saying, "live your life," which had come from a friend in Spain). He hopes one day to own his own hotel, but for that, you need a sizable sum of money, and for Yohan, the road to that money was the Mula Ring. He had never left Cuba before and had no family abroad to provide help with a trip, but fortunately had someone *de confianza* (trusted) in Havana willing to vouch for his inclusion in these informal networks. For those with more limited capital, expertise, or other resources, "strong kinship ties can substitute, providing greater entrepreneurial or informal work opportunities" in informal (post)socialist economies (Karjanen 2014, 109).

100 · Part II. Circulating Value

A friend of the hiring *negociante* (businessman) had moved to Moscow a few years previously to set up a hostel targeting Cuban mules, which was to be Yohan's destination. There are similar businesses to be found in all the sites around the Mula Ring, most notably in Guyana, Panama, Russia, and Mexico. A dozen or so rooms, each with six bunk beds, host mules who travel there in teams (*equipos*) along with their negociante, who is financially responsible for the whole trip. Teams can vary in size from two or three people to half of the plane, although it is best to try to keep it to one buying team per room for security purposes. Theft between rival teams is not unheard of; in Georgetown, Guyana, I observed fistfights break out between different groups on more than one occasion, usually started by accusations of theft.

And so Yohan set off to Moscow on Christmas Eve, with five others, dressed in a T-Shirt, with no coat. For most mulas, the work provides a first opportunity to see the outside world and learn at their negociante's hip how this particular social world works, with the hope that if they save up a bit, they, too, can return one day with their own pack of mules. For professional mules who are being employed by someone else, space and weight are the two premiums, so they take absolutely nothing with them. The negociante buys the necessary items for his team upon arrival (in this case mercifully including a jacket against the Russian winter), all of which is left behind at the end to maximize space for bringing stuff back to Cuba. Some Cuban mula hostels have started renting out clothing and toiletries to teams to make the most of the discarded items at the end (and Abu, the Guyanese owner of a Cuban hostel I spent time at in Georgetown, had taken this one step further, providing Cuban chefs in the canteen, free translators and security guards to escort buyers around the dangerous streets, and a guaranteed "fast track" through exit customs courtesy of a few friends he had at the airport).

Upon arrival, the work is hard. A typical day might be 5 a.m. to 1 a.m. the following morning, with no free time to explore. Each hostel room has its own dedicated minivan and (Cuban) driver to take the teams to the various warehouses that sell merchandise at wholesale prices. While the teams are away, another (Cuban) security guard monitors the hostel to ensure teams do not steal from one another. The work is extremely competitive, as each team tries to arrive at the warehouse before the others to get the best deals. The mula's role is to physically carry all the things the negociante decides to buy over the course of the day. Emphasis is placed upon the role of young men as "carrying bodies" (*cuerpos de carga*) in this context, where it is their

Figure 3.2. A taxi/hostel service "solo Cubano" (only for Cubans) in Guyana. Photo by author, July 2018.

ability to carry weight without complaint, combined with a lack of "personal features" (*rasgos personales*) such as might attract attention from the authorities, that makes them attractive for the work.

Whether on the streets of Colón (Panama), Georgetown (Guyana), Moscow (Russia), or Cancún (Mexico), Cuban mulas are easily discernible as they huddle in groups, dragging black bin bags of merchandise along behind them. Likewise, they stand out in airports across the region, wearing many layers of clothing and up to ten sombreros, with sunglasses perched on top, and buttons sewn onto those—all to maximize space, and therefore profit. "Part of being a good mula is knowing how to make the most of all that, so you put the tightest layers on first and build them up, then walk around like you're constipated!" Yohan told me. Again, emphasis remains on their ability to physically transport the maximum number of items possible.

Merchants in Russia, in turn, need a supply of mint-condition dollars to trade with Chinese and Indian buyers, and so these are typically carried from Miami to Cuba by tour guides who have easy and frequent access in and out of the country, and then traded in Cuba, levying a long-reaching

102 · Part II. Circulating Value

network of contacts, before being carried to Russia for exchange there. All in all, each mula will bring back around US$3,000 of merchandise. As Yohan told me,

> The golden rule is any price you pay in Russia, you have to be able to sell for at least triple here in Cuba for it to be worth it. So a sweater worth US$1 there must sell for at least $3 CUC here . . . often you can sell it for $10 CUC here, though, which is why it's worth it.

With the cost of flights and boarding, the *negociante* will likely pay around US$5,000 per mula in his team. The work is also highly gendered; many negociantes will not employ women, as they are perceived as lacking the physical strength to carry 120 pounds on their backs and can cause security issues.[10]

At the end of the day, the team is collected by the Cuban guide and goes back to the room, where hours are spent removing anything that could add weight. Yohan was adamant that of 120lb of clothing, up to 10lb could be "unnecessary extras," with the resulting litter ending up at knee-height across the room. The items are usually slept upon through the course of the week for added security, until the space between bunks is filled and the teams turn to packing up the suitcases. Anything with an edge, like shoes, goes in the middle (to make it less identifiable by airport security); shoelaces are removed to squeeze other shoes inside, and underwear inside that. The packers work in concentric circles "like a little nest," filling from the outside in to create perfectly spherical bundles that can be rolled rather than lifted; clothing must be screwed up into little balls, rather than folded or rolled to prevent airport staff from counting the number of items on scanned images. The entire package is then wrapped in tight blue plastic "like a little bomb ready to explode."

Different locations offer different incentives for mule teams, and in Russia, the big money is in fake branded clothing and handbags. Various mules insisted to me that the quality of fake brands in Russia was far higher than in Guyana, and less regulated than in Panama, and thus could fetch a higher price back in Cuba. In this regard, there is also a hierarchy of destinations; those with less money to invest (or who had already used up their annual 120lb import allowance)[11] would travel to Guyana to buy cheaper clothing to be sold off at lower rates back in Cuba. To be able to take a whole team to Russia required significant financial input of anywhere from around US$20,000, which in turn required substantial social capital or confianza

Figure 3.3. Mulas about to start packing the goods in Guyana. Photo credit: Crónicas de una compra en GUYANA!!!, Nestor Siré 2018.

to acquire. Meanwhile, smaller teams or individuals can travel to places like Guyana or Panama more easily, starting at around US$1,000 per person.

In 2017 almost 1,000 Cubans were traveling to Guyana a week, with a buying power estimated at GYD$ 400 million (US$2 million) annually in the Guyanese part of the trade network alone (Semple 2016). Meanwhile, Yani, who runs a store in Hialeah that targets Cuban mulas, comfortably takes in US$10,000-$15,000 a month; her store is one of 129 I counted there that specifically cater to this clientele. "And then, of course, you have the agencies, the flights, the shipping companies, all the people working as mules, the people who sort out [*resuelven*] visas . . . it's a whole economy [*economía completa*]." All these places have Cubans and locals alike running satellite businesses that depend on his movement of people—something that struck Yani as impressive evidence of Cubans' economic agency in the

Figure 3.4. Store targeting Cuban mulas in Colón, Panama with a play on the words "Cuba" and *"barato"* ("cheap"). Photo by author, June 2018.

wider world: "as an international network it must be worth billions of dollars, embargo or no embargo!"

Meanwhile, Yohan was certainly learning from the best; his negociante, a man in his late thirties with a penchant for thick golden chains and imported sugary drinks,[12] had started out when he inherited a Havana apartment worth US$25,000 from his grandmother.[13] He sold it to produce the money for the first trip, and to sell everything as quickly as possible when he got back to Cuba he passed everything to his wife, who in turn sold it all to a friend (who would then sell it off piece by piece for a further small profit). He reinvested the money and lent $4,000 to a "brother-friend." After a few years of working their way around the network, they had together recently bought an *almendrón* (a vintage car selling for up to US$40,000 in Cuba) to work as taxi drivers and tour guides for tourists in Havana.

As for Yohan, he saved the US$200 he earned from his week as a mula (equivalent to a year's official state-paid salary for many Cubans) and sees his hard-won trip out of Cuba as a way of improving his life on the island—not, as might be expected, as a way of leaving "poverty" behind him. Of his first and only trip abroad so far, his main memory is of his final evening in

Figure 3.5. Cubans waiting to board a flight back home from Georgetown, Guyana, with their goods. Photo by author, July 2018.

Moscow, when he was allowed twenty minutes to visit the fabled McDonald's he had grown up hearing so much about. "I was so excited about it, and it was so awful, it didn't taste of anything! I took my bite of your capitalism and longed for my rice and beans [*añoraba mis moros y cristianos*]." For Yohan, the Mula Ring offered the opportunity to gain a reputation for himself at home as a person who could procure much-needed items, and also gave him greater access to the visible tropes of a society increasingly infatuated with brand culture and material consumption (Holbraad 2017; Ryer 2017), which might get him access to places reserved typically for visiting tourists, and where he hoped to have his upcoming wedding photoshoot with his fiancée.

Mobilizing New and Old Networks and Hierarchies

Part of the social richness and complexity of the Mula Ring is that different groups of people can interact with it in different ways. There is a complex hierarchy determining who can travel as a mula to where, much of which also maps onto older hierarchies of class and ethnicity in Cuba. Those with grandparents who came from Spain during the Civil War (1936–1939), for example, can often apply for Spanish citizenship, which in turn opens doors to other countries in the European Union and Latin America. Until the

Figure 3.6. Shop sign in Miami advertising merchandise made in Peru to be sold in Cuba. Photo by author, June 2018.

changes in U.S. immigration policy for Cubans in 2017 and the partial closure of embassy services in Havana in 2018, those with family in the U.S. (where the diaspora has also historically been of white and middle-upper-class origins) could apply for an American visa to visit their relatives, and then be financially supported by those relatives while they waited a year for residency papers in the U.S. Consequently, those on the island of white or European ethnicity are more likely to have the opportunity to obtain a visa to travel abroad, and to have sources of money from abroad to fund these trips. Those with five-year U.S. visas were at this time a particularly privileged sub-group, as they could cross the border as often as they liked, and so were uniquely positioned to carry some items (such as hard currency) that could not be procured elsewhere.[14]

The one location in the Mula Ring that provides an exception to this rule is Guyana, which does not require a visa for Cubans, and is much nearer and therefore cheaper to visit than the only other unrestricted option (Russia does not require visas of Cubans either, but the flights are expensive). For some Cubans of mixed ethnic origins, who may not have material or financial support from relatives overseas, but who want to get into the Mula Ring circuit, Guyana is therefore the most accessible option, albeit a potentially perilous one. In Guyana, white Cubans often stand out as ethnically distinct and are known to carry large sums of cash on their persons, and so are frequent targets of theft, violence, and even police harassment ("The Constabulary Ranks Are Harassing Cuban Shoppers" 2017), while Afro-Cubans are perhaps less visibly distinctive to the local population. Likewise, mulas who travel to Panama must cross gang-controlled areas in Colón to make it to the tax-free Zona Libre shopping area, to the backdrop of occasional crackles of gunfire.[15]

Regardless of the various power structures that enable or limit different Cubans' trajectories abroad, the most crucial aspect of the circulation network in fact relies on social capital in Cuba. Once the items have been obtained, they must be sold by employing a lengthy network of contacts and mediated by the moral code of confianza. This is also the moment at which the ring crosses over from a more male-oriented domain to a female-gendered space, as these items are often sold and bought by women in private households. Even when not conducted in a private dwelling, such exchange always happens in enclosed spaces. I have vivid memories of spending a hot and airless day sitting with a female friend in her stifling office at a major government building in Havana; over the course of the day various female friends visited her, to carry out, I presumed, some bureaucratic function of daily life. Each would visit the bathroom before leaving the office, which introduced a welcome breeze into the corridor as the door swung behind them. After an hour or two, I realized my friend in fact had a plastic bin bag of clothing under her desk, which she was selling to the public from inside her office, and they were visiting the bathroom to try the garments on.

In this regard the emergence of the Mula Ring aligns with the *casa/calle* (literally home/street, or public/private) division in Cuba, which has long been considered a legacy of Spanish colonialism in Latin America (Härkönen 2014, 18; Rosendahl 1997, 58–62). Indeed, Anna Pertierra has described the

> gendered process of re-localization which took place during and after the Special Period, in which the household was re-signified for Cuban women. The daily lives of women in post-Soviet Cuba center upon the household in terms of activities, income and social status, to a degree that might seem surprising given the socialist revolution's promotion of equality of the sexes and more than four decades of provision of extensive state services. (2008, 744)

108 · Part II. Circulating Value

In the Mula Ring the men are typically sent out into the public domain to acquire material items, before returning to the private domain where the women distribute and exchange the items of value, leveraging their own considerable social capital in the interest of the family economic unit. Both males and females mobilize kinship networks in various guises respectively to fulfill these roles. While both work in strongly gendered spheres, there is arguably more female agency and power at play here than Pertierra allows for; the circulation of material items from privately run household shops is certainly akin to gendered female roles of family care, nutrition, provision, and social gossip, but these roles are also actively employed by women to assert control over the economic regulation of the household. As the vehicles for the circulation of items, women capitalize their social and kin relations to economically support themselves and their families, and in so doing wield real economic power, albeit in a highly gendered context (Cieślewska 2014; Pertierra 2008; Safa 1995; C.A. Smith 2005; Sutton 1992). Indeed, similar observations were made in the case of informal distributive networks in Jamaica and Haiti in the 1950s, where the "middlemen" were generally women who could leverage their kinship relations to move products on, while simultaneously balancing duties of family care (Mintz 1956, 20–21).

My friend Helman's mother Mislei and sister Lisette were just one example of this. Lisette was earning the equivalent of US$14 a month in her state job, but her friend regularly traveled as a mula. Roughly once a month, Lisette bought the contents of his most recent trip, and took it home to her mother. They sorted through everything on the floor of the family apartment; if it was bulk-bought and low-quality clothing, Lisette might simply sell everything to a friend. As the items were "decent" this time, with (counterfeit) brand names, she spaced them out around the room, and messaged a few friends. Over the next day or so, various friends called round to try clothes on and hold up handbags to the cracked mirror balanced on a worn sofa in the corner of the room. Some could not afford the price that Lisette had set, and the special few who had a long-standing relationship of confianza were allowed to buy at a slightly higher price on credit, with an agreement to pay in installments (*a plazo*) over the coming months.[16]

Meanwhile Mislei, who is in her late sixties and knows little of the latest fashions, is an excellent seamstress, and, for a small fee, would alter clothing, or sew on fake branded logos, the materials for which also came from abroad. She kept all the scraps to make accessories like children's *pionero* bandannas and socks,[17] which she could also sell to mothers in neighboring apartments. Even here, then, in a legal example of self-employed private entrepreneurship (i.e., the sale of a product produced by one's own labor), the tools and materials for this labor were acquired illegally *"por la izquierda"* (see also Y. M. Concepción 2016). From time to time, Lisette also managed to source various dog treats and shampoos, which she could resell to her next-door neighbor, who ran a veterinary practice from his front room. Any jewelry was also set aside to be given to a cousin, who later resold it for a profit to tourists in Martinique when he traveled there. All in all, Lisette and Mislei topped up their monthly income by up to US$400.

Notions of kinship are frequently invoked in these arrangements of exchange (visiting buyers would frequently call Mislei *mamá*), and for the most part male and female realms remain separate. Crossing over into a different gendered space can be a dangerous process, as Lisette was quick to warn me, given the number of solicitations I received (with my privileged non-Cuban, non-American passport status) to work as a mula myself. Lisette's (Cuban) friend, for example, was working as a mula in Mexico when she was asked by an unknown man to deliver a birthday card to Cuba. The envelope in fact contained a forged seal for falsifying official documents, and Lisette's friend was sent to a Cuban prison for three years. This can perhaps be interpreted as a deliberately dishonest invocation of kinship and confianza within a gendered space where, because of her status as unprotected by her own kin, Lisette's friend fell victim to the unregulated illegal activity that can also prosper in these informal networks.

Although manifested and mobilized in different ways according to gender, what is clear is that the confianza that enables and is reinforced by this Mula Ring is itself aiding the emergence of new class structures within Cuba. Those who can leverage their social networks to succeed in this emerging economy can gain economic status and political prestige, which in turn can signal better education, better jobs, or even better marriage prospects (Bastian 2018). In short, a tranche of the nouveau riche is emerging alongside these networks, accompanied by new regimes of symbolic meaning as aesthetic choices (overtly valuing items acquired abroad) to demarcate these emerging classes of prestige in new forms of cultural hegemony (Bourdieu 1984).

Conclusion

In this chapter I have outlined a newly emerging informal network of transnational circulation that I call the Mula Ring. This network is the primary way in which Cubans from all sections of society acquire material items, either directly or indirectly, and as such is a substantial economic force both on the island and in its diasporas. Many of those embedded in these transnational networks are mobilizing these relations to exert considerable economic power, as well as local sociopolitical prestige, which in turn is forging new socialities while a new hegemonic cultural order is becoming increasingly conspicuous (Eckstein 2003) While these networks by no means represent one coherent culturally recognized "system," as Malinowki's Kula Ring so iconically does, a focus upon them nonetheless reveals how Cubans have long operated on a transnational and globalized economic stage. While there are certainly new power dialectics emerging through increased remittance flows from the diaspora, these flows in fact operate in multiple directions, not just from the diaspora toward the island. Defying the expectations of many, some Cubans on the island exert considerable agency both on and off the island due to the way in which they leverage social capital to navigate this network.

The Mula Ring in turn draws upon more traditional modalities of social life in Cuba, many of which are highly gendered (as explored in chapter 2). Traditional Cuban and Caribbean binaries of public and private come to the fore once again (Safa 2008, 321; Stoner 1991), although not necessarily always to the detriment of female agency, as might be presumed. My research reveals how women are key to the success of these informal networks of circulation, and indeed, the traditionally female sphere of "gossip" (*chisme*) and information exchange is in fact of crucial importance to its success, as has been found in other Caribbean and postsocialist contexts (Cieślewska 2014; Sasunkevich 2016; C. A. Smith 2005). Moreover, the need for such networks to operate in private spaces due to state restrictions arguably enables women like Lisette and Mislei to wield some considerable economic power and cultural capital.

The emergence and consolidation of these networks since around 2010, drawing upon trajectories from the previous two decades, is in turn fostering the rise of a new socioeconomic class in Cuba, and perhaps even an increasing focus upon aesthetics of individualism, arguably in defiance of the very ideals of the socialist revolution under which Cuba still formally operates. Although impossible to quantify, these nouveaux riches are exerting considerable influence on many aspects of social life, from education opportunities and local politics to family, fashion, and home ownership, and thus participation in such networks can lead to prestige and expanding spheres of personhood, as with Kula exchange (Munn 1987). Yohan's negociante, for example, had successfully navigated the ring to create a new life for himself and his family, as well as to enhance his role and influence in his community. Moreover, as we saw in chapter 1, these increasing disparities between emerging modes of value and more hegemonic notions of success are increasingly being exported into the Hialeah diaspora, sometimes in turn creating further conflict.

In a void of state regulation, these new networks self-govern using a long-standing moral regime, confianza, which likely predates the revolution but took hold across society during Cuba's Special Period of economic hardship, offering an alternate social code to that provided by the official state. From a period of socioeconomic rupture, new rules of the game are emerging, the navigation of which can lead to considerable success (which, as discussed in chapter 1, is itself a concept interpreted in specific ways at a local level). This confianza mobilizes extended kinship ties invoked either through blood relation or equivalent (as presented in chapter 2) and can be leveraged within the network as social capital, for both good and ill. This nascent system still draws upon older forms of Cuban sociality, including notions of reciprocity, yet has adapted over recent decades to material scarcity and economic hardship.

In this light, the Mula Ring can arguably be seen as a dynamic and creative indigenous approach to combat the political and economic isolationist course officially taken by and/or imposed upon Cuba over the past six decades. By no means merely a Caribbean version of the famous Kula Ring, the Cuban Mula Ring instead vividly demonstrates the deeply imbricated connection of economic processes, in various guises, to culture in multiple and complex ways. By tracing the informal material flows that constitute Cuba's extensive transnational presence at the beginning of the twenty-first century, we also confront evolving dynamics of gender, relatedness, and personhood. Moreover, in many instances it is through an actor's capacity to creatively mobilize the interstitial spaces between formal and informal economies, public and private, local and global, and so forth, that this Cuban world is most successfully navigated. Most significantly, the Mula Ring demonstrates how local actors can navigate decades of socioeconomic and political rupture, in turn reconstructing society in a new, dynamic way, working around the multiple barriers placed in their way. In this regard, the expansiveness of the Mula Ring—its focus upon the beyond—is arguably a powerful bottom-up response to decades of economic and political forces of constriction imposed from above.

4

The "e-Mula Ring"

Digital Networks between Havana and the Cuban Diaspora

Just as Cuba has experienced decades of material scarcity—resulting in the domestic inventiveness in circumventing such limitations that I presented in the last chapter as an emerging "Mula Ring"—so, too, have Cubans struggled to acquire digital items, thanks to both the U.S. embargo and the Cuban government's own restrictive internet policies. In this chapter, I explore the ways in which this resourcefulness in circulating and generating new cultural forms across spaces of social rupture maps over from the material world into an emerging digital sphere, with marked parallels to the informal networks of material circulation already outlined in this book.

Cuba's peer-to-peer digital file sharing network *el paquete* ("the package") has gained global attention (García Martínez 2017; Helft 2015; San Pedro 2015; Parish 2018), viewed as a domestic response to this widespread scarcity of internet access, and even an inventive answer to Netflix (Ayuso 2015) from an island that remains prohibited from officially consuming much international online content. The network has grown and consolidated itself since around 2014 to become the primary source of online information and entertainment for most Cubans across the island. Indeed, some even consider it to be the island's largest (unofficial) employer (Fazekas and Marshall 2016; Press 2015).

This curated database of digital content circulates hand-to-hand across the island through USB sticks and hard drives, including thousands of hours of international TV shows and movies, video games, music and music videos, sports matches, e-books and magazines, cell phone applications, antivirus updates, and classified advertisements. Altogether the content amounts to up to one terabyte per week, although few Cubans purchase the entire thing. The popularity and ubiquity of this network is such that while in 2015 it was distributed on a weekly basis, crossing the island every Monday morning with bus drivers and pilots, by 2017 it had already become a daily phenomenon, with content copied, recopied, and sold across networks of *paqueteros* ("packagers"), who in turn were distributing the material for a profit in their local area. The cost of subscribing to the paquete varied from neighborhood to neighborhood and dealer to dealer, but prices could be as low as two Cuban pesos (10 cents) for an episode of a show, thus allowing Cubans to "transform their offline digital devices and television set into the equivalent of cloud-enabled, data-rich smart phones and TVs" (Henken 2017, 433).

For the most part, compilers of this digital content have been treading a delicate line of legality, and the unwritten rule for participation without unpleasant consequences has been that no politics or pornography can be included. Meanwhile, revenue comes back through two avenues: payments from subscribers on the one hand, and also paid advertisements from local private businesses on the other. Most operate legally under a set of licenses for self-employed work (Henken and Ritter 2014; Ritter 2014), although many of these licenses were frozen in 2017, and private advertising remains illegal on the island. Alongside its international content, since 2013 the network has also facilitated the distribution of independently produced Cuban content, including journalism, music, and domestic TV shows and film, allowing new genres and voices to be circulated more widely through the public sphere (Henken 2017).

While el paquete has been largely fetishized by the wider world as a surprising digital quirk in an otherwise "analogue" place characterized as stuck in the past (Nelson 2016), it in fact does not represent anything drastically new to Cuban societal organization. Indeed, el paquete is arguably the archetypal Cuban response to a scarcity of digital content, and in this regard, it is the latest iteration of what has long been a local approach to obtaining both material and digital goods on the island. Informal networks have been crucial to most aspects of Cuban consumption for decades, becoming the definitive manner in which the problems of everyday life are resolved (see D. J. Fernández 2000, 29–32; Henken 2005). The acquisition of goods through informal means is entirely standard practice to Cubans, who consider it "normal or even admirable behavior that is not necessarily a disavowal of the Cuban state or of the socialist economy" (Pertierra 2012, 402). This attitude of resourcefulness dominates a myriad of aspects of Cuban everyday life, from sourcing groceries to getting from place to place, as has been typical in many post-Soviet economies (Centeno and Portes

2006; Morris and Polese 2014). Moreover, such practices of informal music circulation are common in many lower-income countries and communities (Boudreault-Fournier 2017; Manuel 2014; Schoon 2016; Steingo 2015; Stern 2014). In this chapter I argue that el paquete can best be understood as a digital extension of the same social practices that have forged the Mula Ring over a decade; both are informal networks that observe local practices of gender, power, and kinship to circulate valued material-digital items across transnational Cuban communities.

The Internet in Cuba

The Cuban internet has long been characterized by government censorship, self-censorship, high costs, and slow speeds, along with a frail infrastructure of access. More recent transformations have provided internet access to some of Cuba's population, but this has been inadequate for the needs (and wants) of most citizens, and so numerous workarounds have been created, which are the main topic of discussion in this chapter. Nonetheless, internet access does exist, and it is worth briefly tracing the genesis of that and positioning it in the official political framework within which citizens must operate and navigate on the island.

Cuba adopted a limited-access internet policy in 1996, but this was not widely accessible to the public, and it relied on slow and expensive technology. In 2013, an undersea cable connected Cuba to Venezuela, and Cuba's government allowed the opening of public access to the internet within cybercafes, and the possibility of accessing email followed shortly after, in 2014. A year later, thirty-five public Wi-Fi hot spots were opened across the island, where Cubans and foreigners alike could pay (initially five CUC, or US$5 for one hour of access, later falling to US$1 per hour) to get online by queueing at a government-operated booth and buying a scratch card that provided login details that would be linked to either a national ID number or a foreign passport. Numerous entrepreneurial activities developed around these public spaces of connectivity, including the reselling of access cards to other people nearby, although such activity was and remains illegal.

By 2016, this had expanded across two hundred locations throughout the country, and in the same year, ETECSA, the Cuban government's telecommunications monopoly, launched *Nauta Hogar* ("Home Surfer"), allowing limited home internet access to some residents of Old Havana (the main area where tourists stay). In December 2018, the government also launched a 3G internet service for cell phones, which in 2019 was upgraded to 4G in some areas, although this mobile data was prohibitively expensive for the majority of Cubans, with prices starting from US$4 for 100 gigabytes. As of January 2021, a Cuban would have to pay nearly ten times the monthly official minimum wage (adjusted to 2,100 Cuban *pesos* or US$84) for full-time internet access at home. Since 2014, it has also been possible for people abroad to pay for internet access for Cubans on the island, and in practice this is how many of my interlocutors were able to fund their internet access.

The internet in Cuba remains "arguably the worst in Latin America and the Caribbean—minimal, slow, and unfree" (Press 2021, 33), and in 2018 Freedom House ranked it sixty-first (of sixty-five) in the world, with only China, Iran, Ethiopia, and Syria ranking lower. As of 2019, internet penetration in Cuba was estimated at 68 percent (according to figures from the International Telecommunication Union), and while it still has the lowest cell-phone penetration rate in Latin America, the number of people with access to a cell phone more than doubled between 2014 and 2019 (reaching six million, or 53 percent of the population, according to data reported by Freedom House [*Cuba: Freedom on the Net 2021 Country Report* 2021]). Devices that use GPS or satellite technologies are explicitly prohibited in Cuba, however, and there are still restrictions on owning modems, wireless faxes, and satellite dishes.

Until 2019 (by which time I had finished my fieldwork), the Cuban government largely tolerated the existence of alternative methods of accessing digital content, such as *el paquete semanal* (the weekly package) and the SNET (street) networks that I will refer to in this chapter and have described at length elsewhere (Cearns 2021a, 2021b, 2021c), although these networks were largely subject to self-censorship (Escobar 2017). Since 2019, however, government officials have increasingly taken over the services and much of the content offered by these networks (particularly the SNET networks), permitting access to the content only from the Youth Computer Clubs located in all Cuban cities, or through the government-run equivalent to el paquete semanal, known as *La Mochila* (the backpack) (Farrell 2021). In so doing, the administrative autonomy is gradually being removed from these previously non-political and community-based networks of content distribution, and some have interpreted this as an increase in censorship of digital content in the country (Cimpanu 2021).

ETECSA commonly blocks dissident or independent news outlets, and some foreign news outlets (particularly those based in Miami with regular coverage of Cuba, such as *El Nuevo Herald*) have also reportedly been blocked in Cuba as of December 2020, although much international news

Part II. Circulating Value

coverage (such as the BBC, El País, etc.) remains accessible (Padrón Cueto 2020). Social media accounts such as Facebook, Twitter, and WhatsApp were temporarily blocked by the government following protests in Cuba in July 2021 (Marsh and Culliford 2021). Meanwhile, the introduction of a new law in July 2019 explicitly prohibits the hosting of a website on a foreign server, or the circulation of "information contrary to the social interest, morals, good customs, and integrity of people" (Decree Law 370).

A Short History of el Paquete

El paquete's genesis actually goes back several decades to the 1970s and '80s, when Cubans first started to find ways to circulate foreign films, magazines, and music that did not air on state-run TV. My friend Nestor has vivid childhood memories of helping his grandfather, who had a side-business of renting out books and movies:

> He had this great passion for cinema . . . so as an alternative means of income he started renting out magazines, books, and films in the '70s. The earliest memory that I have of that part of the business was a big wooden trunk he had for all the magazines. And I remember another person would come from another city to swap with my grandfather. The thing was, you'd have a hundred or a hundred and fifty books and a group of customers, so when your customers had read everything, you had to do something, so to get around that problem my grandfather would circulate materials with someone in another city. They used to communicate between themselves, like networks, and like that it grew . . . a network to distribute and interchange materials. . . . At that time the other way of getting hold of magazines and so forth was the ones left behind by tourists or visiting relatives in hotels. People would laminate them so they lasted longer and rent them out. . . . At the same time, cassette tapes started to circulate, and my grandfather exchanged all 200 of his books for eight VHS tapes. People loved that you could watch something more than once, and from that moment the business started to grow. All of the sections you now see on el paquete, like sport and soap operas, started out on the cassettes, and just like you go to the film banks now, you could go and rent out a tape. (Interview, Havana, February 2018)

Throughout the 1980s, ship workers, touring musicians, and plane pilots would bring in Betamaxes from abroad either to sell or rent out: word would go around as to who had what, and people would make copies for themselves.[1] In 1991 the Cuban government installed an antenna on the roof of the Hotel Havana Libre so that tourists and diplomats could watch ten American channels, and locals quickly found a way to catch and (illegally) repeat the signal in the neighborhood and record shows to (illegally) sell to others. The Cuban diaspora in Miami also made the most of this development and started broadcasting radio and television programs through satellite dishes facing out across the sea, in the hope of transmitting alternative sources of news to the island.[2] This practice continues to this day, with many of the more affluent Havana households owning a parabolic antenna to catch the signal from Spanish-speaking channels in nearby South Florida. Some also repeat the signal to their neighbors and make a profit in the process by charging a monthly fee. As of 2021, the import or ownership of parabolic antennas remains illegal in Cuba, and the authorities regularly pursue individuals who use this equipment (Rodríguez 2021). Nonetheless, much of this equipment makes its way into Cuba in travelers' suitcases, and nowadays it is also much easier to get hold of a computer, a smartphone, or an antenna within Cuba via various classified advertisement groups and networks (of which more later in this chapter), often (although not always) paid for with the support of remittances from overseas.

Indeed, some households in Havana are in fact more connected to American media networks than those in Miami itself. In November 2017 I was asked to give a lecture about el paquete at Florida International University in Miami; the event was widely attended and resulted in short interviews on various Spanish-language local television stations afterward. As my Miami household could not afford cable TV, I never saw the footage, but to my surprise, a friend's grandmother in Havana saw the coverage later that night on the local news and convinced a neighbor to send me some of the clips she had recorded via his workplace email address (which had greater bandwidth for sending images). And so, ironically, I was ultimately able to see coverage of my own Miami lecture about el paquete courtesy of an elderly lady in Havana and her deftness with a USB stick.

In the 1990s, the Cuban government's response to the Special Period of economic crisis was to open the island to economic remittances, primarily from the diaspora in Miami—but, as Albert Laguna has shown, this move also had the "unwanted effect of creating an opening for 'cultural remittances' that fuel[ed] the transnational imaginary on the island" (2017, 159). While Cubans had managed to access some limited foreign content before this time, it was during the 1990s that the floodgates were truly opened to

118 · Part II. Circulating Value

foreign media content. This was also when Kike first started to send video content back to his family in Havana. Kike had been the cameraman who filmed much of my el paquete lecture on behalf of one of the major Spanish-language Miami channels, and the following week, he confided to me over a coffee that he had been secretly making copies of television content at work for decades and sending them to Havana.

This had begun in 1992 when he had first gone back to Havana to visit relatives; he took with him some cassettes of music and was struck by how delighted they were with them. In fact, a line formed outside the door as neighbors reserved slots to listen to the cassettes of Willy Chirino music.[3] Upon his return to Miami, Kike started making short movies of Miami on his camcorder to send back to his relatives, with a voiceover explaining what they were looking at. Episodes included "How to use a microwave" and "Planes taking off from the runway across from my office." Kike explained to me,

> Since I worked for Telemundo at the time, I had access to the original tapes, so if I was editing something I thought was good, I'd make a copy to Betamax or VHS and then I put them all together at home. Once I'd got a few together, I'd send them over with someone who was going, and we'd label them as "wedding videos" in case anyone in the airport asked.

As there was limited communication between families on and off the island at that time, Kike also expanded into making movies of people talking to camera about their lives, so that they could send "video diaries" to their relatives. "It was very, very emotional, you know? People hadn't seen their mother for 25 years, so on camera they'd hold up their newborn baby and say here, 'This is your grandson.'" Such audiovisual remittances allowed separated families in many cases to see and hear one another for the first time in years, but also to confront alternative Cuban lives. They become not merely a way of staying in touch, but also "an integral part of how Cubans on and off the island produce and negotiate their respective subjectivities" (Knauer 2009, 165).

While most of el paquete's content originally came from abroad (through various clandestine means, probably including Kike's efforts), nowadays the majority of the content is actually downloaded in Havana itself. Some is downloaded through special internet accounts granted to university staff, party members, and the like, which are less restricted, while the rest is downloaded on hotel computers through the night, when the available

The "e-Mula Ring": Digital Networks between Havana and the Cuban Diaspora · 119

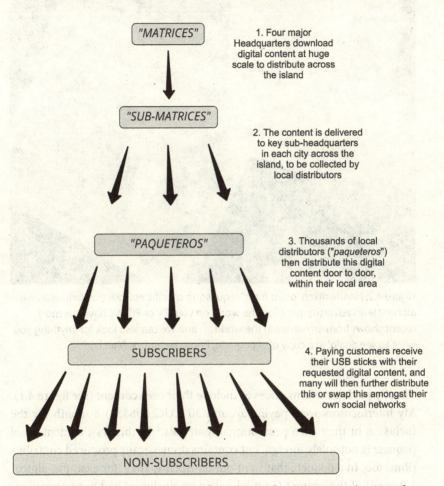

Figure 4.1. Diagram showing structure of distribution for *el paquete* at the time of fieldwork, in 2018.

bandwidth is typically greater (Cearns 2021b; Fowler 2019). The *matrices* (headquarters) of the major producers and distributors of el paquete have sufficient technical equipment to be able to copy multiple files at the same time, enabling them to reproduce el paquete on a mass scale that was impossible even just a few years before my fieldwork began. Meanwhile, as production of el paquete centralized into four major "houses" or matrices, local artists, filmmakers, journalists, businesses, and musicians also started

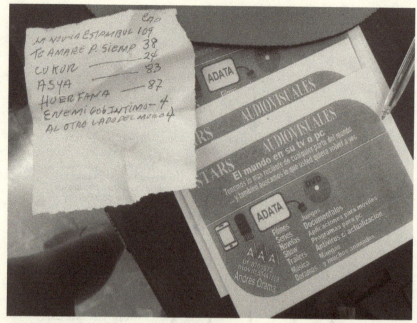

Figure 4.2. Handwritten "order form" requesting specific episodes of various shows, alongside an advertisement for "the world on your TV or PC: We have the most recent shows from anywhere in the world ... and we can also look for anything you want to see again" in a copy of el paquete. Photo by author, March 2018.

directly paying these matrices to include their own content (see figure 4.1). My interlocutors were paying around 30 CUC (US$30) a month for the inclusion of their own promotional materials.[4] In this way, content on el paquete is not solely foreign, but contains domestically produced contributions, too. In a paquete that went out on April 1, 2019, for example, almost 5 percent of the content (approximately 40 gigabytes) had been created on the island itself (Cearns 2021b).

Notably, this emerging arena of circulation is also largely dominated by demographics that traditionally have not occupied primary positions in Cuban cultural production: many of the paqueteros I encountered were young, not university-educated, and of Afro-Cuban descent. Those who developed and contributed domestic content also frequently came from more marginalized groups, including youth from impoverished urban neighborhoods (Mónica 2017), young Afro-Cuban men and women (Levine 2020; Whynacht 2009), and communities of queer or trans activists (Speakman 2021; Stout 2014a). International content was also not necessarily solely

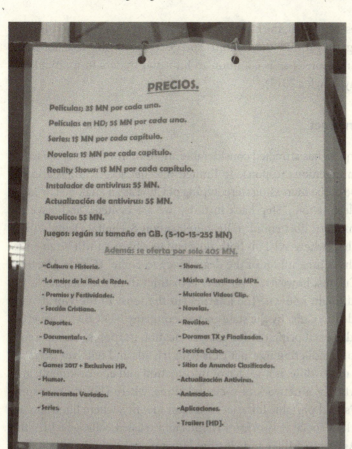

Figure 4.3. Price list displayed in the window of a *paquetero*'s home in El Cerro, Havana. "MN" stands for *moneda nacional,* i.e., Cuban pesos. Photo by author, March 2018.

American; in fact, Asian programs, such as Korean *dorama,* Turkish soap operas, and Japanese *manga* and *anime,* were becoming increasingly popular (S. F. Concepción 2021), as were other Latin American genres such as Mexican and Brazilian *telenovelas*. Most of this content was available with Spanish subtitles or is dubbed (Köhn 2019, 111), although some viewers also consumed language-learning materials through el paquete so as to better follow their favorite show (Humphreys 2021). This can arguably be seen as a legacy of socialist cosmopolitan cultural policies that encouraged the consumption of world cinema and distribution (Iordanova 2003), resulting in a contemporary audience across Cuba that is well-versed in a variety of

Part II. Circulating Value

filmic genres. Moreover, the most successful paqueteros are those culturally fluent enough in various social idioms and genres to be able to tailor packages to their clientele, as is common to informal traders in multicultural settings (Rhys-Taylor 2013).

A Parallel Internet

While el paquete has attracted considerable attention from across the world for being an ingenious response to limited internet access, it has also become a trope of the increasing stereotyping of Cuba as an analogue or "digital detox" destination. "Step back in time," we are invited, "and leave the stresses of modern life behind" ("Rest, Relaxation & Digital Detox" 2019), while in Cuba, "where Wi-Fi is both slow and terrible, you will be an emissary from the future, a hint of the degeneracy to come" (García Martínez 2017). To Cubans, however, el paquete is distinct from the internet as the wider world might know it. The internet (in the sense of the World Wide Web, provided in Cuba by the state-owned company ETECSA) is slow, expensive, and is used primarily for communication purposes, such as sending emails or conducting internet calls with friends and relatives overseas. El paquete, meanwhile, is a source of information and entertainment, and, most importantly, a network of social relations, where USB sticks assume the role of "social portable libraries of Cuban identity, where librarians are a latticework of social networks of friends and trusted colleagues" (Astley 2016, 16). As Daniel Miller and Heather Horst point out in their manifesto for a digital anthropology, "the importance of cultural relativism and the global nature of our encounter with the digital" is to negate "assumptions that the digital is necessarily homogenizing," and thus a digital anthropological lens onto such phenomena as el paquete might allow us to explore "the illusions we retain of a non-mediated, noncultural, predigital world" (2012, 3, 12). Digital technology exists within wider social networks that include analogue and other media technologies, and Cuba's paquete is a prime example of how digital practices are extensions of preexisting social and material worlds, constructed by agents who are situated in cultural specificities.

Perhaps most striking about el paquete as a digital network is its visible reliance upon the material, which is so often presented as juxtaposed with the digital or virtual nature of the online world. Often, especially when working smoothly, the materiality of the digital remains invisible to the user—yet, as danah boyd emphasizes, the architecture of a particular environment matters (boyd 2011, 37; Crowdy 2015), and nowhere more visibly (or tangibly) than in the case of Cuba.

Vincente Morin Aguado (2015) has seen USBs in Cuba as "the people's Internet," but el paquete would perhaps be better understood as a parallel internet that has developed in its own unique techno-social and economic setting. There was nothing predetermined in the 1990s about the way the World Wide Web would develop to become a product through which users' personal data is harnessed and remobilized for the financial gain of large corporations (Zuboff 2019), nor is there anything inevitable about the assertion that Cuba's internet will morph into the identical sibling of Google "when things change" (Johnstone 2019). Indeed, el paquete arguably harnesses some features of what the wider world knows as the internet; its success and profit are also mediated by the harnessing of social data, only in this case, that is face-to-face knowledge of customers by astute paqueteros who serve their surrounding neighborhoods. Yet in other regards it manifests itself differently; notions of ownership and property are distinct (as will be discussed later), as are conceptualizations of authentic or "original" content, and the interface of state and citizen through mutual surveillance. Most of the content is subject to self-censorship, and thus for many years circulation of el paquete was open in Cuba, without any particular intervention from the state. As my Cuban friend Carlos once put it to me after a few beers, "You all get so high and mighty about your free internet, but do you think Google is any different? They watch every move you make, and they profit from it. So it's all a matter of perspective."

In this light, el paquete can be considered an ingenious response to a particular moment in time, when private business licenses are obtainable and yet material (and digital) things still often circulate locally through older networks of distribution that were consolidated under socialism (see chapter 3). El paquete has rendered visible an emerging public space in the Cuban landscape: information and material exchange has always been mediated through social relationships in Cuba and beyond, but this process has manifested itself through new channels of circulation. El paquete represents an "opportunity to synchronize with trends and conversations outside the island" (Laguna 2017, 159), but also within the island, which is arguably equally potent. The transformative power of the internet as interpreted in the wider world is

> not that it allows access to information, but rather that it provides a
> public venue that allows ordinary people to . . . tell their own stories,

to recontextualize existing knowledge and official narratives, and to create their own social networks for sharing ideas. (Bernal 2014, 9)

If in "Western countries," or the Global North, the digital phenomenon has often been accused of generating alienation and individualization among users (Gladwell 2010; Morozov 2011; Nygren and Gidlund 2016), in Cuba, digital access (via el paquete more so than online access) "implies a series of private and relational practices that have contributed to the appropriation of public space by citizens" (Boudreault-Fournier 2019, 751; Liosi 2017). Indeed, this nascent national public space has galvanized and mobilized new discourses across the island, as has been the case for my friend Nestor, whose own artistic work tells us that "el paquete is, in fact, the Cuban public space today and that a gallery as well as a public space should be imagined outside the boundaries of the political and cultural elites" (Mónica 2017).

Curating el Paquete

Nestor is a Cuban artist, originally from Camagüey, but now living and working principally with digital and visual media in Havana. His first artistic interaction with what would later become el paquete was back in 2009, when he created a short film exploring the layers of creativity applied to the audiovisual product by all whose hands it passed through, resulting in a quasi-palimpsestic digital product with multiple authors:

It was about the process my grandfather lived when he rented out disks. He received the film from a matriz in Camagüey, burnt it [i.e., copied it], watched it, and then chose which genre to assign it, which actor to name; he made the cases and chose the information to put on, and then distributed them around the neighborhood, so all that post-production process, which had nothing to do with the actual film itself, was what I made the film about. (Interview, Havana, March 2018)

As a result of this, Nestor met the organizers of one of the major Havana matrices in 2013 and was invited to place his artwork in el paquete itself. He told me,

I didn't like the idea; I wanted to create something more horizontal, so that other artists could also participate, so I used the invitation to create an "online" pirate event, the first in Cuba, and I used el paquete like an online platform to circulate all the artists.

This project eventually became a folder called "!!!Sección A R T E"[5] which goes out in the Omega paquete once a month, circulating the latest artwork by various Cuban artists, as well as well-known art from around the world. Nestor subsequently met the American artist Julia Weist, and together they agreed to curate a project on el paquete at the Queens Museum in New York in 2017–18.

For this project, the artists created a collection of content to insert into Omega's paquete, and then traveled across Cuba to each *sub-matriz* to see how their content was stripped out, altered, or copied in different parts of Cuba. In most cases, the content was removed by local paqueteros who deemed it not to be of interest to their regular clients, but in some cases, Nestor discovered he had enthusiastic followers in even the most geographically remote of places across Cuba. They were also able to observe the way the territorial nature of matrices, sub-matrices, and paqueteros affected how and when content was circulated around emerging power networks. For example, even the controller of domestic flight schedules from Havana airport had considerable agency in this process, and when the first flight to Guantánamo was swapped to arrive before the first Santiago-bound flight, paqueteros realized they could drive their paquetes on a motorbike from Guantánamo to Santiago before the latter's arrival, thus undercutting the market with their own supply of digital content.

In this way, Nestor and Julia's artwork changed as it moved, with each layer of subsequent curation altering the end product. Their artistic practice, mediated by the highly material digital landscape of Cuba, became a practice of texts constantly being reinscribed and reinterpreted by new authors. Noelle Stout has discussed similarly rapid and decentralized distribution of audiovisual materials in Cuba (2014b). Echoing deconstructionist debates of the twentieth century, the text (or artistic work, or indeed, JPEG file) detaches itself from the author(s) and moves beyond his or her control or intention, assuming its position in a public, co-constituted space (Barthes 1977; Sterne 2016).

If following these digital and material flows across Cuba challenged Nestor and Julia's ideas of artistic creation and authorship, exporting el paquete as the centerpiece of their New York exhibition revealed yet further acts of reinterpretation (Hernández Tapia 2017). A further element of their

Figure 4.4. Social call for help transporting hard drives to New York from Havana, November 2017. Source: Nestor Siré.

exhibition was to be a 65-terabyte hard drive, displayed in the gallery, with an entire year's worth of paquetes saved onto what would be the first material archive of this otherwise ephemeral (unarchived) digital library of Cuban popular culture. First, they had to find a way of physically exporting all this data, which could not be sent by email due to the considerable size of the files. In the end, social media was harnessed to recruit tourists, tour guides, mulas and visiting scholars to aid in the attempt.

Once compiled in the museum, American visitors could, for the first time, scroll through a year's worth of Cuban digital content (something that would never be possible in Cuba itself, as hard drives are rewritten again and again to make use of space), and could even buy a piece of their own paquete in the museum gift shop. In this regard, Nestor and Julia exported Cuba's public material-digital space and exhibited it in a public material-digital space in New York. In the process, they, like the paqueteros in Cuba, were able to curate their own package, or parallel internet, and through facilitating the flow of this content from one place to another, were also able to profit from the process.

Figure 4.5. Mugs with an el paquete design, for sale in the Queens Museum gift shop. The design was done by a private agency based in Havana. Photo credit: Hai Zhang, courtesy of Queens Museum.

Making a Name for Oneself

Despite the oft-celebrated decentralizing, do-it-yourself aspect of content production in the digital era, there is a simultaneous and contradictory tendency "toward a certain form of concentration in the industry," as has been evident in various world music scenes (Manuel 2014, 410; Azenha 2006). While el paquete has created a new public space within Cuba, this is not to say that this public space operates as a democracy, just as internet access in no way predetermines democratic organization (Cearns 2021c). Perhaps one of the most dynamic aspects of the consolidation of el paquete as a material and digital network spanning the entire island has been its increasing commoditization and centralization under the emerging hegemonic powers of cultural representation in Cuba: the matrices. In a few short years, two, both based in Havana, had become the major portals through which most digital content consumed in Cuba, both domestic and international, flowed.

The increasing importance of such branding (which is watermarked at the bottom of a significant proportion of digital audiovisual content seen in Cuba) also trickled down to the sub-matrices and paqueteros, who, in a bid to maintain their territories of distribution, competed for customer loyalty. Some individuals have achieved both national and international fame (along with a prized visa to visit the U.S.) due to a combination of their role in the circulation of el paquete and their ability to market themselves as gatekeepers to this world. It is through their social connectedness that these individuals manage to travel beyond themselves, sending forth their digital content across the island and beyond, and so making a name for themselves. In this regard, the head paqueteros operating in Cuba mirror the Trobriand argonauts of the Kula Ring who, through their ability to act as portals between material and social words, expand their personhood and "fame" (Munn 1987). The very materiality of Cuba's parallel internet due to its transportation via USB sticks and hard drives provides further opportunity for these digital argonauts to market their own names; it is common to see both file names and physical hard drives adapted to include the paquetero's trademark.

Perhaps the most famous of all of the paqueteros has been Elio, "El Transportador," whose ability to speak English facilitated interviews in several magazines outside of the island when he left Cuba (Helft 2015). Elio's protégé Danys followed suit a few months later, and eventually moved to Miami via Mexico, where he also gained recognition as an "inventor" of the paquete (Reyes 2016). Interestingly, a few days after my televised Miami lecture on the topic, Danys found and contacted me through Facebook, offering an interview (with his lawyer in attendance) in return for a suggested fee of a few hundred dollars. I politely declined, citing limited PhD funds, but throughout the following year, I received regular communications from him, seeking further conversation and opportunity.

A few months later, in Havana, I bumped into another "founder" of el paquete, who also sought me out. Yino was having some "problems" with the Cuban government and his audiovisual license had been suspended. While his lawyer "resolved" (*resolvía*) the problem for him, he was keen to tell me how he had invented el paquete alongside Elio and Danys, but once they had gained visas to leave, they had "stolen all the credit." He seemed bitter about the fame his former friends Elio and Danys had achieved. But he had a plan to get his fiefdom back once this legal issue had been resolved. "The thing is, they act like they're still running it all, but they're not, there's no way you could do that from outside [*afuera*]. Danys hasn't had any involvement for a few years now, regardless of what he says. But I'm still here, tuned into word on the street [*a tono con la radio bemba*]; you've got to stay connected, you know?"

As a matter of fact, Yino was in the strong position of receiving regular feedback from consumers across the island, enabling him to keep his finger on the pulse of what was popular and what was not. He was receiving numerous emails per week from clients across the island, thanking him for his "great work" (*grandioso trabajo*) and suggesting improvements he could make. One such email he showed me in April 2018 thanked him for "giving the poor Cuban people [*al pobre pueblo cubano*] something to entertain themselves with." This cultivation of personal brand has repeated itself along the paquete food chain, with many ads placed in the classifieds section on el paquete trying to undercut others' business by promoting a uniquely personal service, highlighting individual experience, competitive pricing, selection of content, and willingness to deliver to customers at home.

"Los Piratas del Caribe" and e-Mules

While the consolidation of el paquete as the primary source of digital content in Cuba has, as discussed, fomented an increasing commoditization of digital content associated with personal brand, it also simultaneously invokes parallel movements across Latin America, the Global South, and beyond toward decommoditization, as consumers find ways to share content among themselves. As Miller and Horst point out, "[W]hat does seem clear is that the digital is indeed a further twist to the dialectical screw" (Miller and Horst 2012, 7), insofar as it can simultaneously be more and less commoditizing in its effects. Horst's own ethnographic work (Horst 2011a) has revealed how open-source software and "free culture" in Brazil are more broadly tied to a culture of resistance to hegemonic global culture and traditional patterns of production and ownership. In Brazil, pirated products are almost everywhere, and carry a "particular urgency" as a critique of the injustice of the international market (Dent 2012, 32; Pinheiro-Machado 2017).

The case of el paquete in Cuba has similarly opened these forms of media piracy to a wider demographic, making digital products available to a broad swath of citizens while also, paradoxically, providing them with lucrative business opportunities that often simultaneously seek to deconstruct this "democratization" of assets. Henry Stobart has shown how media piracy in Bolivia might be

> seen to serve the interests of the many traders of contraband goods on both sides of the frontier . . . [and this] might be seen as a symp-

tom of Bolivia's exceptionally informal economy, where money is to be made, even if in very small quantities, from the circulation of goods along trajectories shaped by national imaginaries. (2010, 46)

Likewise, the common perception of Cuba as a somehow exceptional analogue or digitally illiterate place has arguably allowed this informal digital marketplace to quietly grow in Cuba, fomenting local possibilities for ingenuity.

Discussion of music "piracy" has often polarized characterizations as, on the one hand, insidious criminal activity that threatens musical creativity and musicians' livelihoods alongside the production of culture, or, on the other, a legitimate and democratic struggle against hegemonizing corporatism and industry (Knopper 2009; Lessig 2004). In Cuba, el paquete seems to bridge this chasm, both in its capacity to foment public creative production and exchange, and in its disavowal of international notions of ownership and copyright. The complexity of lived social relations surrounding and flowing through such networks as el paquete defies polarizing discourses, for, in reality, actors have their own multiple agendas for participation, which at times can appear contradictory to outsiders.

When I asked Nestor, for example, if he saw the rise of el paquete as signaling a nascent American-style imported capitalism (akin to what I dubbed "Coca-Cola-nialism" in the introduction to this book) in Cuba, he responded,

The problem is, what is capitalism? I imagine it has to do with the idea of consumption. I live in a country where, if I want to find a brand of perfume, or shampoo, it's impossible to consume it, because six months can go by without being able to find it. Everything can disappear in Cuba . . . but if it's about ownership, well, then, maybe we have it right after all. I can buy a paquete this week and gift it to my friends—that doesn't happen in other places. If you bought a cell phone app or a song, your system is made so that you can't share it with other people. That's capitalism. It's complete control, and an impossibility to share. In Cuba, the paquete is a business, and we mustn't forget that, but it's also a business that's so open, not all the earnings are centralized. So talking about consumption in Cuba is a delicate thing.

In so doing, he highlighted two parallel conceptualizations of possession that coexist in present-day Cuba. On the one hand, private ownership is now officially recognized with the introduction of the new constitution in 2019, yet other items are considered *bienes en común* (goods in common ownership), drawing upon socialist notions of public utility and creative commons. Some of my friends viewed el paquete as a daring domestic challenge to American corporate hegemony; one even proudly called himself the digital "pirate of the Caribbean" for plundering lucrative channels of material flow monopolized by colonizing powers, invoking a notion of social banditry (Hobsbawm 2000). Yet, in other instances my interlocutors seemed quick to condense circulation networks and prevent flows to profit personally. Nestor had also embraced the term "pirate," and in fact, as part of his exhibition in the Queens Museum, he placed a publicly browsable copy of *The Pirate Book,* which itself contains an essay about el paquete (Maigret and Roszowska 2015).

Video piracy has undoubtedly enabled people across the Global South to participate in accelerated circuits of global media flows from which they might otherwise have largely been excluded. Examples abound across Latin America, Asia, and Africa, allowing Nigerian audiences, for example, to watch films contemporaneously with audiences in Bogotá or Bangkok (Mattelart 2009). Felicitously, the name of one of the main sites from which international digital content is downloaded in Cuba is eMule, which is a peer-to-peer file sharing site dating back to 2003. The "portable homelands"—to borrow a phrase from Cuban journalist Luis Ortega (1998, 11)—of el paquete thus resonate with the material packages carried back and forth in the Mula Ring (chapter 3) as a means of sourcing and perpetually re-creating cubanidad or local culture from and through another place. Cuban anthropologist Fernando Ortiz suggested a neologism—"transculturation"—as "fundamental and indispensable for an understanding of Cuba" (1947, 103), describing the process of transition from one culture to another as involving the syncretic fusion of various elements (see also Palmié 2013, 95). It is possible to see both the material flows facilitated by the Mula Ring and the digital/material flows of el paquete as a continuation of this transcultural practice, which posits cubanidad in the creative process of identity formation that stems from constant encounters and fusion with the other. Participation in such networks becomes a part of participating in Cuba, or a shared project of inventiveness and resolution that is seen as a defining mutual feature of this shared community.

In his ethnography of media piracy in Nigeria, Brian Larkin points out that while piracy has connected Nigerians to "the globalized world, it does so by emphasizing [their] marginalization at the same time" (2004, 308).

132 · Part II. Circulating Value

Similarly in Cuba, el paquete is more than "just a bunch of bootleg stuff from outside Cuba. It's a media ecosystem unto itself" (Parish 2018)—but by participating in this ecosystem of flow, Cubans are at once both connected to a public font of cubanidad and reminded of their own liminality in this network, which operates through those who have the facility to travel abroad, either in person or online, to procure such content. A study of the informal economy of digital media reveals the (often underground) channels through which cultural globalization operates. The routes taken by pirated cultural products are those of "globalization from below" (Basch et al. 1994; Portes 1999), and in this light, everyday Cubans arguably mobilize more agency than might first be thought in shaping transnational circuits of digital media.

Copyright, Copyleft

A striking characteristic of the digital age is the almost effortless capability it provides to create multiple identical copies of material, which in turn has fundamental implications for notions of ownership, copyright, and what it means to copy. Scholars have cited the distinction between "original" and "copy" as needing ethnographic development in terms of local conceptions of "piracy" and "originality" (Aguiar 2013; Vann 2006). El paquete provides just such an instance where media is copied on a massive scale, yet also re-authored in the process, with the individual attributions of the matriz or paquetero attaching themselves palimpsestically to the product through the insertion of branded watermarks, advertising, and subtitles. In this way, many of my Cuban interlocutors advertised *un producto original* (an original product), despite the fact the vast majority was copied from someone else, who copied it from someone else, who copied it from the internet.

The very word "piracy" suggests an illegal act, yet anthropological research has thematized resistance, subversion, and the creation of non-hegemonic circuits for the circulation and flow of culture through the infringement of copyright restrictions (A. M. Ochoa 2003; Chang 2004; Bosch 2010; J. Miller 2012). The sharing of digital assets can challenge hegemonic notions of ownership and property (Commaerts 2011), as has also become evident in a large movement toward open digital access (Kelty 2008; Coleman and Golub 2008; Coleman 2012). This becomes even more resonant in the case of Cuba, where "copyright" as a concept is not granted the same weight as in many other parts of the world. If "to oppose copyright is to oppose capitalism" (Söderberg 2002), Cuba has a long trajectory of either denying copyright as a concept, or not enforcing it in a bid to undermine nearby capitalizing (and possibly colonializing) projects in the U.S. and beyond.

Artistic production has long been fundamental to the revolutionary project in Cuba, and as such was considered a communal effort, as opposed to an expression of individualism or the sole property of an author. For this reason, many artists in Cuba are still considered state employees, as opposed to the self-employed or freelance nature of the career in many other parts of the world. With the advent of electronic and digital technologies of reproduction,

> the global reach of the mass media, and the transnational circulation of mass culture, the culture industries—which rely on creative labor and a general respect for intellectual property rights—have become export industries fundamental to the expansion of capitalism and related hegemonic projects. (Hernandez-Reguant 2004, 10)

This confronts the Cuban socialist project with new challenges regarding recognition of individual property. Moreover, the rise of el paquete has proved problematic, insofar as it generates surplus value through further creative input (or labor) by additional parties:

> In the case of music, this value is created through its reinterpretation, in "sampling," "versions," and "remixes"; through its circulation in broadcasting and advertising; and in some cases, through its mere consumptive use, via a jukebox or Internet downloads. This is all crucial for understanding the intersections of Cuban late socialist structures and capitalist practices, for under neoliberal capitalism, capital is created not only through productive labor, but also through the circulation, use, and consumption of products as well as through speculation—in this case, with mass-cultural products that are also copyrights. (Hernandez-Reguant 2004, 11).

Nonetheless, networks like el paquete also present some advantages to the Cuban state project. On the one hand, they facilitate the marketing of Cuban cultural production, both across the island and abroad (as will be discussed presently) through transnational commercial networks. Moreover, the consumption and circulation of digital content through new public spaces arguably undermines the hegemonic status of international and

134 · Part II. Circulating Value

capitalizing "intellectual property"; in this regard, the flow of digital products as "bienes en común," to borrow Nestor's earlier phrase, is arguably entirely in line with the Cuban revolutionary project, which seeks to disrupt the progression of capitalist power structures (Cearns 2021c).

Ariana Hernandez-Reguant argues for the Cuban culture industries as a sort of border zone "structured by the interests of a new array of stakeholders, both state and corporate" (2004, 2). El paquete, as the latest iteration of a Cuban culture industry, can be and has been mobilized in multiple directions: both as a litmus test as to the existence of imported neoliberal capitalist practices, and, simultaneously, as evidence of resistance to global hegemonic patterns of top-down ownership. If el paquete is a border zone, it bridges not only formulations of international and domestic, capitalist and socialist, but also confronts conceptualizations of what it is to be Cuban.

The e-Mula Ring

In chapter 3, I described how, through what I call the Mula Ring, circuits of material flow both mirror and actively shape formulations of Cuban identity. These flows connect Cubans on the island with the diaspora, but these flows also move in both directions. Paradoxically, Cubans on the island perform their cubanidad by accessing material items that originate outside of Cuba, evidencing their social connectedness in networks of kinship (chapter 2) and reciprocity. As will be explored in chapters 5 and 6, Cubans in the diaspora invoke much the same thing in the opposite direction: they source items from the island itself to feel a connection their homeland and the Cuban "essence," which comes from the very earth itself.

Digital media are no exception to this rule, perhaps particularly in Cuba, where the digital is so tangibly material in its everyday manifestation. The media in el paquete contribute to the imagining of a nation as a shared community through the production of homogeneous discourses of identity and culture, and in the case of Cuba, I argue that the locus of this identity is poised between the island itself and the diaspora. Transnational media "reach a borderless audience of nationals and non-nationals and disrupt that romantic notion of . . . one national media for each national culture" (Alonso and Oiarzabal 2010, 8), exposing a globalizing cultural landscape under constant negotiation. Moreover, as we will see presently, the material in el paquete clearly speaks to parallel audiences and its value is positioned precisely in the back-and-forth between these communities. Just as circulation is crucial in Kula exchange for the production of culture, mula exchange enables transnational digital circulation through the networks of el paquete, producing a transnational culture in so doing.

Charles Tilly (1990) makes a strong case that it is not people who migrate, but networks, so it is perhaps unsurprising that more recent Cuban immigrants to Miami (and especially Hialeah) should continue to have a desire to partake of el paquete, which I have described here as the largest current social network on the island. While this is by no means a widespread practice, a few recent arrivals (from circa 2015–present) are doing just that. With increased restrictions on Cuban artists visiting Miami to perform for their diasporic fans (Salomon 2020), the circulation of el paquete in the diaspora has expanded yet further. By 2018 there were video stores in Hialeah that mirrored the paquetero shops in Havana, right down to their aesthetic, with laminated menus of content by genre, just as paqueteros display in their windows and stairwells in Havana.

Jaynir is originally from Pinar del Rio in the west of Cuba and emigrated to Hialeah eleven years ago. He runs a small video rental store in a strip mall next to a Cuban clothing store (of the variety that sells cheap *ropa china* or "Chinese-made clothing" to mulas), a Cuban coffee *ventanita,* a shipping (to Cuba) agency, and opposite a botánica selling religious items mostly imported from Cuba. His store closely mirrored the aesthetics of paquete stores in Cuba, with products placed in homemade paper jackets with subtitles or dubbing in explicitly Cuban Spanish ("I used to download the standard Spanish ones, but I got complaints about all the th-th-ths").[6] On the back wall, he had a large display of current Cuban shows, including a TV screen playing a recent episode of *Vivir del Cuento,* Cuba's most popular comedy show. When I asked him how he kept his stock up to date, he replied "I have trustworthy friends [*amigos de confianza*] who go back and forth a lot, and they load up hard drives for me so I can copy the stuff here." At that moment a nurse came in on her lunch break, looking for something to take home for her mother to watch. "Do you have any more of those Cuban talk shows? She loved those, she said it made her feel like she was back home again." It is in this way that some migrants "take advantage of digital technologies to follow the 'pulse' of their countries in some cases more closely than many of those who remained at home" (Mejía Estévez 2009).

It was not just nostalgia for Cuba that brought in customers seeking content imported from the island, however. My filmmaker friends Ana and Rafael, who also lived in Hialeah, had been accustomed to a rich variety

Figure 4.6. President Obama participating on the Cuban national comedy sketch show *Vivir del Cuento* (2016), and explicitly addressing both Cubans "and their relatives."

of international media content through el paquete back when they lived in Havana. They had not even had to pay very often, as their friends at the prestigious art school Instituto Superior de Arte (ISA) had circulated content among themselves, granting them ample access to both domestic and international artistic content. Ana devoured everything, from BBC documentaries to "Scandi noir" and thought-provoking French cinema. That kind of content was hard to come by in the U.S., and also expensive to access; in reality, it required either a cable connection that was out of their budget, given they were on less-than-minimum-wage jobs while they awaited green card paperwork, or a fast Wi-Fi connection at home, when both only had small amounts of data through their cell phones. Once Ana's paperwork came through, she was considering applying to do a postgraduate course in documentary film, and so she took to sourcing international content as study material through Hialeah stores and friends who could sell or share the content through flash drives, imported from Cuba, where copyright restrictions went unobserved.

The gradually emerging import/export business of el paquete between Havana and Miami is only the latest manifestation of a process revealing the media landscapes of the two places to be inextricably linked. Albert Laguna has shown how Cubans newly arrived in Miami continue to follow the work of their favorite comedian—a character called Panfilo, played by Luis Silva—back in Cuba so as not to miss out on what is going on back home (2017, 135). Indeed, the cultural importance of Panfilo's show *Vivir del Cuento* back on the island is such that in 2016, Obama chose it as his platform to speak directly to the Cuban people (see "Obama Visitó a Panfilo" 2016). I would also argue his choice was just as much about communicating with the Hialeah diaspora as with Cubans on the island itself.

In the show, Obama plays dominoes with the main characters, with various tongue-in-cheek jokes aimed at both Cuba and the U.S. For example, one character shows him how to mix the dominoes, or *darles agua,* but "not too much water as you can't always find it," alluding to the material shortages on the island. He then discovers he's been "blocked" in by a bigger player and the "game has reached an impasse," alluding to the embargo (*bloqueo*) the U.S. imposes on Cuba. Panfilo excitedly says that it is good that relations are being restored (as are the streets through which Obama is to be driven to the baseball stadium, he coyly points out). With the help of Obama, the impasse is broken and Panfilo wins the game, while Obama takes the opportunity to ask him to tell all the Cuban people *and their relatives* how grateful he is to have been given the opportunity to visit the island—the first American president to do so in sixty years (see figure 4.6).

Cubans on the island also avidly follow comedy sketches produced by Miami-based Cubans such as Los Pichy Boys (Laguna 2017, 188) through el paquete, and these sketches often draw upon social tropes that only those most connected with the cultural landscapes in both places could understand. The humor of Los Pichy Boys depends upon intimate and ongoing ties to the island; one video, "Los Piratas del Caribe," reenacts Disney character Captain Jack Sparrow stealing a Cuban "Caribe" brand television and presenting it to his girlfriend as an expensive plasma TV (Laguna 2017, 188). Another video deals with the experiences of recent Cuban arrivals to Miami, such as their video "iPhone Cubano: asiri" (Laguna 2017, 196), which plays on confusion regarding Apple's "siri" feature, and a pun with Cuban (contemporary) slang *asere* ("close friend"), alluding to how internet-enabled smart phones might resolve problems in Miami, but in Cuba, it is to social networks of friends that one turns for up-to-date information. They also have another video in which Miami Cubans attempt to send their grandmother's body back to Cuba for burial wrapped up in plastic via a mula, spoofing the volume of mulas carrying goods back and forth and the oft-heard desire to be buried in one's home soil (see chapter 6).

Increasingly, content producers on both sides of the Florida Straits are aware of a dual audience, as their diasporic content is downloaded from YouTube or Miami television channels for consumption via el paquete, and Cuban shows on the island are imported into Miami for consumption by

138 · Part II. Circulating Value

recent arrivals. In large part, this is a way of staying connected with friends and relatives "on the other side"; all around the world, relatives phone one another to say, "Did you see the latest episode of . . . ?" and Cubans are no different in this respect. Some Cuban media producers have even started to make a good living from this interaction between island and diaspora; Cuban comedian Robertico has a comedy club in Vedado (Havana) that is beyond the financial means of most locals, but that attracts a steady clientele visiting from Miami thanks to his material circulating both on YouTube and through el paquete (re-downloaded again in Havana from YouTube). Subsequently he is regularly invited to present shows to sell-out audiences in Miami (Laguna 2017, 179). Others have started targeting their advertising to dual audiences, aware that while the diaspora might spend the money in Cuban stores in Miami, it is often on behalf of relatives on the island. Both Valsan and ¡Ñooo! que barato (stores in Hialeah specializing in selling cheap items for Cubans in the diaspora to send to relatives on the island) have advertised promotions on el paquete; the owner of the latter store, Serafin, once told me he regularly has Miami customers coming in saying they received a phone call from a relative in Cuba to let them know there was a special offer on.

Evidently, then, migrating in a "space of flows" supposes a "much more continuous reality where the meanings of 'origin' and 'destination' are blurred" (Ros 2010, 26). While Cubans on the island may enhance their prestige through obtaining audiovisual materials from overseas, so, too, do immigrants to the Cuban diaspora maintain ties to their homeland through consumption of audiovisual materials. Social capital becomes a "transnational process" as information circulates through "immigrant social networks, along with videos and photos" (Knauer 2009, 160–163) as a form of reverse ethnography, in which each side is observing and participating in the other through digitally mediated encounters. A focus upon diaspora and digital flows reveals nations and identities as dynamic forms that are not only "increasingly difficult to map as bounded communities," but also operate through various networks (Bernal 2014, 1). Such exchanges take place in all walks of Cuban life, and the digital sphere is no exception.

Conclusion

James Clifford's (1994) apt simile situating diaspora in both "roots" and "routes" calls to mind here the term "router," meaning a wired or wireless point of reciprocal connection and digital flow. In the case of digital media in and between Cuba and its Miami diaspora, the two-way flow of information further reveals the mutual formation of Cuban subjectivities earlier presented through the material Mula Ring. The digital, as all material culture, "is more than a substrate; it is becoming a constitutive part of what makes us human" (Miller and Horst 2012, 4), a large part of which, for Cubans on and off the island, requires mutual consumption of and participation in social networks of digital circulation.

This chapter has shown how nascent digital networks in Cuba and its diaspora are providing an emerging public space that both encourages social participation and yet is centralizing itself into an increasingly commoditized platform of fewer voices. This reveals a potential clash between the emerging capitalistic practices and latent socialist ideologies that coexist in Cuban society—something that, to most Cubans, is not problematic, but simply a normal aspect of everyday life. As in the case of pawnshop valuables in chapter 1, notions of ownership flex according to context, and these informal networks of digital circulation build upon long-standing pragmatism and flexibility when it comes to acquisition through participation in social networks.

With the arrival of digital content, Cuba clearly is not morphing into a pseudo-American model of media consumption, as is intimated by some (Fernandes 2017; Nelson 2016; Venegas 2007). Cuba's paquete in some ways points to a parallel model for what the internet could have looked like, emerging from its own particular socioeconomic context. This model arguably forces us to reexamine our own notions of the internet, and where the boundary lies between public and private, state (or corporation) and citizen (consumer), authorship and "authenticity" or originality. Too often, representations of Cuba's digital sphere stem from normative positions premised upon a very specific model of digital connectivity.

Moreover, el paquete does not merely signal the absorption of hegemonic digital and audiovisual culture from the Global North into Cuban praxis; it is also generating new domestic content, and arguably provides consumers with greater variety than its equivalents in the nearby Miami diaspora. Upon closer inspection, this digital network in fact incorporates the wider Cuban diaspora into a reciprocal and transnational flow of cultural identity, and much of the digital content consumed on both sides of the Florida Straits reveals a highly self-conscious awareness of its dual audiences. If "the discussion of national (and diasporic) identity needs to embrace multiple *cubanidades*" (Knauer 2009, 166), it is surely the examination of reciprocal and transnational material-digital flows such as those presented here

140 · Part II. Circulating Value

that provides us with a lens onto the processes of this identity formation. Indeed, the movement of these items becomes key to their ability to bestow a particularly "Cuban" quality upon the owner or holder—something that becomes even more apparent in the case of antiques, explored in the next chapter.

III

Returning Value

5

"Back to the Future"

Nostalgia, Authenticity, and the Antiques Trade between Miami and Havana

"The problem for these people," said Francisco as we wandered around one of Miami's many stores specializing in Cuban antiques, "is that for them, Cuba is dead, and my Cuba is alive." His words resonated through months of my fieldwork experiences, when I had repeatedly encountered conflicting notions of the past, mobilized in distinct ways by different cohorts of Cubans in my different fieldsites through their encounters with material relics representing horizons both lost and found. According to George Marcus,

> multi-sited research is designed around chains, paths, threads, conjunctions, or juxtapositions of locations in which the ethnographer establishes some form of literal presence, with an explicit posited logic of association of connection among sites that in fact defines the argument of the ethnography. (1995, 105)

The guiding threads through this book have been material items, the emotional trajectories they convey, and the people who convey them. Given the multiple layers of agency and symbolism that can be exerted through and by material things, it seems appropriate now to turn to their own temporal trajectories, the histories they narrate, and the histories they silence. The "sociospatial life of stuff" (Foster 2006, 285), when tracked back and forth across Cuban worlds not only through space but through time, is, I argue, an evocative lens onto not only the past, but also present and future contestations regarding what it means to be Cuban.

This chapter traces antique material items back and forth between Miami and Havana, charting the motivations, justifications, and emotional

144 · Part III. Returning Value

trajectories of various actors who, to a substantive degree, define their life narratives in terms of this flow. I address the politics of remembering—as well as forgetting—in the forging of diasporic and national identities to consider how hegemonic gazes onto Cuba itself reproduce themselves through material things, as well how individual justifications and motivations are asserted within this material world both in Havana and in Miami. Finally, drawing on Kopytoff's (1986) proposal of cultural biographies of things, I suggest that in this instance, antique things act in ways that people cannot; just as in the case of el paquete in the last chapter, their ability to simultaneously count as inert "things" while summoning the affective stories and resonance of people uniquely positions them to flow back and forth across a patrolled geopolitical border.

Remembering to Forget

In characterizing the role of memory as a force of distortion, sublimation, and appropriation in a postwar landscape in continental Europe, Tony Judt has argued that it "bequeathed to the post-war era an identity that was fundamentally false, dependent upon the erection of an unnatural and unsustainable frontier between past and present in European public memory" (1992, 84). Judt's phrasing resonates with current contestations over collective memory among the Cuban diaspora in Miami, where distinct generations or waves of migrants from Cuba have arrived with their own memories and narratives of "the Cuban experience," each finding others' memoryscapes to be false distortions of the "real" Cuba they knew. Rather than looking at memory as some form of archive of historical fact, my focus here is more on the work of memory-as-legitimation, for in Miami and in Havana, memory is wielded as a political force to include and exclude. Among an older diasporic generation of Cuban exiles in Miami, this frontier between past and present is a founding tenet of their collective identity, carefully documented and preserved through material artifacts that narrate specific curated versions of past and present, "before" and "after." Thus, my interest here is not so much in any veracity in the historicity of these objects and the narratives they convey—and in this chapter we will see many layerings of "false" narratives in the sense Tony Judt suggests—but more in how and why these narratives are constructed and transported in a way more reminiscent of what Svetlana Boym terms "restorative nostalgia" (2001), or in the assertion of narratives of past heritage to naturalize contemporary power structures.

Susanne Küchler has argued we have "to do away with the idea that the past is 'stored' in a distant, 'foreign' place waiting to be opened up through selective recollection" (Ingold 1996, 183), yet, ironically, it seemed to me time and time again that this was precisely what many of my interlocutors in Miami were setting out to do, quite literally preserving a curated notion of a Cuban past in a foreign place. For many, as self-identifying "exiles" from their homeland, a common discourse of remembering seemingly innocuous things such as brand names, products, and other everyday material trivia was a substantive part of what remained to them of their Cuban identities, which, in following decades, had been under siege both from the American identities of their newly acquired homeland and the remobilization of a Cuban identity in wider hegemonic discourses toward postrevolutionary Cuba, Che Guevara, and "*hasta la victoria siempre.*"[1] A similar significance of the material tropes of yesteryear has been documented in other communities where seismic shifts in identity politics have occurred, especially in the postsocialist world (Blum 2000; Bach 2002).

As such, a healthy market has opened up in Miami, with various stores specializing in Cuban antiques, vintage, and memorabilia catering to a sizable clientele of Cuban exiles (and their children, grandchildren, and even great-grandchildren) who, in their retirement, are seeking material ways to "reconnect" with their "stolen" pasts from before the revolution. Paul Connerton has described the high prestige of memory among "enemies of totalitarianism," where "every act of recollection, every attempt to disinter and reconstitute the past, [is] perceived as an act of principled opposition to state power" (2006, 317). For the aging "exile" generation of the Cuban diaspora in Miami in particular, many of their material (re)encounters with their pasts are also ideological statements of the present and future, and their purchase and subsequent display in the home of such items declare a certain solidarity with what they consider the "true" or "free" Cuba (situated in the diaspora).

Just as Miami's Cuban exiles select memories in a communal act of remembering through evocative material objects, so, too, do they selectively forget other aspects of their shared past. While forgetting is often characterized as an act of loss, it can itself be a creative process, through which identity can be affirmed (Dijck 2007). In her work on kinship and identity politics among Malays on the island of Langkawi, for example, Janet Carsten (1995a) found the act of forgetting to be as central to identity formation as the act of remembering. In the case of the Cuban exile community in Miami, a "structural amnesia" (Barnes 1947; Connerton 2017) regarding any

146 · Part III. Returning Value

potential ills of Cuban society prior to the revolution (for example, prostitution, military dictatorships, corruption, poverty, or racism) has ensured the continuing cementing of a community in present exile, bound by its longing for an invented (or curated) past. This selective memory surrounding details of a shared past has become tantamount to a hegemonic origin myth in Miami, which serves simultaneously to include those who shared this loss and exclude those later generations of immigrants whose memories of Cuban history have been different. Such memories serve as another terrain on which questions of hierarchy and power differential between different waves of Cuban migrants can be battled over, carving up Cuban identity along boundaries of class, race, and political ideology.

In Miami, these shared structures of memory in turn find their manifestation in various shops and museum sites, which become physical, tangible shrines of memorialization to a collective loss. Drawing on work by Pierre Nora, Didier Maleuvre has written of the West's "invention of the past," modernity's "rise of heritage" and "concomitant Eurocentric urges to build places of memory [*lieux de mémoire*] because there are no more real environments of memory [*milieux de mémoire*]" (Maleuvre 1999, 59; Nora 1989). These can be viewed as contemporary acts of repossession, in which the dream to both define and repossess one's lost heritage endures. In this way, the sites commemorating a shared heritage in Miami that I present throughout this chapter have arguably become shrines for "civilizing rituals" (Duncan 1995) in a secular world, where antique phone books from 1958 Havana or old Cuban photographs serve as relics of a lamented lost Zion (or Havana).

While this speaks to a strong sense of national identity, it also expands beyond these parameters. As transnational, diasporic subjects who now recognize themselves as participants in multiple communities, it is perhaps unsurprising that these Cuban exiles should narrate this shared past specifically at sites of arrival or entry. Miami's Freedom Tower, which in the 1960s was where Cuban immigrants were processed upon arrival, was closed at the time of my fieldwork for redevelopment as the Cuban American Historical Museum, to house material artifacts narrating this generation's exile and subsequent assimilation in Miami. Most of the commercial and museum spaces celebrating these material links to "the homeland" are clustered around entry points into the Little Havana district, which was where the generation of Old Cubans first settled, and there is a sizable exhibition of artifacts at the Cuban Heritage Collection at the University of Miami, which in turn might be considered a more symbolic locus for arrival and departure.

Shopping in a "Graveyard for Cuba"

Despite having left Cuba over fifty years ago, Pilar had only set up her Cuban memorabilia store a few years before I met her. She had moved to Venezuela for a few years, and suffered such acute homesickness and nostalgia for cubanidad that she set up an online Cuban food store first—"nostalgia starts in the stomach you know, you feel it in your gut"—before expanding into her current property in Little Havana in Miami. Her shop of over 3,000 items celebrating various tropes of Cuban culture visibly overwhelmed several of the other first-time visitors who stepped through the front door during my first visit. Most of the items were fairly cheap gifts that might be bought as a joke present for a Cuban diaspora relative: bumper plates saying "Honk if you're Cuban," domino sets, and mojito glasses were among the cheaper items she had out on display in the front room.

But toward the back of the store was a side room where she housed her "special collection": a veritable treasure trove of antique objects all purportedly dating back to before the revolution in Cuba. The room was crammed full of old school tiepins, photos, and faded documents, little sacks of Cuban sugar and soil, and miniature Coca-Cola bottles (containing some likely rather flat soda) that were, crucially, also from before 1959. Most of the items had been brought over in exiles' suitcases in the 1960s, and subsequently donated or sold to her as the succession of years brought about a few home clear-outs. Others had quite obviously come from Cuba more recently, including, much to Pilar's pride, the original brass doorknocker from Havana's capitol building, etched with "República de Cuba, 1929." "I don't always ask too closely about the provenance of all my items," Pilar grinned at me as she caught me inspecting it. A few years before, she claimed, a young Cuban man had shown up at her front door with a suitcase full of antique items from Cuba. "I get them all the time, they get hold of this stuff there, and I don't ask too many questions about how, and they show up here trying to sell it to me," she said. Pilar usually did not bite, but on this occasion, she could tell it was the real deal.

I wasn't sure if I should buy it at first, as it was probably stolen, but then I thought, you know what? This is really historic, and it belonged

148 · Part III. Returning Value

to the free Cubans from before the revolution. And the free Cubans are here now, so in a way, this is our birthright. Plus, at what he was asking for it, it was a steal!

"It's a very powerful and solemn room, this one," she whispered, surveying the piles of stuff. "Every day somebody will come in here and find something that makes them cry or laugh; material things have the power to do that." On one occasion, several years earlier, a man had come into the store and was looking at a photograph Pilar's husband had acquired of his school class from 1953. The man had looked at it intensely for a while, before turning to him and saying the date on the photograph must have been wrong; it was from 1956. When asked how he knew, the man replied that he had been the teacher of that class; fifty-five years later, teacher and pupil were reunited in a small shop in Miami. "I've never seen anything like it!" said Pilar, "the tears were just streaming down my husband's face. We have his old teacher over for dinner once a month now, and to think we'd all been here all that time without knowing!"

Indeed, for Pilar the store is not just a shop, but rather a museum dedicated to Cuban heritage. "You see, you can probably go and see the school your grandparents went to, but we had that taken from us. All our heritage has to be through these things, because there is no other way of teaching our children and our grandchildren about their heritage." As such, Pilar encourages local schools to bring children on field trips to learn about Cuban history, and revels in taking out selected items and "presenting them with their past." She also allows elderly Alzheimer's and dementia patients to come and touch the items. "It's a beautiful thing to see; by [them] touching the things, you help them keep in touch with who they are."

Most of all, Pilar sees her store as an educational experience, and is proud to spend at times four to five hours a day "teaching" Cubans visiting from the island about their heritage. "So many of them come in and don't recognize any of the signs of Cuba! This is their cultural heritage, and they feel completely betrayed that they don't know about it, so I see it as my responsibility to help them reconnect with what's been stolen from all of us." For Pilar, patriotism and national identity are things to be instilled in people when they are very young, and material artifacts help in this educational process.

Feeling Cuban is the thing that unites us all. It doesn't matter where you were born, and if our children don't have those memories—we have to implant them. My daughter has never been to Cuba, but she feels the same pain I do, and the pain that represents exile is what you see here in this store.

Such is the symbolic weight of holding an item from Cuba (representing a specific version of cubanidad from before 1959) in one's own hands, Pilar also on occasion rents out items to loyal customers who wish to showcase them at a family gathering or party. A particular traditional *guayabera* shirt that was made in Havana's famous El Encanto store over sixty years ago is often lent out, in a protective glass case, as the centerpiece for *quinceañeras* or birthday parties to provide a touch of "authenticity." Such rituals surrounding the artifact as a site of cultural authenticity bring to mind the Aboriginal Tjuringa described by Claude Lévi-Strauss (1966), which are placed at the center of ceremonies of cultural identity to stress their capacity to store cultural memory and identity. Pilar gave another friend several old school tiepins to put in her father's coffin, so that he could lie at rest with a piece of his Cuban childhood (see also chapter 6). For charitable acts such as this, and her ongoing efforts to "preserve" Cuban heritage, Pilar is widely recognized in "the community" (*la comunidad*), and, indeed, the street adjacent to her store will soon be renamed after her—another physical memorial to a specific rhetoric of Cuban heritage within Miami.

Not all Cubans agree with Pilar's portrayal of the Cuban past, however, and as such, her store can be a site of spiritual and emotional (and, on rare occasions, also physical) conflict and turmoil. After several months of visiting the store and getting to know the owner, I decided to return with a close friend of mine, who had himself only moved to Miami from Cuba three years before. Francisco was outright offended by Pilar's shrine to Cuba before 1959 and saw it as a violent assault on his own identity: "They've kidnapped our history! These people, for example, were fascists!" he said, brandishing a faded picture of Cuban politicians in the 1920s in my face.

When I come into a store like this I realize I must be French or something, because apparently I'm not Cuban! These people talk as if everything before the revolution was perfect, as if they had everything they wanted and nothing ever went wrong. It's such a lie, they've completely reinvented the truth.

His disdain was only heightened when he spotted a display cabinet containing a copy of Havana's 1958 phonebook (see figure 5.1), with an editorial gloss added by Pilar, reading,

If there's a way of knowing or remembering the abundance of Cuba in the 1940s and 50s, there's no better than the phonebook from Havana in 1958. In its yellow pages you will find ads for the products and services that existed in Cuba in that beautiful period: cars (of all makes), textile and clothing stores, laboratories, shops, glasses, food, etc. Whatever was consumed in the USA and in Europe, we also had in Cuba. Nothing was lacking! Everything was in abundance... until the arrival of the Communist Plague!

For Yessi, a twenty-something-year-old employee at the store who had also recently arrived from Cuba, the store was a site of tense encounters as well. On less than minimum wage, she told me (somewhat sardonically) that she was going through Miami's "reeducation program" ("*programa de reeducación*"), where, bit by bit, she was being taught to "remember" her "true" stance on the Cuban historical narrative. She had moved to Miami

Figure 5.1. Havana phonebook from 1958, for sale in Pilar's store. Photo by author, November 2017.

with her young son to find work and had been working in the store for a few months, more often than not out back, cleaning the customer toilet (which had Fidel Castro's face painted in the bowl). When I asked her why she'd come to work here, of all places, she beckoned me over to a corner away from the customers, and said, "I really don't like it! People here have very particular opinions about Cuba, really, really bad ones. As if it's our fault! It's not like I ever had a choice in the matter, I'm 23, that Cuba's all I've ever known!" With the utmost diplomacy, she caught my eye and said, "It's a distinct version of Cuba, and working here, believe me, I hear it all. But this tropical crap [*esa mierda tropical*] has nothing to do with where I'm from," she muttered, rolling her eyes. "Have you noticed how she calls herself *directora*, rather than the owner?" she asked, referring to Pilar's decision to represent herself as a cultural figure within the community, rather than a business owner. "'*Ay Dios!*" [For heaven's sake!]. Returning to my friend Francisco, we wandered back to the antiques room. "Poor José Martí," he said sadly, surveying the rows of cheap busts of the Cuban martyr on sale, "he's the prostitute of Cuban history."[2]

> She doesn't even have a coherent selection—this statue that she has with the pre-revolutionary stuff is definitely more modern than she thinks it is. This is like a graveyard for Cuba, a graveyard of relics. I guess this is where Cuba has come to die!

Sites of Preservation

Pilar's store, like many others dotted around Little Havana in Miami, was a curious mixture of memorabilia shop and museum of artifacts, taking the form of almost a personal shrine presided over by a charismatic individual with a specific ideological outlook. As such, it closely resembles the private museums to the former GDR described by Jonathan Bach in his work on *Ostalgie* and material culture in Eastern Germany (2015, 2017). Bach depicts store/museums, privately funded, with cluttered thematic rooms claiming to authentically represent a vanished (and often idealized) form of life. These spaces offer visitors the ability to touch objects ("*Geschichte zum Anfassen*" or "History to Touch") as an interactive, informal, and tactile approach to representing the quotidian, which, Bach argues, also reunites ex-GDR citizens with a way of "working through the past" in a tactile and empowering way, amid general feelings of powerlessness stemming from the loss of a way of life. Taken together, these informal private museums

152 · Part III. Returning Value

represent generational and epochal memories that form the kind of "we-identity" often associated with the political memory of nations, but also associated with a collective politics of forgetting that excludes as much as it includes.

"For better or for worse, Miami is Cuba's archive, and most things end up coming here where there's a desire to preserve everything, or at least a version of it," noted another friend, Julio, as we walked over to the Cuban Heritage Collection together. Material and digital cultural artifacts have a powerful role in the canonization of memory, as they are often used as media through which a culture is documented and curated (Connerton 2006, 317). While Pilar's store and others like it are private and informal spaces of heritage preservation, Miami's formal institution for documenting and narrating exiled Cubans' versions of Cuban history through material artifacts is the Cuban Heritage Collection, housed at the University of Miami. The collection is home to many items, including books, postcards, periodicals, official and personal manuscripts, maps, photographs, and digital material, largely (although not entirely) dating to before the revolution. Everything in the collection is either directly from Cuba, deals in some way with life on the island, or has meaning for and is related to members of the global Cuban diaspora. The material includes items from the colonial past to the present.

The significance of the Cuban Heritage Collection to a diasporic community constantly trying to define itself in the light of new waves of immigration to Miami is underlined by the continuous support it has received from members of the Cuban community based in Miami and elsewhere. The act of donating an item to this prestigious institution for communal use and appreciation is a way of participating in an effort to "shift from forming part of a dispersed and private, though distinctive, Cuban American reminiscing, to become added to resources for institutionalized public memory" (Lohmeier and Pentzold 2014, 8). As such, donating is seen as an act not just of preservation, but also of creation in the face of a dissolving material culture and a transforming community. Anxieties over the loss not only of Cuba, but also of the diasporic Cuban community so energetically built in the 1960s and 70s as new waves of immigrants from Cuba and beyond arrived, propel efforts to preserve, project, and cement heritage forms before they are lost "again." A renewed energy has therefore gone into resurrecting institutionalized sites of communal remembrance, with several new museum spaces opening in just a few years (2016–2020). A "mnemoscape" (Lankauskas 2014) of private collections and stores has expanded outward into several publicly funded museums (including the American Museum of the Cuban Diaspora and the Cuban American Heritage Museum, as well as the announcement of a new Casa Cuba at Florida International University in 2018), due in no small part to several wealthy benevolent donors.[3] This move toward institutionalizing public memory in Cuban Miami might be seen as a direct reaction to increasing confrontations with alternative discourses and memories of Cuban identity and heritage, which vie for hegemonic status in the official narrative of the diaspora.

All-Consuming Nostalgia

The term "nostalgia," drawing on Greek *nostos* ("return to the native land") and *algos* ("grief"), has been in use since the seventeenth century, when it denoted a physical complaint common to those who "once away from their native land . . . languished, wasted away and even perished" (Lowenthal 1985, 10). It was presented to me by my participants frequently as both a collective and an affective phenomenon. Much of the literature addressing the transition from socialism to a postsocialist form of capitalism across Eastern Europe in the 1990s has charted how affective forms of nostalgia have cemented and become increasingly institutionalized and commodified within cultural memoryscapes. Jonathan Bach, for example, has argued that in East Germany the phenomenon of Ostalgie is "a collective phenomenon that emerges through the effects of commodification, which transforms everyday objects into nostalgia objects and enables their circulation and recombination with contemporary debates, tropes, and symbols" (2017, 17–18). As with the Cuban exodus in the early 1960s, in East Germany many felt that there was "no time to say goodbye"; objects became the things with which actors constructed their own mourning, and thus symbolically transcend a cultural death. In the words of Alexei Yurchak, "everything was forever, until it was no more" (2005). Moreover, nostalgia posited in material culture becomes instrumental in constructing a shared future (Angé and Berliner 2014; Boym 2001; Piot 2010).

The Miami Cuban diaspora's reception of their collective trauma has also become a commodified experience that can be ticketed for general admission at an annual fair—rather like the *Ostprodukte* antique fairs enjoyed in East Germany (Bach 2017, 39)—which, for $12 admission, hosts a ream of material ephemera simultaneously lamenting and celebrating the tangible aspects of loss under one expo-center roof. In 2018, the fair was celebrating its twentieth anniversary, and was held in the heart of Cuban Miami, on

Figure 5.2. Cuban diaspora visiting the Nostalgia Fair, walking the streets of Havana and reminiscing. Photo by author, May 2018.

8th St. in Westchester. I went along on a Friday night, and found myself in a large hall, surrounded for the most part by Cuban exiles in their 60s and 70s, who had come to Miami as young children, and had fairly scanty memories of actually being on the island itself. Many had brought children and grandchildren along to "show them" their own past; as with the nostalgia-themed memorabilia stores elsewhere in Miami, the fair focused upon the more sensorial aspects of nostalgia that are most missed: touch, smell, taste, sound. Visitors could walk a short length of a reconstructed seafront promenade Malecón (although this version had been decorated with graffiti saying "Free the press!") and pause to take selfies in front of a vast printout of Havana's cathedral. Large street maps of Havana and Santiago de Cuba had been printed on the floor, so that visitors could quite literally walk the streets they once knew, pointing out landmarks to one another with one hand while reminiscing, with a Bacardí mojito clasped in the other.[4] An old man sat at a piano in the corner, bashing out rousing versions of old tunes from the 1940s and '50s, to a backdrop of large posters celebrating various landmark achievements of human history (although none, I noted, from after 1959, after which point time has seemingly stood still).

At various strategic points around the room were low tables set up as stalls, where locals were selling antiques and memorabilia relating to Cuban nostalgia. Many of the items were identical to those I had seen in stores such as Pilar's, but one stall in particular had a huge amount of stock, ranging from sixteenth-century manuscripts to signed photos from the 1950s, and everything in between. Various visitors were leafing through booklets, occasionally asking a man in his seventies what price he wanted. When met with an extortionate answer, most briskly backed away to seek out mojitos and *pastelitos* from the nearby food truck. I, however, went over to strike up a conversation with the man, whom I recognized as Ernesto, the owner of Miami's most renowned Cuban antiques store, in prime position on 8th St., which I had found to my dismay to be permanently closed up with padlocks.

It turned out that Ernesto, who by his own estimates had over $60,000 of stock, was slightly paranoid about break-ins or retaliatory attacks from the Cuban government, and so chose to feign a permanent state of closure; visits were by appointment only, for serious buyers. Ernesto and his 93-year-old mother, who both energetically used social media to campaign for Donald Trump and the Republican Party as well as other right-wing causes, were concerned that retribution from the leftist Cuban government could be delivered personally to their door at any time. On his table at the fair Ernesto had only items dating from pre-1959, which was of no surprise to me and in line with the wider ideological stance taken by most collectors I had come across in Miami; indeed, he particularly liked investing in anything that might help win the ideological war against the leftists who had stolen his homeland.

Of all the objects in his possession, his favorite was a book, which he himself compared to *Mein Kampf* in its political leanings, that he claimed had been written by Hitler's right-hand-man before being given to Fidel Castro, and then consequently gifted to Che Guevara with an annotating instruction on "how to destroy a country," dated to before the Cuban revolution. This, for Ernesto, was proof that Castro had set out to destroy Cuba, and as such it was of incredible symbolic, emotional, and ideological potency. "As far as I'm concerned," he told me, "the embargo never existed, because people have always known how to circumvent it, and the Cubans have always played that to their advantage." He was convinced the Cuban government was now trying to take advantage of the exiled community once more by permitting Cubans to smuggle out the patrimony that had been stolen from them 60 years earlier, only to resell it to them in Miami. "If they're determined to rob us twice, I'll play them at their own game!" he barked. "I consider myself the savior of Cuban patrimony. They don't care about anything from before 1959, so I am saving our history and preserving the future."

Over the months that followed, it gradually emerged that Ernesto in fact did not have quite such a polarized view on relations with Cuba as I had first thought. While at the fair he had openly scorned anyone who was willing to visit or conduct a dialogue with the island, by the time we were munching pastelitos at a well-known Cuban café on 8th Street a few months later, he was openly boasting about all the business contacts he had there, some of whom went back and forth a lot, more often than not carrying items for him. "It's absolutely incredible what I can find!" he told me excitedly, "although it's not like it was. Now that they have more internet access, they're more likely to want the market price for the stuff." But Ernesto had even had people make an appointment with him in Miami to "order" the collection of items that had been lost to them in Cuba; he would then get in touch with his contacts in Havana and, on occasion, the item would be "found" and transported (for a hefty price) to its "rightful owners" in Miami.

I gradually started to understand what he had meant back at the fair that day, when he had said he would play the Cuban government "at their own game." For Ernesto in fact did sell many items from after the revolution . . . just not in Miami, where doing so could put even the most careful person at risk of some kind of retribution. Instead, he sold his stuff online and at fairs from Chicago to Seattle, where he found (to his great dislike) that consumer expectations of Cuba were in fact synonymous with t-shirts bearing Che Guevara's face. As Ernesto justified it to me, selling tropes of Cuba post-1959 for profit was the ultimate way to recoup some of the loss his family had suffered because of people like Che and Fidel. In this revelation I found Ernesto, like many other Cuban antique dealers in Miami, to be a curious mixture of ideology and pragmatism: While he was staunchly opposed to the revolution and committed to re-narrating his particular brand of Cuban history through the curation of antique items he collected, he also took no issue with (quietly) buying items that epitomized the very things he stood against, when it appeared to suit him—something that, as with Pilar and her doorknocker, he justified in politicized terms. At times these seeming contradictions would even spill out of his mouth in one succinct turn of phrase, such as his assertion:

I don't allow politics to affect my business too much, the only color I care about here is green [i.e., dollars]. But you know, they stole all of our stuff and now they send it back through with these Cuban boys to try and sell it back to us at an inflated rate. So I'm going to do the same with their stuff.

Ernesto, like many of the dealers in his circle, had also noted that there was a good deal of money to be made not only from nostalgia in Miami, but also from nostalgia in Cuba itself, often mobilized in a different way. One of his more recent clients was a wealthy businessman still living in Havana, who had a wife and children in Orlando, Florida. He sent them regular remittances from Cuba to top up the state benefits on which they subsisted in the U.S., and eventually sent them down to Miami to purchase Cuban antiques from Ernesto, paid for with money from Cuba, to be sent back to him in Havana to decorate a restaurant he would be opening there.

Picking up the Pieces of Cuban History

At the stall next to Ernesto's, I found Pablo, a police officer from central Florida who also made a decent living on the side collecting and trading in antique coins from Cuba. His parents had left shortly after the revolution, and it was only a few years ago that Pablo had become interested in collecting Cuban coins as a way of reconnecting with his family roots. Like Ernesto, Pablo was keen to show me his collections, and whipped out a suitcase full of old silver coins, drawing several other nearby men over to glimpse inside. Where Pablo differed from Ernesto, however, was his stance on present-day Cuba; he had first gone to the island on his own to visit a few years before, and rather than defining his life in terms of loss, he instead saw his status spanning the categories of both Cuban and American as a unique opportunity in a changing marketplace, his bicultural fluency meaning he could navigate "both worlds," as well as parallel nostalgias, to his advantage.

Pablo had started to visit Cuba more frequently on buying trips, acquiring antiques to bring back and sell online, or to sell to other traders like Ernesto who would not visit the island themselves, but who needed someone who would. On his last trip he had befriended some Cuban divers and paid them to find one of Cuba's 400 coastal shipwrecks; they had chipped a hoard of early nineteenth century silver coins away from the bedrock, badly weathered, which Pablo had then bought from them for a reportedly meager price. To counter any difficulties in carrying them out of the country, Pablo had made sure to be documented arriving in Cuba with old coins (which he sold to various wealthy collectors or antique shops in Havana);

158 · Part III. Returning Value

as far as the authorities were concerned, he was leaving with the same collection. It is illegal to remove cultural patrimony from the island without permission and documentation from the authorities, but, when necessary, staff at the Cultural Office in Havana could be "incentivized" (for $30) to stamp the required documentation, Pablo told me.[5] "It works out pretty efficiently because I can sell in both directions, and there aren't many people who can compete with me at that." Ironically, this also meant that Pablo was frequently handling items that, having been taken from the U.S. or Spain to Cuba in the eighteenth and nineteenth centuries, had then been carried out of Cuba to the U.S. in the twentieth century, bought by him, and carried back into Cuba again in the twenty-first century, to be sold to foreign tourists who would take them back to Europe or the U.S. At each stage of the item's journey, it would be imbued with a new level of affective meaning, which in turn shifted across the decades with the changing relationships among the U.S., Cuba, and Spain. Moreover, these items were able to plot the life stories and trajectories of (now-deceased) Cubans in a way that most modern-day Cubans currently cannot.

At this point, an older Cuban man at the fair pulled the briefcase toward him to take a look at the shipwreck coins, and expressed amazement that Pablo had in his possession items that had been taken from Cuban waters. Pablo clearly hoped that their status as having come from Cuba would add a layer of affective value to the bounty, but, as it happened, on this occasion the man took offense. "You see?" Pablo said to me, "some people are fascinated by the relics I can bring them from their home country, but others get jealous that I can access something that's lost to them." Similar emotions passed across Ernesto's face as he looked through Pablo's stock for a bargain. "Yeah, Pablo has a lot of interesting stuff, he goes to Cuba a lot," he said, with what I interpreted as flickers of envy, scorn, and loss in his expression.

Pablo also saw no problem in dealing with items from after the revolution, and proudly (albeit cautiously) showed me a 2017 mint-condition coin with Fidel Castro's face etched on it, minted the previous year in Mongolia and thus purchasable online without breaking the embargo. At this point, another young Cuban American in his twenties revealed he also had a secret stash of contemporary Cuban coins. Both men had become interested in coin-collecting after a lifetime of hearing parents reminisce about a place that they themselves had no tangible knowledge or experience of. But as time wore on, they had become frustrated that this history never expanded. "What about what's happened on the island since they left?" Pablo asked, wide-eyed.

They're all so obsessive, like they want to be unhappy. Whereas this gives me joy—it's my way of connecting with something I didn't have as a child. So this is a way of constructing or reconstructing that history, and making it a bit more tangible for those of us who didn't experience it. I guess it's my way of staking out my claim, 'cause you know, I'm Cuban too.

He was also honest enough to point out that it made good business sense, too, so long as he was careful whom he spoke to. "Eventually things will change, and this marketplace will explode. There is so much emotion there, and so much history, so I'm going to be in prime position for when that change comes. Being a police officer is increasingly my side job!"

The act of collecting is evidently about material consumption and acquisition, but here we see how it also posits value in a material artifact's contribution to a collective whole, and its own biography of circulation (Kopytoff 1986). The contestation and negotiation I witnessed at the Cuba Nostalgia Fair, as well as at the various shops/museums across Miami specializing in antiques and memorabilia, focused on what should or should not merit inclusion within the category of "Cuban." This related to whether or not an individual was born on the island, but also to their "diasporic generational" status (Eckstein and Berg 2015). Pablo's relationship with cubanidad, while equally affective and potent within his life narrative, held a distinct ideological stance from that of Ernesto or, no doubt, his own parents. Both Pablo and Ernesto (as well as Pilar from the nostalgia store earlier in this chapter) saw material consumption not just as an act of devouring, but also of accumulating, preserving, and, ultimately, curating not only one's own identity but also that of others, in line with the view of a collector as "a heroic and selfless savior of objects rather than an acquisitive and selfish consumer" (Belk 2006, 534). All were devout collectors, and, in their distinct ways, purists. For Pilar, anything post-1959 was without value; for Ernesto, it was of retributive value; while for Pablo, an item was of value precisely for its ability to complete his collection. "I don't understand why they all want to sully this with politics" he confided, shaking his head. "Either you're a collector, in which case you want a full collection, or not. Why would you just stop at 1958?"

The Past Is a Foreign Country

David Lowenthal notably characterized the past as a "foreign country," mobilizing a model whereby he defined past as different from the present, and as an "ever more foreign realm, yet one increasingly infused by the present" (1985, xxv). Others have moved from this discussion toward an understanding of heritage as the creation of a future, which certainly resonates with the (re)creation of shared memory- and heritage-scapes among generations of Cuban diaspora in Miami. Yet a consideration of the meaning of shared pasts (presents and futures) for my interlocutors in the diaspora posed questions of how we can understand the past, and who owns it, when it is quite literally *in a foreign country*. Whose is it to claim, curate, and mobilize when different groups of people have equal claims on an identity? And in the contestations that follow, how is a hegemonic discourse narrating such histories established and promulgated? In this sense, notions of heritage and nostalgia can become weapons in an ideological battleground, akin perhaps to Daphne Berdahl's portrayal of the role of nostalgia and Ostprodukte between East and West Germany, whereby material artifacts gain the agency to symbolize unification or rejection of "the other," and to Svetlana Boym's work on the mobilization of nostalgia in a utopian past to create a future (Berdahl 1999; Boym 2001). Heritage as invoked through material culture becomes a mechanism for both inclusion and exclusion. Nostalgia sets up an "ethical mechanism" for the evaluation of authenticity that can be "political conservative" (Dawdy 2016, 145).

Considering material items in diasporic settings further complicates such questions, as artifacts assert different identities and narratives in parallel. Moreover, scholars have shown how many immigrants in fact experience their national identity more keenly from the outside, or in other words, mobilize their pasts more when in a foreign country. Deanna Barenboim (2018), for example, has described how Mexican migrants from the Yucatán peninsula "learn" their heritage upon arrival in the diaspora in California, where the material culture of a shared past is incorporated into new lives in the U.S. Indeed, a whole industry surrounds the importance and symbolism of such items, with businesses specializing solely in couriering these items by truck from Mérida to San Francisco, often preordered by diasporic relatives from people back home through WhatsApp or Facebook. Material items as evocations of heritage and past thus speak to a "diasporic state of mind" whereby "through long-distance memories, attachments and senses

Nostalgia, Authenticity, and the Antiques Trade between Miami and Havana · 161

of belonging migrants experience home and away simultaneously" (Ang 2011, 86).

In this light, Denis Byrne's notion of "heritage corridors" (2016a, 2016b) is a helpful one when conceptualizing the transnational connectivity between migrant heritage sites and overseas locales, as well as the two-directional flow of ideas, things, people, and capital that is so materially evident between Havana and Miami. Old things do not have a fixed heritage, but rather "offer one means of ameliorating alienation" (Dawdy 2016, 117) through their capacity to mobilize affective values that can in turn be shaped to the ideologies present on either side of the "corridor." Moreover, it is precisely the ability of these items to move back and forth along this corridor that imbues them with their particular value; their ability to move physically (a possibility which to so many people is prohibited) and to assert flexible identities on either side in different contexts speaks to their powerful status, symbolism, and agency. The layers of meaning that can accumulate in some such objects, in particular those that have moved back and forth several times in different periods of history, further speaks to just how mutable notions of heritage and past can be, pointing to this "corridor" as a web or "zone of entanglement," as Ingold envisions it (Ingold 2008). For Sharon Lee Dawdy, antique objects become "dialectical" in their ability to "bring the past and the present into a charged proximity that changes both" (2016, 117), and when seen against the map of their movements shuttling back and forth along these corridors or zones of entanglement, antiques becomes objects that, "circulating as a possession possessed by no one, prompt people to think of one another" (Brown 2003, 124).

Inventing Tradition

Just as I have already described to be the case in Miami, material artifacts imbued with historic or nostalgic value are also highly prized in Havana. Visits to friends' houses invariably revealed antique furniture, vintage lamps or crumbling books; such things were kept, cared for, and restored (whenever materially possible) partly because they might have been passed down through the family and thus had some affective value, partly because they were invariably of a higher quality than any newer items that might have been purchased in Havana, and partly because newer items were, of course, rather hard to come by. Old things, by contrast, are in fact rather easy to come by in Cuba, given the island was once a destination for Europe

162 · Part III. Returning Value

and America's bourgeois travelers and their extensive luggage, and Cubans have developed a knack for restoring and renovating all kinds of old things rather than throw them away (Pertierra 2011). Affect and pragmatism by necessity weave a close tapestry in daily life in Havana.

Havana has also seen its own explosion in private store/museum spaces, in part fueled by a boom in tourism in which tourists who equate Cuba with a fetishized image of yesteryear wish to buy a piece of that fantasy, and private restaurants and hotels opening up across Havana also wish to source vintage items with a "patina aesthetic" (Dawdy 2016) to decorate trendy new hipster spaces catering to this clientele. This, combined with a greater number of flights connecting Havana with Miami, and therefore a greater ability to sell to a diasporic market as well, has meant that antique traders, restorers, and collectors can do a bustling trade in Havana.

One such history buff was Luis, who was a priest, and found the social connections that job afforded him highly useful when it came to hearing about antique items on the grapevine, acquiring them, and reselling them. Whenever he got a tip-off that there was something interesting worth investigating, he would call me up and we would step out together, Luis striding confidently through the streets and markets, greeting men as he went and informing them of any recent purchases he had made that might interest them. "Everyone in Cuba is a collector at heart," he said. "You just have to find out what tune they dance to." On this occasion, we were headed to a woman's house in Chinatown to inspect some valuables she claimed her family had hidden away for decades. On route Luis took us past one of the official state stores for antique furniture, large hardwood wardrobes and escritoires lined up along the pavement out front. The items had paper tickets attached with high prices: one wardrobe I noticed was set at over US$1000, although Luis assured me that if you spoke to the employees on the street rather than inside, you could easily get that price down to $400. Around the corner, a few men had lined up a series of antique chair legs along the wall, squinting at them to work out which would best replace the worn legs on a broken antique chair they were fixing.

When we arrived at the apartment in question, a middle-aged woman with heavily plucked eyebrows led us inside. "We might not look rich, we Cubans, but a lot of our wealth is in our *salones,*" she said to me, as Luis inspected a heavy porcelain lamp from the turn of the nineteenth century that the family claimed they had had for decades and was worth many hundreds of dollars because of the "legacy and emotional value" it represented to her family. "What she didn't tell you was that her grandmother was probably the maid to some wealthy family that fled and [she] stole the lamp in the first place," said Luis, laughing, once we had headed out of the apartment and down the crumbling stairs. "People have got wise that a family story to tug at the heartstrings [*palanca*] puts up the value, even if they have to slightly reinvent a story from someone else!" With a little storytelling, artifacts "can stand in for the dead, for past traumas, for social stratigraphy, and for fictive ancestry" (Dawdy 2016, 117). In reality, many of the artifacts in Havana's antiques markets had probably been stolen or plundered at some point in their history, whether in the nineteenth century, the twentieth, or the twenty-first, to be packaged and sold in Miami, like the doorknocker from Havana's National Capitol Building that I saw in Pilar's store. Havana is home to several "antiques houses" as well, some catering to tourists (most notably the one in the Old Town near where many hotels are situated), while others cater to collectors and dealers like Luis, who know most others on the circuit.

One such house was a large imposing colonial building in the affluent El Vedado neighborhood, converted into a shop/museum where every room was quite literally filled to the ceiling with old items. Chairs, tables, sofas, gilt mirrors, record players, cigar boxes, grandfather clocks and pocket watches, photographic cameras, swords and sabers, and 1970s socialist posters clung to every possible surface, with Louis XIV furniture crammed in next to baseball bats signed by Fidel Castro. The owners slept among the items wherever they could find space, and cats crawled from between statues of the Virgin Mary and menorahs (clearly at one point removed from churches and synagogues), yowling for scraps.

The antiques business, I was told, works in a sort of pyramid in Havana. At the bottom are *los buscadores,* or the searchers, who go house-to-house sourcing items. They typically sell to middlemen like Luis, who sells to collectors such as Víctor, who runs this particular house. Víctor in turn sells online, taking payment by credit card via his son based in Canada, as well as to visiting tourists or collectors like Pablo who are over from Miami. At each stage of the process, further layers of "inalienability" are added to the artifact, with the result that, for its very inalienability, or inherent relation to some personal trajectory or another, it is in fact more commoditized as its market value increases (Appadurai 1986; Dawdy 2016; Weiner 1992). The value of the item resides in its relation to an often-invented story that establishes familial and national narratives to anchor the thing in time and space (see also the discussion of value and pawnshops in chapter 1). The porcelain lamp, for example, that the family so prized for its supposedly having been

164 · Part III. Returning Value

"handed down through time" had been taken from another family, who had prized it for tying them to their bourgeois roots in France. Had Luis bought it, he could no doubt have added a further layer of sentiment by selling it to a diasporic Cuban in Miami as a "reencounter" with their lost family heritage in Havana. Or he might have sold it to Víctor, who might have sold it to a visiting French tourist hoping to carry it back to France as a material window into an "unchanged world" now lost to her in modern-day France. Beth Notar offers a parallel example of these layers of representative symbolism that objects can invoke, describing a Swiss woman visiting China to have them paint copies of Monet to sell in France as "authentic" souvenirs to visiting Asian tourists (2006, 64).

Indeed, to cater to this long and complex chain of relations to material artifacts representing (or indeed inventing) lost heritages, some Cubans have started importing "antiques" from Spain and Russia to resell to tourists visiting from America, or to new restaurants in Havana that want to present an "authentic Cuban" experience without the price tag associated with it. Old furniture, porcelain, and cigar boxes are in fact much cheaper and easier to find in Spain, yet their value is increased for being *Cuban*, hence collectors buy them (often with money sent as remittances from relatives in the Cuban diaspora to begin with), import them, add a personalizing story ("My grandmother brought this from Spain when she fled the Civil War" is a common example), and then have them shipped to Miami or sell them (Stubbs 2014). Again, there are parallels with Notar's ethnography of souvenir-sellers in southwest China, who added familial stories to artifacts to enrich their value, when they had in fact been purchased from a factory only a week earlier (2006, 79).

Heritage marketing insists upon a focus on the unique and personal characteristics of things to bestow authenticity, which sits in tension with the mass consumption and commoditization that simultaneously operate within this marketplace. The point here, though, is that even in cases where historicity—or "patina"—is faked, this does not alter an object's authenticity in terms of its "evocative efficacy" (Dawdy 2016, 139). Regardless of any supposed distinction between real and counterfeit, these items nonetheless engender affects among those who acquire them (Copeman and da Col 2018; Navaro-Yashin 2007). The invocation of nostalgia through emphasis on the aesthetics and narratives of a curated past bridges these tensions and allows the object to speak to buyers' emotional need to "remember" their pasts tangibly. Paul Connerton has written that "people are not the only things to vanish. The material culture of former lives does too. Indeed, it disappears more rapidly as the value attached to it diminishes" (2006, 316). So, too, it would seem, can the opposite be true. Historical things and the heritage they represent can also be created as their value increases, and differing sources of their inherent value are brought to the surface and mobilized in different ways by different subsets of Cubans on either side of the corridor.

Conclusion

In this chapter we have seen how material things can assert multiple affective symbolisms and narratives simultaneously, according to the ideological, temporal, and emotional contexts within which they are mobilized. The "heritage corridor" between Cuba and its diaspora in Miami is a salient example of one such situation, where material items assume new layers of meaning in a normative transnational and generational battleground over identity, memory, and the past. In their preoccupation with remembering, curating, memorializing, and forgetting the past, people on both sides in fact reveal their acute anxiety not with the past so much as with the present and the future. Contested identities and anxieties over authenticity are of equal concern in Miami, where new waves of migration and old scars shape what is included within the hegemonic marker of Cuban, and also in Havana, where socioeconomic shifts and new waves of tourism are similarly affecting what it means to be (or perform) authentically Cuban on the island.

Ironically, communities in both Miami and Havana seek to fossilize and commoditize their distinct notions of the past in reaction to the isolationist course they have both officially charted throughout decades. The exile community in Miami has consistently maintained its distinction from other Latino diasporas in the region, narrating this through its communal heritage of trauma and loss, as represented through material cultures that are mobilized to reproduce these narratives for new generations. Accounts of other Cuban diasporas both in the U.S. and Spain have found a similar preoccupation with nostalgia, and an idealization of what life was like "before" (Andrews-Swann 2011; Berg 2014). Meanwhile Cuba's "opening" to the world and to increased tourism in the past two decades has also meant that capitalization of fetishized notions of a Cuba stuck in the past is becoming a necessary strategy to derive income from the performance of a romanticized authenticity "unaffected by modernity," which is increasingly the object of tourist desire the world over (MacCannell 2013). In this light, the preoccupation with authenticity, heritage, and countering narratives of the past in both Miami and Havana reveals "the negotiation of parallel authenticities in tension" (Theodossopoulos 2013, 339).

While the ethnographic vignettes presented here have revealed very different motivations, justifications, and emotional trajectories of those involved in these networks, the constant factor is the ability these objects have to move between places in a way that most people in this particular social world cannot (due to either emotional or political obstacles). In so doing, they have a means of speaking to different groups of Cubans in different ways, mobilizing powerful affective values to traverse the Cuban world. As such, I see such objects as palimpsestic in their ability to acquire and accumulate different heritages, nostalgias, and pasts, while evoking a unique authenticity that renders them valuable. The fact that some of these items are not, in fact, authentic in the sense of being "genuinely" old, but are instead fakes, forgeries, counterfeits, etc., does not matter here, because it does not prohibit them from invoking a community that consciously constructs its own authenticity through materialized continuity with an imagined past.

A commodity chain analysis of the heritage corridor between Miami and Cuba reveals how antiques as commodities are deliberately imbued with "inalienable" qualities (Weiner 1992)—even if these themselves must be somewhat manufactured—each time they move back and forth along this corridor, showing how consumers and sellers on both sides (re)enchant this network, ascribing their own layers of affective meaning to these totemic material items that bestow authentic identity upon the owner or holder (Jamieson 1999). These layers of meaning in turn reveal the normative battleground over identity that exists not only between Miami and Cuba, but between generations (both biological and diasporic) in both places. If the locus of the power to participate in that battle is the material objects themselves, then the ownership of one becomes an important way of asserting oneself as Cuban. Moreover, through this case study of antique items and their authenticity realized through transnational travel, we see the embedded possibilities of objects' semiotic flexibility to act in ways that people in this context cannot. These objects have the power to evoke memory and pasts that people are prevented from returning to (whether temporally or geographically), and thus mobilize emotional agencies through their portability and capacity to return home, in a way that few Cubans in the diaspora can emulate.

6

Patria en Muerte

Making Death Matter

"To die for the motherland is to live"[1] proclaims a lyric from the Cuban national anthem "La Bayamesa" (1868), a phrase that, as I will illustrate through this chapter, still resonates strongly with Cubans to this day, both on the island and in the diaspora. It is no coincidence that the Cuban revolution of the twentieth century took up the call to arms in its own much-cited slogan, "Homeland or Death!"[2] Yet, ironically, for many Cubans exiled to the Miami diaspora, the *patria* ("homeland")[3] is only to be regained *en* or through *muerte* ("death"); this final rite of passage forms a crucial moment of identification as Cuban, in particular for those whose lives have, in their majority, been experienced outside of the island. The question of dying Cuban is a difficult one for the diaspora in Miami: What does it mean to live in Miami but to die Cuban?

To be buried in the diaspora is, for many of Miami's aging Cubans, a worryingly permanent state of exile, as well as an inherently political statement. Consequently, as many of the first wave of Cuban exiles died in the 1990s, they started to include wishes in their will to be exhumed and returned materially to their homeland soil "when Cuba is free." During my own fieldwork in Miami, I heard of the death of an elderly Cuban man who had wished to be returned to his native soil for burial, but whose family—who strongly resented Cuba's socialist government—could not bring themselves to permit it. The family found itself in a moral bind: They felt obligated to meet their grandfather's wishes, but strongly resisted dealing with any "traitor" who would be willing to return to Cuba with his cremated remains. And so, instead, they mobilized a by now familiar Cuban inventiveness to resolve the situation, and set off in a car headed for Tampa, six hours to the north. There they visited the Parque Amigos de José Martí in Ybor City,

168 · Part III. Returning Value

which had been the epicenter of the original Cuban diaspora in Florida at the end of the nineteenth century. This tiny communal park was in fact donated to the Republic of Cuba in 1956, three years before the revolution, and legally remains the property of Cuba to this day, albeit administered by the City of Tampa in Florida (Guzzo 2017). The park contains soil taken from each of Cuba's provinces before the revolution and scattered over the Floridian earth, and so, late one evening, the grandchildren of this family crept through the gate with a plastic beach bucket and spade and shoveled in a few fistfuls of soil from a neglected corner near the railing. This was promptly driven back to Miami and scattered over their grandfather's coffin as it was buried in Little Havana. Evidently most of this soil had never been anywhere near Cuba, yet by coming from land that legally *belonged* to Cuba, and even better, that somehow materially predated Cuba's "fall" to socialism, this soil had agency to return the deceased man back "home."

While this is a remarkable story even within the context of Cuban Miami, it points to the ways in which death in its "material facticity" (Heidegger 2010) becomes a quite literal embodiment of life; it was necessary to render this man's experiences of life in exile valid through his death, and the very materiality and trajectory of the soil, which had itself charted a life course similar to that of his own body, became the tool through which this could be effected. Post-death consumption practices reveal much of the way people curate and express their lives, and as such, posit them firmly within a cultural idiom. The ontological and material implications of death on personhood and society also point to the power relations that regulate such formations (Forde and Hume 2018). In the case of Cuban culture, this book has argued that it is impossible to be Cuban without the flow of material items between Cuban communities across the world, principally between the major diasporic community in Miami and Cuba's capital, Havana. It is perhaps unsurprising, then, that "dying Cuban" should not be so very different from being or "living Cuban," and is a highly material concern.

In this chapter, an ethnographic exploration of the materiality of "dying Cuban" reveals once again how these two places are not only highly interconnected, but in fact mutually constitutive. This interconnectedness and material fluidity gains momentum at key Cuban life moments or rites of passage, such as birth, a girl's fifteenth birthday, marriage, or major illness, as we saw in the case of Lilia and Milagros's family in chapter 2. Rather than focusing upon the ritual of death as a rite of passage, then, this chapter instead argues that the materialities of death become perhaps the foremost

Patria en Muerte: Making Death Matter · 169

manifestation of Cuban identity construction in its current transnational setting. In the most literal of senses, the material matter of death matters.

The Matter of Death in Havana

Prior to the revolution, funeral homes in Havana were privately owned and typically filled with Catholic symbols; indeed, all cemeteries were in fact owned by the Catholic church. These were co-opted by the state in the 1960s and funeral homes passed into state ownership, as they remain to this day. Given most funeral homes lack refrigeration, wakes typically take place very shortly after death, and usually involve members of the family staying up (with the body) throughout the night to "keep it company" (*acompañarle*). All bodies receive make-up and are usually dressed in the smartest clothing that can be found; Heidi Härkönen gives the example of a balding man's body being dressed with a wig, with an aim "not to make his body look like it was in life, but better" (2014, 174). A well-cared-for body is testimony to love and care from relatives in life, while a neglected body might point to a lack of social connectivity. Death in its materiality therefore emphasizes the position of a person as socially connected, both within a family and within the broader notion of family as the Cuban people. "Cubans live their lives embedded in networks of social relations and close kinship connections and that is how they die as well" (Härkönen 2014, 176), and this is demonstrated, as in life, through ongoing and reciprocated material care (see chapter 2).

The main cemetery in Havana is the Cementerio de Colón, a vast necropolis in the west of the city that resembles a city in its own right, laid out in a grid with streets of mausoleums and whole sections dedicated to different parts of society. Bodies are initially placed in vaults (*nichos*) for two years while they decompose, at which point they are removed, usually free of flesh (although not always, on which more later), and the bones are sprinkled with talc, wrapped in cloth, and then placed in an ossuary to be conserved. The first funeral is a social event where friends and kin alike pay their respects, while the second funeral—where the bones are removed (*sacar los huesos*)—is typically attended only by close kin for what is a far more solemn (and sometimes grim) affair. Robert Hertz proposes that the ritual of secondary burial marks the completion of the burial process, with the final interment of the material remains of the deceased marking a return to normal life for the living, and an emphasis upon a "final" resting place

170 · Part III. Returning Value

as opposed to the temporary or "liminal" state of the body before it (Hertz 1960, 77–84; Huntington and Metcalf 1979; Metcalf 1981; Miles 1965). This is the point when close relatives visibly confront the fact that their loved one is no longer in a recognizable form, and that they have been reduced to matter (Campkin 2013; Douglas 1991; Hallam and Hockey 2001; Hockey et al. 2010).

These rows of vaults do indeed have, as Ruth Behar describes in a parallel Spanish example, "an amazing anticipatory quality" (1991, 364), while also being reflective of the socialist ideology of all being equal in death, as in life. Nonetheless, death continues to differentiate people by wealth, residence or place, achievement, and particularly notions of origin in Havana, for after death there is a "strong attempt to take a person's body to where s/he is seen to truly belong" (Härkönen 2014, 180). This is usually understood as a material and spiritual connection to place. For some, this is being transported back to the region of Cuba where they were born,[4] while for others, as we shall see, this involves transnational journeys of both bodies and things. It is broadly agreed that being buried where one was born links the beginning and end of life, closing the circle. Furthermore, the burial site (after the secondary burial) becomes a marker of identity not just through place but also through kin; a family tomb is the ultimate way to unite family beyond death.

While this is the most typical format for death in Havana, there are, of course, myriad ways to die, which in turn mirror and are shaped by various Cuban cosmologies. "Shaped by colonial, post-colonial histories and now neoliberal orders, Caribbean bodies are ciphers from where life, death and the afterlife are understood" (Arroyo-Martínez 2018, 337), and merely walking across the cemetery and observing material items left in strategic places reveals a host of parallel Cuban practices influenced by traditions in Palo, Ifá, and Santería,[5] as well as material evidence of those with relatives in the diaspora who maintain material ties of care. For many Cubans, questions of spirituality are not a situation of either/or, and respects may be paid to the dead while observing aspects of socialist, Catholic, and Afro-Cuban funeral rites, often in combination. Altars, dolls, statuettes, and other forms of representing the dead may be found placed in both the cemetery and on the street, in what Diana Espírito Santo calls "the locus of myriad intersections of cosmologies" (2018, 214). The dead regularly invoke themselves through matter: consumable items such as plates of food, alcohol, and cigarettes, for example, become further places where the dead may be acknowledged. These items in and of themselves also trace stories; material items have trajectories that become key in representing and invoking an identity, especially in a diasporic context (of which, more later). Thus, Todd Ramón Ochoa's description of the Palo dead, for example, as being best understood in "metaphors of fluids, flows, tides, and waves" (2010, 14) is also an apt one when considering what death (and therefore life) means in a context in which Cuban identity in its myriad forms is constituted through movement and migration, flow and flux.

The Matter of Death in Miami ("Next Year in Havana")

The process of dying and remembering the dead is markedly different in the U.S., where the funeral industry is geared not only toward profit but also sanitization, whereby the idea of picking up and moving a relatives' bones or other material signs of decay would likely be met with horror (Douglas 1991). Focus is often on the

> elaborate avoidance, both in word and deed, of the brute facts of death. The majority of deaths now occur in hospitals, where the fiction of probable recovery is often maintained until a person is near the point of death. The corpse is then promptly removed without the aid of the bereaved, who see it again only under very special circumstances, after it has been primped up to appear as if asleep. Coffins are selected for their superior padding, as if comfort mattered to the corpse. We speak of the deceased as having "passed on"; we describe the premises of the death specialist with the cozy-sounding terms "funeral parlor" or "funeral home"; we comment how "well" the embalmed corpse looks lying in the "slumber room"; and so on. This endless shying away from confrontation with mortality is undeniably a marked feature of American culture. (Huntington and Metcalf 1979, 201)

If a body is to be viewed, there is a requirement that it first be embalmed (at a cost of around $700) by a qualified mortician in what might be interpreted as an increasing medicalization of death and its subsequent banishment to the realm of scientific expertise; death becomes reduced to its unavoidably biological finiteness. This is part of what Jessica Mitford (1963) attacks as widespread profiteering through selling unnecessarily expensive services and goods to a captive American clientele under great stress, creating a realm of labor around the human body as "thing" to be dealt with, tantamount to a political economy of death (Feeley-Harnik 1984).

172 · Part III. Returning Value

While there are degrees of this process that are enshrined in law in the U.S. and are thus unaccommodating to cultural variance in the marking of death, the Cuban diaspora in Miami has nonetheless adapted American funerary traditions to incorporate at least some of their own cultural processes of death. Richard Huntingdon and Peter Metcalf maintain that while the U.S. has continued to receive immigrants from many different cultural backgrounds, "the majority have adopted American deathways, just as they have absorbed other aspects of national culture." Had it been otherwise, they argue, "institutions would surely have sprung up to cater for their needs [which] shows that funerals somehow fit into a peculiarly American ideology" (Huntington and Metcalf 1979, 200). A short drive along 8th Street through the Little Havana district of Miami, however, would quickly dispel such notions. Here, clustered around the community heart of Café Versailles,[6] are at least a dozen Cuban American funeral parlors, all catering most explicitly to a Cuban(American) clientele, and many of which are continuations of well-known funeral businesses that operated in Havana before the revolution (Härkönen 2011a, 269).

Part of the key to these businesses' ongoing success is that they understand the central symbolic role of death among the Cuban diaspora, and in particular, among the exile generation. For many, the process of becoming exiled from their native Cuba was already tantamount to a death, at least in its social or emotional (as opposed to biological) sense of rupture, as Carlos Eire depicts in his own autobiography of leaving for South Florida as a child:

I left behind my parents, my entire family, all of my possessions, and my native land, and at this moment I don't really know whether I'll see any of them ever again. In other words, I've just died. I've passed through the burning silence that strips you bare of everything you've ever been. (2010, 1)

Such emotional loss can even be expressed in terms of a physical interment or spiritual purgatory, as in the lyrics of the song written by Luis Aguilé and performed by Cuban American singer Gloria Estefan, "Cuando salí de Cuba" ("When I Left Cuba"):

Nunca podré morirme	I can never die
Mi corazón, no lo tengo aquí	I don't have my heart here [with me]
. . . Cuando salí de Cuba	. . . When I left Cuba
Dejé enterrado mi corazón	I left my heart buried

As the years in exile went by, this sense of loss only increased, and the imminent reality of biological death in exile hit home, combined with a "shameful" inability to tend to the material needs of both living and deceased relatives back home in Havana. Exiles living in Miami have been haunted by the memories of their "unfulfilled deep filial obligations" (Wyndham and Read 2010, 14) for much of their lives, and as they have aged, many have become preoccupied with the dichotomy between their own future American resting place and that of their ancestors back in Cuba.

A significant proportion of the Cuban exile community that has died in Miami has been buried in Woodlawn Park Cemetery, on 8th Street between Little Havana and the equally Cuban neighborhood of Westchester. It is large and spacious, with large stone tombs and mausoleums spaced out across neatly manicured green turf; a smooth tarmac road winds between the graves so that relatives can drive from one to the other without getting out to walk in the hot Miami sun. Here, bodies are buried in large, heavy wooden coffins, as in the American tradition, with an engraved headstone marking a person's place of rest. An emphasis remains upon kinship through death—where possible, families are buried together. Larger or more notable Cuban American families have constructed stone mausoleums with the family surname engraved in large print, replicas of the family tombs that lie abandoned back in Havana's Colón Cemetery. The family names of the deceased are sometimes pared down to two or three, rather than as many as half a dozen (as is often the case in the Spanish style), in what Marivic Wyndham and Peter Read call an unspoken "Well, that will do for now, until we get back to Cuba" (2010, 15). As much as mourning a buried presence, Woodlawn is also a memorial to absence—of relatives buried on the other side of the sea, and of longed-for lives unlived.

Ashes to Ashes

I first heard about Victor—a businessman based in Little Havana—while talking to the owner of the neighborhood's longest-standing Cuban funeral parlor, which traced its lineage back to a family business that had opened in Havana before the revolution, and then "reopened" in Miami in the 1960s. This funeral home claimed many of the exile community's most prominent members among its clientele. Staunchly anti-Castroist, the owners had vowed never to benefit the Cuban state with their business acumen, and so, like most other Cuban funeral parlors in Miami, refused to countenance the idea of repatriating bodies for burial in Cuba, or importing material

174 · Part III. Returning Value

items from the island to assist with a "good" burial in Miami. If I wanted to know about that kind of thing, the "disreputable" Victor, who owned a rival Cuban funeral parlor round the corner, was apparently the person I should talk to.

Intrigued, I set off around the corner, went inside, and took a seat in what appeared to be a large living room full of squishy faded sofas, potted plants, and framed pictures of sunsets scattered across the walls. At one end of the room, a cabinet of urns and plastic orchids was for sale below a flashing neon sign advertising burials in Cuba. Funerals ended simultaneously in two adjoining rooms on the left-hand side, and suddenly the waiting area was filled with somber, black-clad Catholic Nicaraguans on one side, and white-clad Cuban *santeros* (those initiated into the Santería religion) beating out rhythms on drums on the other. Between the groups weaved a portly old Trinidadian man with thick white hair—Victor—who, apparently due to an outdated filial loyalty to the British Empire, was very amenable to chatting with me and my British accent.

Victor was one of those people who buys failing businesses to turn them around and sell them at a profit. In the 1990s he had acquired a struggling Cuban-owned funeral parlor just off 8th Street and renamed it, borrowing the name of a once-famous funeral parlor that had operated in Havana before the revolution. Things turned around for the business when he accepted the county contract to bury unidentified balsero migrants' bodies.[7] Nowadays 90 percent of his customers are Cuban, and Victor is, at least according to him, the only man who is willing and able to provide the service of repatriation, or shipping bodies and cremated remains back to Cuba after death. While not Cuban himself, Victor sees himself as an "honorary Cuban," in part due to his "humanitarian" efforts to serve the needs of more recent (often poorer) arrivals from Cuba (a greater proportion of whom are Afro-Cuban than in earlier generations of Cuban migrants) when their funeral needs cannot or will not be met by more traditional Cuban businesses around the corner.

Victor, who is in his early 70s, is married to Julieta, a 27-year-old Cuban woman recently arrived from the island, to whom he has now given the business. She is able to quickly discern customers according to their diasporic generation, considering their accent, dress sense, and the vocabulary they use, and in this way judges whether or not it would be appropriate to offer repatriation services.[8] In the 1990s, Victor had to charter flights to return bodies to Cuba, or send them via Canada or Mexico, but nowadays he sends them direct, and the bodies or ashes are typically accompanied by an employee to manage the paperwork. This process was made considerably easier upon the acquisition of some government friends who informed him he could circumvent the embargo on "humanitarian grounds," so long as the proper paperwork was in place.

Victor has "teams" in every city in Cuba who receive the bodies and deal with the burials. He pays them well, and told me,

> The reason most people don't manage to make business work in Cuba is they don't understand that you have to look after your own. I make sure they are loyal to me and won't steal from me, because I look after them well. It has to work like a family. They have to be indebted to you.

Arguably, the key to Victor's success has been his ability to tap into the confianza that is so essential to the operation of material flows invoking kin relation (see chapter 3).

> Obviously you have to know the right people, and Julieta accompanies about fourteen bodies a month to Cuba to take care of the people there . . . nobody else here has managed to maintain those links, and that's why no other company can offer the repatriation that we do; it really is the bottom line.

In this way, Victor and his wife are also able to offer tomb restoration services in Cuba (they have teams in place that, for payment, can apparently restore old family pantheons to give Miami exiles some peace of mind), drawing upon the need to invoke family within Cuban conceptualizations of a good death. "The gist of the whole thing is family first," Victor tells me, presenting a gold-trimmed business card with various toll-free numbers including 1–800 FUNERAL, 1–800 CREMATION and 1–800 INGRIEF. "They want to go home because it's the motherland, fatherland, whatever you want to call it." This stratagem is also key to his advertising campaigns; the funeral parlor regularly takes out a half-page slot in the local Spanish-language newspaper *El Nuevo Herald* (albeit ironically publishing the advert in English). One such advertisement, published on January 26, 2015, reads (reproduced here unaltered):

> An open letter from Isla Funeral Homes—Cuban nationals should read this. For twenty years we have serviced Cuban families . . . with opposition, from detractors and running against the wind Isla, has been re-uniting Cuban families in Cuba with deceased loved one

176 · Part III. Returning Value

who died in the United States. While other Hispanic funeral homes worried about the politics: at Isla we focused on families and the humanity. Family like soldiers are not left behind, with a desire to be repatriated to the Fatherland and even in death, even in death. Today we again encourage for your deceased family members to be buried in Cuba. It's free, gratis, for nothing. And you are buried next to family and friends, not, next to perfect strangers in Miami cemeteries, after paying thousands for a simple water-logged hole in the ground. We offer to any Cuban family whose family owns a *panteón* [tomb] in any Cuban cemetery, and which is in disrepair, we will have friend of Isla in Cuba retile, repair and repaint your family's burial heritage. We deliver cremated remains door-to-door in Cuba, and we wish you to consider us anytime you require services to, or bringing loved ones back from Cuba. We are your connection to Cuba. We thank you, the Hispanic women management team.

The ad focuses on a rhetoric of family and kinship within a Cuban community ("family, like soldiers, are not left behind"), set up in opposition to the alien world of the exile land ("buried next to family and friends, not next to perfect strangers in Miami").

The pamphlets neatly piled up on a coffee table by the front door echo similar words, drawing upon kinship and gender ties. Julieta is the visible frontperson of the business. With a sympathetic pat on the shoulder, I watch her pass one of these pamphlets over to a middle-aged Cuban woman who has spent the night accompanying her father's body through a vigil: "Friends don't turn away from friends at the hour of need, call upon your friends here at [. . .] and we will be there for you. We are a team of young, dedicated women who are passionate about connecting families, even after death," it reads. Once the woman has exited to the adjacent car park, Julieta turns and eyes the mess strewn across the sofas where various family members have drifted off over the course of the wake. "The problem here is that people treat this place like their home!" Julieta objected. "People come and sleep on the sofa every night of the week, now it all has to be reupholstered, it's filthy!" When I asked her how she found the business of death in Miami compared to in Cuba, she replied,

Death is an interesting thing here in the U.S. Every aspect of it is a sellable thing, and even after death, people continue to charge—even just for the cemetery plot, you have to keep paying forever. And a lot of Cubans feel like even after decades here they have never fitted in.

They look on from the outside but they're never really part of American society. So even though they live their whole lives here, many of them want to be buried in a place where they're automatically "in."

When I showed Victor's local paper ad to other Cuban friends in Miami, the vast majority were affronted and frankly offended at the idea of sending remains back to Cuba. This was not exclusively because of any political ideology, but more because they felt he was taking advantage of an emotional vulnerability inherent within the Cuban exile community for profit. One friend in fact viewed this as a *"falta de confianza"* ("lack of trust," "betrayal"), citing the way Victor's company had invoked Cuban discourses of kinship and family for his own ends, in what my friend clearly felt was a scam. The fact that his wife was a recent arrival and the business clearly depended upon working relations with the Cuban authorities certainly did not help matters.

Rumors also went around Miami that the whole thing was a farce: one man at a coffee window told me he had a cousin (who had a neighbor . . . who had a friend . . .) in Cuba whose relative had supposedly arrived in a casket, only for them to open it up and discover the body of a complete stranger looking back up at them. He suspected the whole thing had been a way of moving material goods into Cuba, as he had heard the body was also accompanied by stationery, books, and some toiletries. Victor confirmed as much when I next spoke to him, although he said he usually warned customers against sending valuable items inside the casket, as he could not guarantee that only people on his own team would have access.

> People sometimes include photos and things like that, or letters. Or they give stuff to my team to pass to their relatives on the other side when they take urns of ashes, like a childhood object or a watch or something they associated with the relative. I leave that up to them to negotiate.

The legality of this situation is somewhat blurred; Victor or his wife flies to Washington at least once a month to organize forms and death certificates for the transfer on humanitarian grounds, but any further items that might end up going along for the trip would likely be in contravention of the embargo.

Victor's words were still in my mind when, not two weeks later, my friend José forwarded on an email to me that he had just received from an aunt in Cuba. It contained a joke that perfectly mirrored the very scenes I

178 · Part III. Returning Value

had been hearing about from various people in the funeral parlors at which
I had been spending time:

The whole family in Cuba was surprised when a coffin with the corpse
of a beloved aunt arrived from Miami. The body was packed into the
coffin with the face pressed against the glass of the lid. Upon opening
the coffin, the family found a note pinned to the clothes that read:

Dear Mom and Dad:
I am sending the body of Aunt Jimena, for a funeral in Cuba,
as she wanted, sorry for not being able to accompany her, but the
expenses were many, what with all the things that, taking advantage of the circumstances, I am sending to you.
Underneath our aunt, at the bottom of the coffin, you will find
12 cans of "Bumble Bee" tuna, 12 bottles of conditioner and 12
Pantene anti-dandruff shampoos, 12 bottles of Vaseline Intensive
Care (very good for the skin, not for cooking), 12 tubes of Colgate
toothpaste, 12 toothbrushes, 12 cans of beans (Spanish, the very
best), 4 cans of (real) chorizo.
Divide with the family, (without fights!). On Aunt Jimena's
feet are a pair of new Reebok size 9 tennis shoes, they're for Juan
(because we didn't send him anything with Uncle Esteban's body
and he was annoyed). By her head there are 4 pairs of new socks
for Antonio's children in different colors.
Again, please, (no fights!) Aunt Jimena is dressed in 15 Ralph
Lauren sweatshirts: one for Robertito and the others for her
children and grandchildren. She also wears a dozen Wonder Bras,
divide among the women, along with the 20 bottles of Revlon
nail polish that are in the corners of the coffin. Aunt also wears 9
Dockers and 3 Levi's jeans, Dad: keep 3 and give the others to my
brothers.
The Seiko watch that Papa asked for is on her left wrist; she
also wears the earrings, bracelets and rings that Mum asked for.
The chain around her neck is for my cousin Carlota, the 8 pairs of
Chanel stockings are for sharing with my friends and the neighbors, or if you want they can sell them, please do not give them
away cheap, they are expensive.
The dentures that we put in are for grandmother, who's been
toothless for years and can't chew (with these teeth she will be
able to eat bread without first dipping it in the coffee). The bifocal

Patria en Muerte: Making Death Matter · 179

lenses are for Alfredito, because they are of the same degree as the ones he uses. He also gets the Orioles cap she is wearing.

Aunt's hearing aids are for Aunt Carola, they are not exactly what she needs, because they are second hand, but the new ones are very expensive. Auntie's eyes are not real, they are contact lenses, which are for Marcela, she's owed them from her 15th birthday. On her fingers are Lolita's gold rings for her wedding, so that she is super-beautiful on the day.

I hope no one complains this time . . . Don't tell anyone about this and take it all out quickly, before you begin the vigil over the body.

With lots of love: María Dolores.

P.S.: Please get old clothes to dress Aunt Jimena in for the funeral and dedicate a Mass for the repose of her soul, because she helped you even after death. As you can see the box is very good wood, it won't get termites, so take it apart to make legs for Mum's bed and buy Aunt a cheaper coffin, she liked simple things. Take out the glass from the lid and fix the picture of grandmother that broke years ago, a plastic bag will be enough to fix it again. With the coffin lining, which is white satin for 20 dollars a yard, Lolita can make her wedding dress. After the death of Aunt Jimena, Aunt Blanca got very sad and sick, so I believe that soon I will be sending more things.

While the joke clearly exaggerates for effect, its humor lies in the universal recognition among the Cuban community that its content is not so very outlandish, riffing on the much-lauded Cuban trait of *invento* (inventiveness, often involving the circumnavigation of the law to "get by"). The key to Victor and Julieta's success was that they were in the privileged position of being able to navigate the complex bureaucratic nexus of relations that exist around material flows and the embargo between the U.S. and Cuba, and thus were able to connect families materially, much as the mulas in chapter 3 do, in this case citing "humanitarian reasons" to justify their business at what is, so often, an emotional juncture of life.

Moreover, as a non-Cuban, Victor is perhaps more open to various aspects of contemporary Cuban culture than is the exile generation running competitor businesses. Victor, for example, embraces more recent arrivals from Cuba who wish to incorporate elements of Santería traditions into their funeral services: "I won't let them kill a goat in here, but beyond

180 · Part III. Returning Value

that, they bring their bongos and do whatever they like" (his wording, not mine!).[9] Indeed, Victor himself regularly travels to Cuba and brings back (or has his mother-in-law bring back) religious items to resell for Santería burials, including beads, herbs, and horse hair from the island. He tutted when we heard on the radio in my car that a woman had been arrested at the Miami airport for trying to bring in a human skull from Cuba (purportedly for religious purposes). "They should have come and found me; I could have sorted it for them. But people are so stingy. . . ."

Dust to Dust

Perhaps the most in-demand of all the material items Victor and his team imported from Cuba on the return leg of a "drop-off" was soil—*tierra cubana* (Cuban earth). On a monthly basis a member of the team would gather containers of earth from each of Cuba's provinces so that a handful could be scattered over the casket of Cubans as they were buried in Miami. For those who could not afford repatriation, had no relatives left on the island to care for a grave, or were ideologically resistant to returning while socialism remained on the island, this was a compromise that meant they could still be buried where they were from. In Victor's words, "Cubans are very . . . Cuban. There's something important, almost mystical, to them about coming from Cuban soil." Victor himself had got into some problems a few years back when the white soil from an eastern region of Cuba was initially mistaken at the Miami airport for cocaine; moreover, it also broke the agricultural rules of the U.S. border, but others still supplied him when it was needed. "It's amazing, the emotion you see on people's faces, when I bring out a vial of red Pinar soil!"[10]

In his ethnography of priests and cremation rites in Banaras, Jonathan Parry depicts how mourners often bring the ashes of deceased kinsmen to submerge in the waters of the Ganges, which is a site imbued with spiritual or holy qualities (1994, 97). Leonie Kellaher's work has also documented a preoccupation with disposing of human ashes in places of spiritual significance, albeit perhaps in a less formal regard, such as depositing the material remains of male kin in an English football stadium (Hockey et al. 2005, 2006, 2011; Kellaher and Worpole 2016). While for many Cubans, the equivalent would also be preferable—where possible, many Cubans would wish to have their bodies or ashes returned to Cuba-as-spiritual-home either immediately or in a potential post-Castro future—the next best thing is to bring Cuba to them to imbue their final resting place in exile with this spiritual homeliness. In the Cuban case it is also arguably mulas, rather than priests, who facilitate this equivalent last rite in the Cuban world by acting as physical portals between material and spiritual realms for the departing souls of the dead.

> Physical movement through material spaces also operates metaphorically within rites of passage to convey movement within social and cosmological space . . . thus it is through spatial movement and orientation that the body is ritually transformed. (Hallam and Hockey 2001, 180)

Agents such as mulas or Victor's "teams" play crucial roles in enabling this. Mulas here operate as portals between social worlds, and in this regard, at least, they provide a provocative (and perhaps surprising) parallel to Parry's priests on the River Ganges.

"Next Year in Miami"

It was late in the evening when my friend Elián received the call from his sister in Camagüey, central Cuba. We were sitting out on his Hialeah patio, smoking and swatting at mosquitos. The family would be removing his father's bones (*sacando los huesos*) tomorrow for secondary burial, and Elián mother wanted him to be there. At such short notice, the flights would be expensive, and Elián was unsure he would be able to afford the fare along with the presents he would inevitably have to take with him for relatives and neighbors. While I retrieved some citronella candles from inside, he set about phoning trusted friends (*amigos de confianza*) in Hialeah who might be able to arrange a free fare back to Cuba for him as a mula. At such short notice, this would be the most cost-effective way of quickly making the trip there and back.

An hour later it was all arranged, and early the following morning he set off for the Miami airport to find a woman with pink sunglasses and a baseball cap, for whom he would deliver a suitcase to a neighborhood near where his mother and sister lived in Cuba. She would pay the return airfare and the baggage cost, as well as any taxi fares, in return for the safe delivery of some medicine and clothing to her elderly family members on the island, and Elián would be able to attend his father's exhumation and final interment. Elián's face was a mixture of emotions as he set off for security; he had missed his father's funeral, and this would be his final chance to say goodbye. Not only that, his own move to Miami three years earlier had

182 · Part III. Returning Value

been a death of sorts for the family. When Elián was a teenager, his older brother had gone missing at sea during an attempt to flee Cuba on a raft for the shores of South Florida and was presumed dead. His parents had never been the same again, and the topic of Miami was a tense one among the family. "Next year in Miami," his brother had long repeated before disappearing, in a poignant parallel to the "next year in Havana" that echoes across exiles' Cuban American dinner tables in Miami, which itself echoes "L'Shana Haba'ah B'Yerushalayim" ("Next year in Jerusalem"), often sung at the end of the Passover service in Judaism to evoke exile and displacement. Eventually his father had lost his second son to Miami's bright lights, too, and it grieved Elián that his decision to seek economic security had caused his father further pain.

His brother had always longed to go to a football match in Miami but had never had the chance. When he left home for the final time, he had been wearing a football jersey. And so, before leaving the house for the airport, Elián grabbed a jersey from his laundry which sported the logo of his university's team in Miami. His brother's body had been lost to the waves, but by taking some symbolic token of him from Miami back to Cuba, he hoped to "right the wrong" ("*corregir el mal*") that his parents had suffered to some degree, and reunite some aspect of his brother, who in his mind had died in Miami, with his parents back in Cuba. As a mula, he was limited in what he could personally carry back to Cuba, and so he wore the shirt, with the intention of placing it in the ossuary with his father's bones when they were interred in the cemetery, and then returning to Miami in a shirt of his father's, to bring something of him for his brother. If exhumation is "a practice through which memories of the dead are consolidated [where] the dead are . . . reconstituted, materially" (Hallam and Hockey 2001, 192), Elián's wish was to unite the strands of separated kin in Miami and Cuba in a material act of paying homage to his father and brother. In becoming a mula, he sought the opportunity to effect material and spiritual closure for his family.

Seeds of Change

In her account of the Bangladeshi diaspora importing foodstuffs into the U.K., Katy Gardner depicts a complex relationship between homeland and diaspora that cannot be reduced to simple polar opposites involving economic power located in the latter and powerlessness in the former. Through concepts of *desh* (the homeland) and *bidesh* (the diaspora), she explains how the homeland is "more than just a physical mass of land, trees and rivers"; it is the locus of one's social group. "Home is where one's kinsfolk are" (1993, 5). Meanwhile *bidesh* represents the material and economic power of the diaspora; she emphasizes that "local mental maps involve a geography of power, in which locations are points along a continuum, with different types of empowerment to be found in each" (Gardner 1993, 5).

Deshi products, especially products that undergo processes of embodiment (like fish and rice), are imported into the *bidesh* so that their consumption denotes not only nourishment of a physical nature, but also of a spiritual and emotional nature. Death ultimately casts any juxtaposition of *desh/bidesh* into new light, as *desh* becomes "the place where one truly belongs, the locus of spirituality and the self" (Gardner 2002, 191), manifested materially through products physically formed in the homeland itself. The construction of domestic spaces of kinship as sacred, versus the profane space of *bideshi* mercantilism, is played out transnationally when decisions are taken regarding where to bury the bodies of kin.

The parallels in the case of Miami and Havana are striking; over the course of my fieldwork, Cubans regularly cited the quasi-spiritual nature of anything and everything that was "*de tierra cubana*" (from the Cuban earth). Avocados grown on trees planted from a Cuban seed were softer, beans were more wholesome, herbs were holier, and tobacco seeds were stronger. Indeed, there is an entire industry in both Little Havana and down in Key West (Florida) dedicated to the perpetuation of this legend of "de tierra cubana." Despite the impossibility of selling Cuban cigars in Miami (due to the restrictions of the embargo), many stores advertise them. Upon visiting a cigar factory in Miami, I eventually found out they qualify as "Cuban" by virtue of the fact that they are made from tobacco seeds that were supposedly collected from plants in Cuba, but then taken to Nicaragua (which apparently has the most similar soil-type to that of Cuba's western Pinar province), where the presence of a Cuban overseer at the plantation bestows additional Cubanness (cubanidad) to the production process, before they are shipped to Miami for sale. Numerous times I observed Cuban Americans take a deep drag and smile with satisfaction, saying, "*Esto sí es el sabor de mi tierra*" ("That's the taste of my land"; see also Stubbs 2014).

Within the cosmology of the Cuban diaspora, *la patria* (akin here to Gardner's *desh*) evidently has spiritual or sacred qualities that, through mere tangential consumption (such as the smoking of a cigar made from tobacco leaves grown in Nicaragua from seeds that were harvested originally in Cuba), can bestow value, even at considerable distance. The con-

Figure 6.1. Dominican cigars made from "Cuban seeds" for sale in Key West, Florida. Photo by author, July 2018.

siderable rupture undergone by this community is best navigated with the aid of material links back to a homeland and core identity, in this case effected by seed and soil. The owner of the funeral parlor who had originally pointed me in Victor's direction estimated that as many as 40 percent of his customers had a desire to be taken back to Cuba, either as ashes or bones to be reinterred. "It's something about the Cuban earth [*la tierra cubana*], it's a spiritual thing, it calls to us [*llama*]." The power and agency of Cuban earth and movement have been discussed in reference to traditions of Santería, Ifá, and Palo before (Espírito Santo 2018; A. Fernandez 2014; Holbraad 2007; T. R. Ochoa 2010), yet clearly the sacred quality of Cuban earth and its derivatives also extends beyond Afro-Cuban cosmologies into a broader understanding of what constitutes being Cuban for many of my interlocutors.

Figure 6.2. Shrine to St. Lazarus containing a Cuban cigar, in a tree in a parking lot in Miami. Photo by author, April 2018.

Conclusion

Memorializing Matters

Given the intensely social construction of places of memorial and burial, it is perhaps unsurprising that sites of death in both Miami and Havana should also betray distinct ideological stances. While this chapter has demonstrated the importance of actual material transfer, such transfers inevitably also convey political and ideological layers of meaning that speak beyond the material confines of shrines and cemeteries. Death, as arguably the most permanent rite of passage, is particularly evocative as a representation of life, and the physical body or remains become quite literal flags or "stakes in the ground" in an ongoing ideological battle between fractured Cuban communities on either side of the Florida Straits.

As in chapter 5, where material items acquired and were at times co-opted by specific curated versions of history and memory, memorials and burial sites in both Havana and Miami point to deep-set anxieties regarding what it means to be Cuban. Where does true cubanidad ("Cuban identity") reside? Is it rooted in the soil, or can it be separated from its constituent material parts? These were questions that many of the people I encountered during my fieldwork seemed to be wrestling with, and for this reason, cemeteries and memorials have become sites of contested identity, battlegrounds over cubanidad. Death highlights both the complete interconnectedness of Miami and Cuba (this chapter has presented items carried in both directions to facilitate "good" Cuban deaths), and also, paradoxically, the rhetoric of separation that keeps the two apart. One cannot help but conclude that those Cubans who opt to have their ashes scattered in the sea of the Florida Straits, midway between Miami and Cuba, may have found the easiest option.

Anxieties over identity are evident in the prominent positioning of Cuban flags across Woodlawn Park Cemetery, as well as by the memorial to the Cuban patriot dead in Little Havana. Indeed, this memorial is accompanied by a proud inscription explaining that the shrine itself was constructed using soil taken from each of Cuba's "seven" provinces,[11] in a conscious remobilization of Cuban earth to commemorate the shed blood of "true" Cubans. Palm trees line the memorial, and each is planted in soil also taken from individual provinces of Cuba, to provide shade for the eternal rest of the souls they commemorate.

The introduction of material items invoking cultural ties to other places is nothing new in Cuban memorials; Chinese influences have, for example, been identified in the material culture of Afro-Cuban shrines, narrating long cultural ties between these diasporic identities (Holbraad 2010; Tsang 2015). Diana Espírito Santo has said Cuban religious travelers who construct

> long-term translocal ties with practitioners in Cuba see their practice as constituted in the travel event . . . [Their] transitional *caminos* [paths] are thus geontologies, sacred religious sites produced in the complex geopolitics of moving through different nations, politics, and spiritual assemblages. (2018, 225–226)

This is clearly applicable beyond an Afro-Cuban or even explicitly spiritual setting. As demonstrated in this and preceding chapters, Cuban identity is in large part derived from and expressed through material networks of flow; a concept of geontologies speaks to Cuban death—just as life—as experienced always through a lens of geographical flux and flow.

In Miami, Cuban Americans seek to rest with a piece of home, which is imbued with an almost sacred capacity to bestow kinship and selfhood. Yet equally in Havana, palliative patients rely on the material care displayed by relatives in the diaspora, and in death, some Cubans seek reunion with lost or departed loved ones in the diaspora through material relics and tokens. Moreover, in some cases, the physical transferal of bodily remains from one place to another not only marks the permanence of death, but also permits other material flows (such as items in the coffin), which facilitate ongoing life and demonstrate reciprocated material care. James Clifford's by now familiar homonym of *routes* and *roots* in relation to diaspora (1994) emphasizes the ways in which every form of rootedness and dwelling already presupposes travel, but this is even more symbolic when one thinks of where (and how) one finally puts down roots at the end of an uprooted life. Perhaps most importantly, the rite of passage of death accentuates what is so crucial in Cuban life, which is a strong sense of home and family (both in an affinal kin sense and a nationalistic sense), experienced through material care. As such, this rite of passage as a final performance of cultural identity points to the anxieties and emotional trajectories of Cuban life more than any other point in the life cycle, demonstrating a magnetic force of simultaneous attraction and repulsion between the island and its diaspora.

Conclusion

Constructing Cuban Culture
from the Cracks of Society

In November 2018, the city of Miami unveiled a new flag for the Little Havana neighborhood, comprising a rooster atop the merged flags of the U.S. and Cuba, with 22 other Latin American flags around the border, and the words "Little Havana, U.S.A.: the one with freedom" written in capital letters across the bottom. The flag was designed by Miami city commissioner Joe Carollo, and, in his own words, was meant to symbolize a banner of inclusivity to represent the whole community of Little Havana (Holly 2018). The move was met with opposition on many fronts, however, with one local film director tweeting "Miami politics is just a big dumb crooked cockfight." The commissioner then launched a return attack, declaring these critics admirers of Fidel Castro, and adding, "It's amazing that a simple phrase that speaks of freedom brings all the rats out of the sewer" (Pentón 2018). Within days, the argument had exploded across social media networks and local newspapers, as various cohorts of diasporic Cubans in Miami argued over who and what should be included within such symbolic visions of a Cuban community.

In the wider political context of Miami, this debate hardly seemed surprising. The city has long been a fractured place, especially along ethnic and socioeconomic class lines (Grenier and Stepick 1992; Portes and Stepick 1993; Stepick 1994b)—yet, despite this, there has also long been a rhetorical attempt to present the Cuban diaspora as a unified community. Much has been written about the Cuban diaspora's shared experience of exile (Campa 2000; Rieff 1993; Tweed 1997), which in turn has contributed to a largely accepted ideology of another hegemonic and "authentic" Cuban identity, existing away from the island itself, yet always drawing meaning from its

Figure 7.1. A (rather undiverse) selection of Miami City and Little Havana community representatives unveil the neighborhood's new flag, November 30, 2018. Source: City of Miami Twitter Account (@CityofMiami), https://twitter.com/CityofMiami/status/1068554279986827264?s=20&t=z3V9ya1LEayvRXftMmAOdw.

relation to the island (as demonstrated most tangibly through the transfers of antiques in chapter 5, and seeds and soil in chapter 6). Yet this book has largely focused upon those, both in Cuba and the Miami diaspora, who live in between dominant imaginaries framed by the rigid nationalism of both official island and traditional exile discourses; migrants who maintain links across communities while at the same time endeavoring to "carve out their own paths and reinvent themselves throughout the world" (Silot Bravo 2016, 159). In so doing, it contributes to a growing body of literature addressing the challenges of ambiguity and uncertainty in day-to-day Cuban life, both on the island and in the diaspora (Bastian 2018; Cubas 2007; Del Real and Pertierra 2008; Holbraad 2017; Pérez Firmat 2012; Weinreb 2009).

The considerable ruptures experienced by Cubans not just in recent decades since the revolution, but also across history—from colonialization and slavery to struggles for independence and beyond—thus go some way to demonstrating how generative such processes can be in producing culture. If there was one thing that seemed to unite all my interlocutors across fieldsites, it was their vehemence that Cuban culture (however they defined this) was unique, special, unparalleled. "Life on the hyphen," a "city on the

190 · Circulating Culture

edge": various apt images have been proposed to encapsulate the everyday lives of the betwixt and between of Cuban and American cultures (Pérez Firmat 2012; Portes and Stepick 1993), yet most have also presented this sense of rupture as a loss or breakage from some core element of identity, the "natural" locus of which remains centered on the island of Cuba. Descriptions of the Cuban American experience have this in common with wider discourses on diaspora and migration, whereby "routes" and "roots" still point to an origin of departure, a point disappearing over a horizon (Clifford 1994, 1999). They fail to capture what is coming into view: the way such rupture or flux generates newly emerging cultural forms, which seemed so dynamic and abundant to me throughout my fieldwork. "Life on the outside" can in fact be both generative and culturally creative (Cohen 1996).

In this concluding chapter I briefly consider two contrasting ethnographic vignettes in which diasporic Cubans negotiate this sense of cultural rupture through even more concerted efforts to demarcate and perform what counts as "true" Cuban identity. I then refer back to the previous six chapters to draw conclusions as to how Cubans have negotiated decades of societal rupture, and what this might in turn offer up to us as anthropologists in our approach to analytical categories of people and things, flow and flux, and cultural identities.

¿Qué Pasa, U.S.A.?

In the final weeks of my fieldwork in Miami, posters started to go up in all the main overtly Cuban hangouts in town, advertising the return of a much-loved television drama from the 1970s, this time as a staged play that would be performed in a major cultural center in central Miami. ¿Qué Pasa, U.S.A.? was America's first bilingual sitcom, aired on the Public Broadcasting System (PBS) from 1977 to 1980, taped in front of a live audience at Miami's PBS station. The show explored the trials and tribulations of a Cuban American family living in Little Havana as they adapted to a new country and language, and to this day, it remains cherished by many Miamians as a vibrant portrayal of "life on the hyphen" in their both resented and beloved "city on the edge." In fact, when I first arrived in the city to conduct fieldwork, several newly acquired friends insisted I should watch the entire series as my own cultural induction to the city, and as a useful lens onto Cuban humor and the "Spanglish" malapropisms so commonly encountered in Miami.

This theatrical staging, entitled ¿Qué Pasa, U.S.A Today? 40 Years On was to be an update on what had happened to the familiar cast of characters as their lives had continued over decades of considerable cultural and economic change in Miami and would see the original cast return to fulfill the same roles, forty years on. In short, it would be a staged account of the various ways in which Cuban immigrants had traversed subsequent decades of cultural rupture. Billboards promoting the show were placed along the prominent arterial highway of the I-95, while community meeting points for the old exile crowd, such as Café Versailles, hung up ads for the show, which in turn was sponsored by a quintessentially Cuban American coffee brand.

My friend José and I joined what felt like the whole of Cuban Miami on the opening night, which was completely sold out. As I looked around the auditorium, I saw that whole families were attending together, with grandparents and young children alike hanging over the balcony rail to catch a glimpse of these much-loved characters, who for many felt like old family friends or relatives with whom they had not had the opportunity to chat for many years. As the curtain went up, an enormous cheer erupted across the audience; the actors came on stage, and we learned what had happened to them in the intermittent forty years. The once-teenaged Violetta, now with teenaged children of her own and in the middle of a divorce, had returned to Little Havana after twenty-five years living away, only to find that many of her old Cuban haunts in Miami had gone bust and shut down in her absence. Upon returning to Miami, Violetta took over her uncle's old botánica business (a Cuban store selling items for religious worship) and moved back into her old Little Havana home, which was in dire need of updating (cue several much-appreciated jokes about old Cuban-style furniture).

The audience was hanging on the actors' every word; the couple seated in the row behind me was lost in both waves of hysterical laughter and gentle sobs directed into their jacket sleeves. The outpouring of emotion from an almost entirely self-identifying Cuban American audience (whose members had lived in Miami for many decades, and most of whom remembered or had since watched the original series many times over) for these old familiar characters was almost tangible. The play lent itself to its audience as well, comprising an hour-long tribute to the nostalgia so embodied and projected by a particularly loud faction of the exile community in Miami. At the mention of Café Versailles, the audience spontaneously erupted into applause that lasted for a full minute.

But the play also reflected upon the changes experienced by "the Cuban

192 · Circulating Culture

community" (*la comunidad*) in Miami over the intermittent decades. Violetta drily remarked on how 8th Street (the center of Little Havana) was now almost entirely made up of funeral parlors and cemeteries ("I guess the old ones are full up now"—see chapter 6), while characters walked onstage clasping bags bought in Valsan or ¡Ñooo! que barato—cheap stores selling material goods for export to Cuba, often via mulas (see chapter 3). Overwhelmed by the changed state in which they find Miami, the characters sit down on their now-deceased grandmother's sofa and order a pizza from the major American chain Papa John's, which is promptly delivered by a Cuban balsero who migrated in the 1990s and who uses the word *papayón* (meaning papaya, but also a crude sexual innuendo in Spanish). At this moment the stage lights went out, signaling a blackout, and the pizza delivery character quipped, "Don't worry, I only learned to deliver pizzas in *la Yuma*[1]; back in Cuba I was an electrical engineer." This prompted a standing ovation from many of the people seated around me at the back of the hall, and my friend José sprayed his *materva* drink all over himself as he burst out laughing. The pizza delivery guy character, it turned out, was about to go back to Cuba for his honeymoon and promised to return with "authentic souvenirs" to sell in Little Havana to tourists (see chapter 5), prompting a discussion among the characters of Miami's well-known *tema* (issue): whether or not "going back" was morally acceptable.

The play also addressed the recent influx of Venezuelan migrants to Miami; when the grandmother character announces she is inviting an older Venezuelan man round to visit, the rest of the family immediately quizzes him to gauge if he has communist leanings or not. When the grandchildren discover he lives in the wealthy neighborhood of Brickell, where many properties have been bought by recently arrived Venezuelan migrants with significant quantities of cash, they joke, "Brilliant, he must have loads of moolah"—and, to the audience's amusement, the Cuban grandmother misunderstands and admonishes them for thinking he could be a mula, which is to say, likely someone of lower social class (see chapter 3).

In this way the play spoke to palpable tensions and divisions within the expanding Cuban and Latino communities in Miami; indeed, many of the subtle jokes and references in the script could only have made sense within Miami itself. As an updated contemporary version of the same show presenting old characters alongside new generations (in the form of their children), the play spoke directly to the anxieties felt by a generation now aged around sixty and above, as well as the experience of their American-born children fretting about whether or not they qualify as "Cuban." At one point

Conclusion: Constructing Cuban Culture from the Cracks of Society · 193

in the play, the adolescent character Joey answers the door to the pizza delivery guy, who presumes he is American and proceeds to speak in broken English. Joey replies (in Spanish) "No, I'm Cuban!" prompting the delivery guy to ask where he was born. "I was born here, but in my spirit and my soul I'm Cuban," Joey replies fiercely, prompting a wave of applause, cheers, and cries of "*Eso sí!*" ("Yes!") from the audience. Toward the end of the show, the cast paid homage to the now-deceased grandparent characters, and the woman sitting to my left whispered a short blessing in Spanish and crossed herself, reminding me of Gustavo Pérez Firmat's assertion that "Miami is a Cuban city not because of the Cubans who live here but because of the Cubans who have died here. The living can always move away; it is the dead who are a city's truly permanent residents," with no chance of return (1995, 10; see also chapter 6).

As we walked out of the theater, José noted,

You know, they did a pretty good job of steering through some major topics there. I was wondering how they'd do it. There's so much anxiety and discomfort around new migrants moving here, and class conflict and stuff, it was great they managed to make it all funny.

On the basis of the waves of laughter and happy chatter coming from other departing theatergoers around me, I agreed with him. The play's producers had managed to capture a great deal of the rupture and uncertainty experienced by Miami's Cuban exiles over the intermittent decades since the show had gone off air, and there was almost a tangible sense of relief in the humid air as the audience relaxed into a carefully curated performance of a particular aspect of Cuban Miami identity.

¿Qué Pasa, Hialeah?

A few weeks later I found myself having coffee in Hialeah with a Cuban friend from a rather different background from José's. Valeria is in her mid-thirties and was born in Hialeah just a year after her parents arrived from Cuba (via Venezuela) in the late 1980s. Her father had, in fact, already been to Miami before, sent as Cuban intelligence, and in the process had become involved with a Jewish community group that later helped to get him and his pregnant wife to the diaspora via connections in Venezuela.

I'm pretty sure my Dad then went into the drug trade when he got here, because I remember we used to have this concrete safe under

194 · Circulating Culture

the rug on the living room floor, but then after my Mom got ill and died he went back to Cuba and remarried there. Then he got real sick but wouldn't come back to Miami for treatment because we couldn't get his second wife a visa to come, too. I'm still in touch with her, though, and I send her things from time to time.

Valeria had really hated growing up in Hialeah; it was suffocating and incredibly boring. She also found the ever-pervasive Cubanness of Hialeah to be oppressive, combined with her father's interrogation-style technique of questioning where she had been, and with whom.

It was like there was no option to not be Cuban! I was never really into Spanish music, I wanted to listen to Nirvana, and I couldn't wait to get away. I wanted to move up to New York for college, but then my mom got sick. The same year as my dad died, I got a divorce, and finally ended up going up to New York to tend bar for a while and take a bit of a break, before eventually coming back and retraining to be a teacher.

It was only once she had left and then returned to Hialeah that Valeria started to feel a sense of connection with the wider community she had grown up in. "I think I've always had a love-hate relationship with the place, but I also always end up coming back," she added wryly,

and now that I've lost both my parents, there are so many questions I'd want to ask. I'm starting to reconnect more with my Cuban identity, I'm definitely Cuban American, and if I have children I definitely want them to speak Spanish and know what it means to be Cuban.

But she was also adamant her kids would not grow up in "some post-traumatic-stress-disorder household with survivors' guilt." Once, while sipping coffee, she said to me,

I think what it means to be Cuban in Miami is evolving. If you think about it, everyone was an immigrant at some point, and there comes a time when they start calling themselves American. So I want to preserve some of that Cuban culture, but I don't want it to be all-defining like it has been for many people here. There are so many people who would never leave Miami, or even Hialeah, because realistically it doesn't mean anything to be Cuban outside of here. The entire economy of Hialeah is devoted to Cuba, and it's so efficient that the slightest change in Cuba [happens] and we're all so keenly aware of it here.

Conclusion: Constructing Cuban Culture from the Cracks of Society · 195

It was really interesting to be in New York for a while, where being Cuban or Hispanic just meant something totally different.

Upon her return to the Miami area, Valeria started campaigning for Obama in his then-upcoming presidential election, going door-to-door to encourage people to register to vote. "I would have all sorts of really intimate conversations with them on their doorsteps, and that's how I decided to set up ¿Qué Pasa, Hialeah? as a community group to try to get the community's voice, or maybe I should say voices, to be heard in local decision-making." Valeria's choice of community name conspicuously echoed the famous sitcom *¿Qué Pasa, U.S.A?*

That show was all about cultural translation and finding your way in an alien world, and that still resonates with lots of newly arrived Cubans here in Hialeah, who feel really disenfranchised from America but also from that exile community in Miami in general.

Valeria's community group started off by organizing a bike ride across Hialeah to get locals feeling engaged in their community once more. Soon after, they began to apply for public money and grants for public art and to create some dedicated "hip spaces" to promote local culture. The result was the Leah Arts District, which includes several large public murals and some new art studios showcasing local artists and musicians and is fast becoming an alternative locale for tourists to the Miami area seeking "authentic" Cuban and Hispanic culture. "That's something a lot of my generation want to cultivate more of in Hialeah," Valeria told me. "We're young, Cuban, and also American, and we wanted to create a space for all those other versions of identity that I certainly experienced myself as a teenager. You can be Cuban and still like Nirvana!" One of Valeria's friends, for example, is in the process of setting up a *brujería* (witchcraft) market selling artisan local items, tacos, and craft beers. Another has founded an art studio to showcase art reflecting what it is like to be a first-generation American from an immigrant family in Hialeah.

Valeria once observed,

I would probably be a huge disappointment to my parents if they were still alive, because I'm in my mid-thirties and I'm single and I don't have any kids. It's difficult being the first generation; there's a lot of pressure, and sometimes you want to go in two directions at once. . . . The older I get, the more interested I am in my cultural roots, but there are lots of different versions of Cuba, and all of them

196 · Circulating Culture

are played out and imagined here in Miami. There are people who completely lose themselves in it, who define their whole lives by a sense of loss, so I see what I do as a more positive way of embracing some of that and creating something from it. I've already had a lot of grief in my life, so why would I choose to find more?! Hialeah is a lot of different things to different people, and I wanted to celebrate that uprootedness through the cultural events and spaces we co-curate together.

(Re)Constructing Culture

While both José's and Valeria's observations had links to the same TV show and its presentation of Cuban American life, the juxtaposition between these two normative presentations of cubanidad is striking. José and Valeria had very different experiences of being Cuban in Miami, and both had a love-hate relationship with their cultural identities, finding their Cubanness at once claustrophobic and comforting. Yet despite the many differences between their interpretations of what constituted being Cuban, they both agreed that being Cuban, outwardly, was incredibly important. "Seeing is believing," José told me, echoing Yani's remark that you have to "fake it 'til you make it" (chapter 1). This anxiety was mirrored in much of the audience at the theater performance, along with various other encounters I had around Miami, where I consistently found Cubans to be keen, perhaps even anxious, to demarcate what being Cuban meant. The more their position as the major non-American group in Miami was threatened by new waves of Venezuelans, Mexicans, Hondurans, and Guatemalans, the more acutely they performed this cubanidad—as much to themselves as to anyone else, it seemed.

There is a visible and tangible materiality to this cultural category of identity that has echoed throughout this book, from the fluid ownership of valuable items in pawnshops in chapter 1 right through to the often-ostentatious burial ceremonies presented in chapter 6. The opening vignette to this chapter, with the unveiling of a new flag as a symbol of the Cuban community in exile, is just one further example of how, in the face of constant rupture and uncertainty, Cubans in exile have sought to demarcate a sense of identity for themselves in a public-facing and declarative way. The more changeable the environment (and bear in mind my fieldwork saw a transition from President Obama to President Trump, the death of Fidel Castro, and a consequently significant shift in Cuba-U.S. policy), the more

Conclusion: Constructing Cuban Culture from the Cracks of Society · 197

my participants all seemed to want to construct or cement some sense of Cuban identity in a public-facing, and ultimately material, way.

It is in the ordinary, mundane material exchanges of everyday life that what we might call an emerging habitus takes form (Bourdieu 1977, 77–78), from which the cultural performances described at the outset of this chapter then draw their own metacommentary employing recognizable tropes of emerging cultural forms. The interpretations of cubanidad that I was presented with throughout my time in Miami often differed so drastically that I started to see the oft-cited term cubanidad as rather meaningless, and yet, to my interlocutors, it clearly meant everything. The more things changed, the more adamant they were that everything stayed the same (Pertierra 2012). As one participant commented to me during Hurricane Irma in October 2017, "The more the winds buffet you, the more you have to dig deeper with your roots."

Flow and Flux

One of the dominant images of Cuba, especially in the United States, is that of a geographically and politically isolated nation: an "off-bounds place, caught in a retro time-warp of the late 1950s and 1960s, quaint, romantic, shabby chic revolutionary, a sort of social Galapagos" (Damián J Fernández 2005, xiii). This portrait of isolation and Cuban exceptionalism, promulgated both within and off the island itself, presents the island as suspended outside real time and space, beyond the parameters of global social life. First and foremost, this book has sought to deconstruct such fetishistic portrayals of Cuba, ethnographically exploring the myriad ways in which Cuba is not isolated, but in fact highly interconnected with the wider world in every possible regard. Moreover, Cuba has been at a crossroads of global flows for centuries, and is arguably just as connected, if not more so, than ever before.

The representation of Cuba as an isolated, disconnected, or somehow frozen place is largely the workings of political projects that seek to entrench differences between socialism and capitalism. These binaries in turn then map directly onto other oppositions of legal and illegal, American and Cuban, free and oppressed, "here" and "there." Life for Cubans and Cuban Americans is not just "life on a hyphen" (Ciani Forza 2006; Duany 1997; Pérez Firmat 2012; Torres-Queral 1998), but more often life balancing precariously across entrenched binaries. The ethnography presented throughout this book has consistently deconstructed such binaries, however, pointing to how much more ambiguous life in its everyday lived reality is. Moreover, it has often revealed that such ambiguity can in fact be a positive thing; most of my New Cuban interlocutors rarely felt the need to pick a side between capitalism and socialism, American and Cuban. As Martin Holbraad points out, to force such binaries upon them would be an "ethnographic distortion," when such ambiguities might better be understood as "binary equivocation[s]" (2014a, 369–370). My participants were comfortable with picking elements from both as it suited them, carefully navigating paths across these binaries with regularity in the course of a normal day in family life.

In chapter 1, we saw newly arrived Cubans in Hialeah circumventing traditional notions of capitalist ownership to achieve a material success that fitted better with their fluid and transnational lives. In chapter 2, Milagros and her family ignored hegemonic, state-enforced or traditional conceptions of kinship to create their own sense of relatedness across considerable geopolitical and socioeconomic boundaries. The mulas of chapter 3 did not use the Mula Ring as a means of escaping the island to make it to affluent America, but rather as a way of traveling beyond the local to enhance their personhood and conditions of life back in Cuba; likewise, the paqueteros of chapter 4 revealed themselves to be mindful of dual audiences and cultural idioms, both in Miami and Havana. Finally, chapters 5 and 6 both pointed to how, despite reifying rhetoric separating the diaspora and the island, people on both sides of the Florida Straits were navigating an existence that was more ambiguous than this, and that drew meaning from both "sides" in parallel.

The concept of transnational flows as both imaginaries and cultural landscapes has been explored by anthropologists a great deal, usually relating to globalization, modernity, and transnational capitalism. For Arjun Appadurai, the driving force behind contemporary global cultural processes is situated in the tension between tendencies toward cultural homogenization, deriving from the dominance of global flows from the Global North, and cultural heterogenization, resulting from local appropriation of these flows (1990, 95). Similarly, for Aihwa Ong, modernity is situated in local approaches to negotiating the dynamic flow of capital, ideas, goods, and people "in a context of time-space compression" (1999, 16). Ong also points out that relatively less attention was paid to the agents who were part of these transnational flows presented in emerging discourses of transnationalism, migration, diaspora, and globalization in the 1990s (1999, 93). Such gaps were subsequently addressed in the 1990s and 2000s, most particularly by scholars of postsocialism, who explored how people negotiated the shifting cross-currents of cultural and economic flow at home and in transit and upon arrival in new places of residence (Burawoy and Verdery 1999; Mandel and Humphrey 2002), and by scholars of migration and diaspora studies, who revealed the complexities and ambiguities at work in the myriad identities of people living in between and across flows of culture (Burrell 2008; Duany 2002; Horst 2010; Olwig 1993). These ethnographic bodies of work explore the experiences of people on the move who live their entangled lives between cultures and contexts, across borders, and who nevertheless aspire to live coherent, meaningful, and dignified lives in different worlds simultaneously.

These areas of ethnographic work also pointed to the agency of regular people working within and across global flows of transnational capitalism, living their lives in literal and figurative borderlands in sites of political, cultural, and social rupture, where identities converged, coexisted, and sometimes conflicted. From these bodies of work, we come to see the power of counterflow to be just as significant as flow when addressing the concept of culture and citizenship in contexts of ambiguity. This inherent tension is encapsulated in Anna Tsing's notion of "friction," whereby cultures are produced not through unimpeded flow, but rather through "the awkward, unequal, unstable, and creative equalities of interconnection across difference" (2011, 4). Tsing's notion of friction as an inherent productive tension within cross-cultural and long-distance encounters producing culture is crucial to the argument of this book. To it, I also add the concept of flux, which comes to us from the same etymological root as "flow" (Latin: *fluxus*, to flow), but encapsulates also a sense of ongoing or continuous change, of disruptedness, uprootedness, and ambiguity. If "flow" has often hinted at a sense of direction, perhaps even of emerging order, "flux" rather points to a certain chaos; if flow is a transactional moment or event, flux is an overarching state of being, characterized by the productive tensions Tsing includes in her presentation of friction.

I maintain that such a distinction is important to understanding the ethnography I have presented here, which has charted the flows of people and things, both material and digital, but which I hope has gone beyond that to portray a world of disorder from which new rules and social orders can emerge. I have referred to this at times throughout the book as an "emerging habitus," drawing on Pierre Bourdieu's definition of habitus as "the way society becomes deposited in persons in the form of lasting dispositions, or trained capacities and structured propensities to think, feel and act in

200 · Circulating Culture

determinant ways, which then guide them" (Wacquant 2005, 316). Yet it is also distinct from Bourdieu's formulation of "habitus" in three key ways.

First, Bourdieu envisages habitus as a largely reactive, unthinking, and unconscious force for cultural reproduction—one that operates "without any deliberate pursuit of coherence . . . without any conscious concentration" (1984, 170)—yet throughout this book I have described the conscious actions of interlocutors who have set out to manipulate or steer the formation of this emerging habitus. Indeed, at times I have described it as a battleground in my attempt to characterize the agency, strategy, and passion exerted by many of my interlocutors.

Second, for Bourdieu any habitus or social order is also situated in what he calls "distinction" within a social hierarchy, which is established by wielding capital (both material and cultural), and leads to the unconscious acceptance of social difference (1986, 471). The ethnographic material in this book has shown how these class-based manifestations or performances of distinction can be disrupted in transnational settings, and particularly in the communities presented here that span a spectrum of capitalist- and socialist-informed interpretations of socioeconomic class and hierarchy, or distinction.

Third, we get the sense of longevity in Bourdieu's formulation of habitus: it is not fixed or permanent, but changes over long periods of time, something that Appadurai has dubbed the "glacial undertow of habitus" (1991, 200). In the ethnographic context this book deals with, the shifts in cultural identity and expression seem rather quicker than that, more akin to the "quickened beat of improvisation" Appadurai later suggests (1996, 5), where habitus has to be "painstakingly reinforced in the face of life-worlds that are frequently in flux" (1996, 56; see also Handler 2002). The cultural flux associated with the transnational or postnational realm of experience problematizes any search for steady points of reference in terms of tradition, kinship, and cultural identity (Featherstone 2001).

The Mula Ring as presented here is not merely the flow or circulation of items (and people) between supposed binaries of socialism and capitalism, or between physical places and communities, but rather the emergence of new forms of value from interstitial possibility. Nor is it one coherent network unto itself; rather, it is an improvised amalgamation or bricolage of various people's responses to ongoing ambiguity and flux, where rules of life are negotiated and renegotiated in a void of clarity and continuity. This is equally true in the digital world of el paquete and what I call the e-Mula Ring, where Cuban cultural forms can be renegotiated amid a backdrop of ambiguity. This book therefore shows how the circulations and flows of people and material or digital goods is crucial to the expansion and renegotiation of cultural forms, as asserted in various works on globalization, material circulation, and transnationalism. Moreover, the Cuban case arguably goes beyond this, revealing how new regimes of cultural and economic value emerge precisely at moments of material and social flow and counterflow across landscapes of ongoing geopolitical and socioeconomic flux. It is also at this level that what I present here as the Mula Ring parallels the iconic Kula Ring—not just as a network of material circulation, but as a force generative of culture itself, the creation of a wider social world, where structures of identity, personhood, and even kinship—in short, the rules of cubanidad, of sociality—are played out in everyday life, not just in performance or discourse.

Cracking Culture

Perhaps most important of all, this book emphasizes that it is the generative quality of such rupture, and people's agencies in navigating, manipulating, and even wielding the ambiguities inherent in these moments of interstitial possibility, that is most significant in galvanizing the production and expansion of new cultural logics. As the Saint Lucian poet laureate Derek Walcott so beautifully reminds us, this is a skill the people of the Antilles have long honed:

> Break a vase, and the love that reassembles the fragments is stronger than that love which took its symmetry for granted when it was whole. The glue that fits the pieces is the sealing of its original shape. It is such a love that reassembled our African and Asiatic fragments, the cracked heirlooms whose restoration shows its white scars. This gathering of broken pieces is the care and pain of the Antilles, and if the pieces are disparate, ill-fitting, they contain more pain than their original sculpture, those icons and sacred vessels taken for granted in their ancestral places. Antillean art is this restoration of our shattered histories, our shards of vocabulary, our archipelago becoming a synonym for pieces broken off from the original continent. (1993, 809)

This brings to mind the Japanese craft of *kintsugi* ("golden repair"), whereby broken ceramics are mended by applying a mixture of lacquer and gold dust along the crack. Precious metals serve to highlight prior breakages in this transformative repair craft, in contrast to other forms of repair that typically attempt to hide a history of damage or rupture (Iten 2008, 18). The smoothed, golden seams that bind the ceramic pieces together suggest a life of quality, even of beauty, beyond catastrophe, and are "an expression of the binding force that ameliorates the oppositional forces pulling them apart" (Keulemans 2016, 26). For Christy Bartlett, such kintsugi are defined by a sense of "rupture" of "surface and structure" that corresponds to the struggles of life in Japan. She adds, "the vicissitudes of existence over time, to which all humans are susceptible, could not be clearer than in the breaks, knocks, and the shattering to which ceramic ware too is subject" (2008, 11).

For Deleuze and Guattari, meanwhile, the effects of such scars from rupture do not operate in isolation; affect is mediated by materiality, and extends outward from the micropolitical to the macropolitical, operating both upon the individual and upon society and culture (1987, 208–216; 1994, 168). The point I would add to this line of argument is not just that these cracks or ruptures can extend from the realm of the micropolitical to the macropolitical, but also that they can do so in a generative, even a structurally provocative way. If we take kintsugi as a metaphor, or perhaps rather an image we can think through to expand on Walcott's imagery and conceptualize the ways in which new cultural forms emerge, we are directed toward the ways in which affective material items endure rupture, even catastrophe, but can emerge as new forms, which to some might even be more stimulating. The craft of kintsugi emphasizes the appeal of these precious scars, finding cracks to be culturally generative spaces from which new form can emerge, and gives equal aesthetic and structural importance to the edges as to the center: the scars can radiate inward and outward, making it difficult to locate any original point of breakage.

The only shortcoming of this metaphor is that we end up with a receptacle of the same size as we had before—whereas the cultural generation I have described here as coming from the cracks of societal rupture adds up to more than the sum of its pre-ruptured parts. To echo Maurice Merleau-Ponty, "What we call disorder and ruin, others who are younger live as the natural order of things and perhaps with ingenuity they are going to master it precisely because they no longer seek their bearings where we took ours" (1964, 23). Perhaps here we might equate Cuban mulas and their networks of circulation and exchange with the likes of Gaudí, who, when confronted with a load of broken pottery, reconfigured the pieces into a new, more fluid structure that broke the mold altogether.[2] Gaudí's work also arguably draws more on the inherent tension between the brittleness of cracked shards and the malleable fluidity they can form when placed together in a larger col-

Conclusion: Constructing Cuban Culture from the Cracks of Society · 203

lage, in a way reminiscent of the arguments I have made here about the generative interstitial possibilities that lie in the cracks. The imagery of Gaudí's *trencadís* also calls to mind the metaphors so often cited when thinking about the Caribbean—of bricolage, of hybridity, of creolization, of transculturation (Benítez-Rojo 1996; Khan 2001; Ortiz 1940; Palmié 2013; Puri 2004; Réjouis 2014; Trouillot 2002)—all of which discuss (to a greater or a lesser degree) the breaking, mixing, and reshaping of cultural forms into new realms of identity. The normalization of crisis leads to tentative orderings of disorder (Taussig 1992; Vigh 2008), to people actively seeking new bearings in a "situation of emergence" (Bhabha 1994), whereby social life is made sense of, and, as I argue here, perhaps even expands in some horizons as others are curtailed.

As Gaylene Becker has pointed out, the effort to create order has been, in essence, what anthropologists have studied throughout most of the history of the discipline, and it has only been relatively recently that anthropologists have started to focus specifically upon moments of disruption (1997, 5). Yet even when disruptive moments have been observed, they have often been noted more for their capacity to throw cultural phenomena and traditions of continuity into relief. We see this focus on cohesion and continuity inherent in many of the big theories we still work with today: Pierre Bourdieu's (1977, 1984) notion of habitus, to pick one prominent example, proposes a concept of culture that, for the most part, follows a set of rules or traditions or habits, and when these rules are broken, it serves to highlight the rules even more through their very rupture. Michel Foucault's work (1979, 2002) on "regimes" of power and value follows much the same line of thought; we comprehend the boundaries of culture as a hegemonic sphere of operation precisely when these boundaries are transgressed.

Throughout my time in the field, however, I was constantly confronted by participants disagreeing among themselves and negotiating what it meant to be culturally Cuban. Adriana Méndez Rodenas's description of the "radical rupture in the Cuban collective psyche" seems apt to me (2007, 143), given the decades of ongoing economic, familial, cultural, and political rupture that Cubans in all guises have experienced. The commonly held notion that being Cuban means belonging to a "mythopoetic idea" or a "state of mind" (Herrera 2007b, 179) takes Benedict Anderson's (1983) idea of an "imagined community" even further, whereby being "Cuban" can only truly be experienced through this state of disruption, rupture, or flux. There was a general sense among my participants that their history, and in a sense much of their identity, had imploded, the shockwaves of which were still keenly felt in both Miami and Havana. *Lo cubano* ("Cubanness") has become "a performative site of political confrontation, as well as of trauma, desire, and utopia" (Silot Bravo 2016, 20), and as I have demonstrated throughout the chapters of this book, this performative site of contestation inevitably manifests in the material and digital world and the circulation of such items through differing regimes of affective, economic, and political value.

As Michael Taussig so aptly puts it, "What does it take to envisage a society breaking down?" (1992, 17), to which I add, what does it then take to conceive of a society as reconstructing itself from the fragments left behind? What does culture look like in this instance? In this light, it hardly seems surprising that so many commentators upon Cuban culture in the twentieth century have emphasized arboreal metaphors of rootedness, perhaps in response to a sense of uprootedness assuming such a central position in the experience of Cuban identity throughout this period (Duany 1997; Ortiz 1940; Pérez Firmat 1997). In my own research this became particularly clear in the emphasis upon earth, soil, and seeds presented in chapter 6.

In this book I propose that the cracks resonating out from such moments of rupture or uprootedness are precisely the locus of new cultural forms; just as Japanese kintsugi or Catalan trencadís highlight the generation of new aesthetic form from breakage, so, too, have the most dynamic and emerging aspects of contemporary Cuban culture seemingly emerged precisely due to and from these rifts. Chaos has historically been negatively valued in Western discursive tradition because of the prominence of binary logic; if order is good, chaos must be destructive as its conceptual opposite (Becker 1997, 6). Yet in all the material and digital cases presented throughout this book, we have seen what Holbraad et al. describe as the "dual aspect" of rupture, whereby an inherently negative switch-point breaking with existing conditions can also be a positive or dynamic impulse toward redirection, reconstitution, and renewal (2019, 1). This is in keeping with a broader shift in recent anthropological studies to celebrate discontinuity as a moment of potential emergence (Bach 2017; Calis 2017; Freeman 2017; Humphrey 2018; Marshall 2016; Robbins 2007). As this book has demonstrated, the realities of crisis and its surrounding discourse transform the material and moral environments of people going about their lives, which sits in productive tension with a need to fill these cracks with new forms.

Furthermore, in the case of Cuba and its Miami diaspora, there is also a tension between a supposedly homogenizing globalization and the asymmetries of sociopolitically disparate communities shaping these material

Conclusion: Constructing Cuban Culture from the Cracks of Society · 205

flows. This, for Subrata Mitra, "constitutes the process of culture, not to be understood as geographical entities, but as transregional and transnational concepts that mostly come into existence only through contact with others" (2013, 8). This concept of a transnational "space" of cultural production, mitigated by flows and streams of material circulation, therefore draws heavily upon ideas in theories of globalization and also "liminality" as nexuses of productive tension (Burawoy et al. 2000; Harvey 2007). This is not merely a new symptom of modernity and increasing globalization in the Cuban or Caribbean context, however. Cuba is located in a semantic and discursive universe "with many layers of sometimes contradictory historical, cultural, and political meanings" (Lins Ribeiro 2019, 764). The rupture and ambiguity experienced by Cubans in the past six decades has, in fact, been a central theme in much of the Caribbean since colonial times, a long narrative characterized by "competition, movement, fluidity," "overlapping networks of association and exchange," and "multiple identities" (Austin-Broos 1997; Mintz and Price 1976; Ranger 1983, 248; Wardle 2002). For Sidney Mintz, the Caribbean region as we know it marked the invention of a modernity located in overlapping flows; Caribbean peoples were, in his eyes, "the first overseas conscripts of modernity" (Scott 2004, 192). Ambiguity and rupture are a daily aspect of life in Cuba and are entrenched in local culture through oft-cited references to *inventar, sobrevivir, la lucha* ("inventiveness," "survival," "struggle"), and so forth (Del Real and Pertierra 2008). While some scholars have thus situated trends of precarity or ambiguity within globalizing neoliberalism or late capitalism (Jameson 1991; Ong 1999), it is arguable that in a Caribbean context, this is more a "pre-post-modern" condition (Olwig 1993, 7), having evolved from a long-standing position of political, economic, and social in-betweenness over centuries. Ambiguity and discontinuity are, in fact, utterly ordinary in this context (Trouillot 2020). Perhaps, given the region's past of slavery and capitalist colonialism, Caribbean cultural forms have always emerged from these social cracks or interstitial spaces (Olwig 2007, 11).

As Joel Robbins rightly points out, "an argument for rupture as culturally driven cultural change is easier to assert than it is to really work through, for in theoretical terms it is not as simple as one might imagine to construe rupture as a cultural process . . . because culture is generally taken almost by definition to be . . . a force for its own reproduction" (2018, 219). Typically conceived of in terms of structure or tradition, culture is all about "steering social action along well-worn grooves" (Robbins 2018, 219). This is often a

206 · Circulating Culture

tacit assumption, even a departure point, for much ethnographic writing. We anthropologists arrive in our fieldsites to inspect the grooves and draw a map of them.

By contrast, this book has set out to explore how these grooves are carved out in the first place. What does emerging culture in its embryonic and dynamic budding forms look like? In the case of Cuba and its diasporas, charting decades of every conceivable type of experiential rupture, I propose this incipient Mula Ring as the first marks in the ground by way of carving out these grooves. Here we see new cultural forms based upon material circulation and kinship systems that are generated specifically by this fluid and vibrant situation. I do not go so far as to agree with Benjamin Lee and Edward LiPuma however, when they write,

> The advent of circulation-based capitalism, along with the social forms and technologies that complement it, signifies more than a shift in emphasis. It constitutes a new stage in the history of capitalism, in which the national capitalisms that were created from the seventeenth century through the concluding decades of the twentieth are being simultaneously dismantled and reconstructed on a global scale. The effect is to subordinate and eventually efface historically discrete cultures and capitalisms and to create a unified cosmopolitan culture of unimpeded circulation. (2002, 210)

These new pathways or routes, marked out by circulatory flows and counter-flows, echo arguments made about infrastructure, whereby roads, for example, both expand and limit pathways across space; they facilitate ease of travel while simultaneously acting as structures of confinement (Dalakoglou and Harvey 2012; Tsing 2011, 6). Of course, the response to this is that people go off-road, and carve a new path alongside the old. Rather than "subordinating" to the erasure of "discrete cultures," as Lee and LiPuma would have it, I have shown here that people invent, they work around, under, across, and through. Circulation is by no means unimpeded; it is precisely the impediment that is generative of new flows. As Manuel Castells recommends in his latest treatise on neoliberal rupture, then, "given our historical experience, maybe learning to live in chaos would be less harmful than conforming to the discipline of yet another order" (2018, 227).

Akin to Anna Tsing's analogy of frictive roads (2011, 6), I also begin and end this book within an infrastructure that exemplifies the arguments I have presented here. In the prologue and the epilogue, we find ourselves in the Miami airport—a place known to all mulas, a place of the in-between, of arrivals and departures, waiting and rushing, encounters and partings, flow and flux. Like roads, these are places that open up one's horizons while in the same fell swoop limiting them, determining trajectories. Sitting in an airport lounge, looking up at a maze-like network of pipework in the ceiling, one cannot help but think that flow could not exist without pressure and flux; culture would not expand so dynamically without simultaneous forces of societal constriction.

Epilogue

I'm sitting on a worn sofa in Miami Airport, sipping a lukewarm Starbucks coffee while I wait for Pablo to finish his final shift. I had first met him a year earlier, as he checked my passport and "Cuba Ready" stamp before I boarded a flight to Havana. He had moved to Miami from Havana only a few months earlier, having procured a job with Cuban Travel Services, and was gradually settling into his new life in Hialeah. Amid the tensions of the line to board the flight, his bright countenance and jovial manner had seemed a ray of sunshine through an overcast sky. "Soy un jodedor típico" he had chuckled, referring to his teasing sense of humor. "That was actually why I took this job. I thought it would be perfect for me, you know, to bounce up and down the line and put people in the right frame of mind before they start their holiday, I thought I'd be sort of officially greeting people into Cuba. American-style customer service a lo cubano, haha!"

Things hadn't quite turned out that way, though. It turned out that CTS was a middleman for American Airlines to do, in Pablo's words, "their dirty work." This was the company that held the contract with the Cuban government (due to various embargo-related limitations), and Pablo answered to three Cuban officials, whom he described as thinly veiled government operatives stationed within the Miami airport. "In my first week I thought I'd be given customer service training, but I was actually told how to recognize returning Cubans and report this to my seniors." Within a month, he had already been reprimanded by his boss for being too friendly and talking too much to customers.

Prior to getting the job, Pablo had done ad hoc work as a mula, and this newfound legitimate status in Miami was to be a significant boon in his expanding travel possibilities. He would now be able to go back and forth with even greater regularity, allowing him to visit his elderly father in Havana, carry items back to sell, and also benefit from some of the more material comforts of living in the U.S. "In some ways it seemed kind of a natural step, I guess," Pablo laughed. "I'm already pretty well accustomed to the inner workings of an airport, after all!"

But after almost a year of persevering, and having got his green card paperwork through to reside in the U.S. permanently, Pablo had decided it was time to move on. I was on my way back from Guyana and had arranged to meet him in the airport lounge after his final shift. "I think it's about time I tried to establish a normal life for myself," he said, when I asked him what he planned to do next. "So I guess I'll go home, watch some TV, feed the cat, and look for a normal job."

Extract from field note diary, June 2018

A few months later, and I'm hovering near the port in Havana, watching a steady stream of American tourists disembark. Quite by chance, I turn around and walk straight into Pablo. "I thought you were supposed to be in Hialeah, feeding your cat!" I laugh, and he grins somewhat bashfully, pulling at his starched uniform collar in the heat of mid-summer Havana. "I did try for a while," he reports, "but I ended up getting a job working on cruise ships. It's great—I get to entertain people, and to be honest, I missed the back-and-forth in the end. I felt a bit stifled just being in the one place; there was, like, this great pressure to be Cuban enough, and somehow I never quite knew what that meant or something. But now I'm here and there, to and fro, back where I'm supposed to be . . . in between! I guess that must be my 'normal' . . ."

Extract from field note diary, September 2018

Notes

Introduction

1 At the time of my fieldwork (2017–2019), Cuba had two currencies, the CUP or *peso* (roughly twenty of which equated to one U.S. dollar) and the convertible *peso* (CUC) which was roughly equivalent to one U.S. dollar. Neither could be taken off the island, and exchange rates on the island were fixed, including an additional 10 percent tax for those converting U.S. currency. As of January 2021, the convertible *peso* has been removed from circulation, and Cuba now uses only the CUP (*moneda nacional*).

2 The embargo was partially relaxed in 2000 by President Clinton, who introduced a reform allowing for the sale of agricultural goods and medicine to Cuba for humanitarian reasons. This exception remains in place, and in 2020, $176.8 million worth of goods were exported from the U.S. to Cuba, and $14.9 million were imported to the U.S. from Cuba (see "Trade in Goods with Cuba").

3 The Special Period euphemistically refers to the economic hardship experienced in Cuba after the collapse of the Soviet Union in 1991, when many Cubans fled the island, or had to make huge sacrifices to manage even the most basic sustenance. For most Cubans on the island, it has become a common referent in a discourse of "before" and "after," and the period is still regularly cited by Cubans as a time when the rules of moral and social order changed, and questions of *sobrevivir* (survival) and *luchar* (struggle) became paramount (Hernández-Reguant 2009; Powell 2008; Rosendahl 2001).

4 In general, the "exile" generations of Cubans in South Florida have typically voted Republican, and they have proven decisive in several key elections (Girard, Grenier, and Gladwin 2012; Grenier 2006; Salter and Mings 1972).

5 See also Burawoy and Verdery 1999; Buyandelgeriyn 2007, 2008; Creed 1995; Dalakoglou 2012; Humphrey 2002; Kaneff 2002; Lemon 1998; Lindquist 2006; Pine 2002; Ries 2002; Rofel 1999; Schwenkel 2013; and Verdery 2003 on the various difficulties of characterizing a "transition" from socialism.

6 I explain why some of these locations are so relevant more fully in chapter 3, but broadly speaking, they were all countries that offered visas to Cuban visitors, and/or that had semi-regular flights to and from Cuba at the time of fieldwork.

Chapter 1. "Fake It to Make It"

1 Americans often refer to South Florida as "south of the South," alluding to its conservative and racially segregated history under Jim Crow (as in the case of neighboring Georgia, Alabama, etc), and also to its absorption of migrants from Central

212 · Notes to Pages 33–42

and South America. Since its inception, Miami has been a "melting pot" of different cultural groups from across North America, the Caribbean, and Latin America, and remains a highly diverse yet segregated city to this day.

2 Political geographers conventionally distinguish among "boundaries," "borders," and "frontiers," and I broadly follow the conventional distinction throughout this book, whereby "boundaries" and "borders" evoke a precise, linear division "within a restrictive political context" (P. Sahlins 1991, 4), while "frontiers" maintain a more "zonal quality," where there is "blurring, ambiguity and uncertainty" in a broader sociocultural context, even long after the imposition and reification of a political border or boundary (Hannerz 1997, 9). In English, the word "frontier" might bring to mind the American experience of the Western frontier, and all of the cultural, economic, and political interactions that engendered (St. John 2011). It is with this character in mind that I describe Miami as a "frontier space" as well as a boundary; the city marks the port of entry across the border of the United States for countless immigrants, especially from the Caribbean and Latin America, but it also serves as a sort of liminal zone between places of departure and arrival for many of its inhabitants, and in that sense is also a zone of possibility as well as cultural violence.

3 See U.S. Census Bureau data at https://www.census.gov/quickfacts/hialeahcityflorida and https://datausa.io/profile/geo/hialeah-fl/. Accessed January 19, 2020.

4 Greater Miami subdivides into smaller "cities," each of which has its own mayor, and so while Hialeah is geographically located fairly centrally within the Greater Miami-Dade area, it is also its own distinct place, and governs itself.

5 A *botánica* (literally a "plant store") is a store selling religious goods such as folk medicines, herbs, candles, and statues of saints. They are common across many Hispanic American countries and have become increasingly popular in the U.S. as Latino diasporas have increased there.

6 The Virgen de la Caridad del Cobre (Our Lady of Charity) is a popular title for the Virgin Mary in many Catholic traditions and is particularly beloved of Cubans. The "home" church for Cubans in the Miami diaspora is named after her, and thus many exiles also place statues of her in prominent places near their home (see Tweed 1997).

7 For Marx, currency is a "token" (2020, 81) or a semiotic medium of representation that makes possible the form of universal commodity exchange that is the basis of the institution of the capitalist market. It also brings all things "under a common rubric" (Maurer 2006, 16); as a "social technology" (Ingham 2001), it standardises the denominations of value that form the basis of exchange in "modern" societies. Furthermore, according to Simmel (drawing on Marx's ideas), money is an alienating and abstracting technology, insofar as it bequeaths "the absolute freedom from everything personal" (Simmel 1990, 128) as a universal and homogenizing measure of value. Numerous scholars have pursued more nuanced readings of various aspects of the theory of money, challenging ideas of its inalienability (Strathern 1988; Zelizer 1994, 2005), its demands upon timeliness and morality (Parry and Bloch 1989), its universality (Gregory 1997; Hutchinson 1996), and its anonymity and materiality (Foster 1995; Keane 2001), among other things.

Notes to Pages 46–89 · 213

8 See also Murawski (2018) for counter-views on defining "success" in postsocialist contexts.

9 A rite of passage in much of Latin America celebrating a girl's coming of age at fifteen.

10 Moving money back and forth between Cuba and the U.S. is possible, but complicated and subject to various state restrictions, not to mention costly. Whenever possible, it is preferable to enact two transactions: one exchange between relatives from both transacting parties in Cuba, and another between relatives in the U.S. Thus, large purchases, such as property investments, often realistically happen between "kin groups" rather than simply between individuals.

Chapter 2. The Ties That Bind

1 Between 1993–2004, dollar stores were government-owned shops in Cuba that sold goods (that were very hard to find in other stores) in exchange for hard currency. Originally their main clientele was foreigners (such as diplomats) who could pay in U.S. dollars, which were made legal tender in Cuba in 1993, or in Cuban convertible *pesos*. The stores are widely considered to have been a strategy to get much-needed hard currency into the Cuban economy during the Special Period after the economic crash of the Soviet Union. The term "dollar store" still remains in colloquial use in Cuba to mean stores where imported goods can be purchased, even though U.S. dollars ceased to be legal tender in 2004.

2 As already mentioned in earlier chapters, Black Cubans on the island are likely to have both lower incomes and a lower likelihood of having a relative overseas who can send remittances to them. See de la Fuente 2016; Hansing 2018; Wirtz 2017.

3 See, for example, Cabezas 2004, 2009; N. T. Fernandez 2010; Härkönen 2015; Hodge 2001; Lundgren 2011; Simoni 2012; Stout 2014a.

4 There is an extensive literature on diaspora and remittances, but in particular the following reveal parallels with the role of extended kinship I describe in the Cuban case: Åkesson 2011; Amuedo-Dorantes and Pozo 2006; Burman 2006; Fouratt 2017; Ho, Boyle, and Yeoh 2015; King and Vullnetari 2009; Lindley 2009; McKay 2007; Paerregaard 2014; Singh, Cabraal, and Robertson 2010.

Chapter 3. The "Mula Ring"

1 At the time of my fieldwork, self-employed workers (or *cuentapropistas*) could apply for a license to work in one of 127 permitted activities. In February 2021, in part in response to the economic crisis caused by the COVID-19 pandemic, the Cuban government issued a new decree expanding this list to 2,000 activities in which self-employment is allowed. The government also announced that the previous Quota Regime—whereby some businesses were assumed to be so small-scale that they were required to pay a minimal fixed monthly fee, regardless of real income—would be abandoned. In future, self-employed workers will pay a percentage of income tax on a quarterly basis ("Ordinaria No. 94," *Gaceta Oficial De La República De Cuba, Ministerio De Justicia* 2021).

2 There is a substantial literature exploring issues of informality in the former Soviet

214 · Notes to Pages 90–97

Union and the independent nations in Eastern Europe that succeeded it, much of which deals with similar issues to those I discuss here. See Bruns and Miggelbrink 2011; Burawoy and Verdery 1999; Fehérváry 2011; Hass 2011; Henig and Makovicky 2017; Karjanen 2014; Knudsen 2015; Mandel and Humphrey 2002; Pine 2002; Sasunkevich 2014; M. Wagner 2011.

3 A common refrain heard on the streets of Havana is "*Todo aquí es por la izquierda.*" Literally "Everything here is from/by the left [hand]," this is a common idiom in Cuban Spanish which suggests money changing hands, as it would be in English, under the table or behind closed doors. As far as I know, it has no correlation to any (coincidental) association of Cuban socialism with leftism. Interestingly, though, there are parallel metaphors in other (post)socialist societies, such as *na lewo* ("on the left") in Polish discourse, and Francis Pine (2015, 33) documents a strikingly similar sentiment in a phrase from one of her participants: "*Tutaj nic nie jest wolno, ale wyzystko jest możliwe*" ("Here nothing is allowed, but everything is possible").

4 Nonetheless, this is a pun that has been made more than once: most recently in an arguably rather unempathetic account of the effects of the COVID-19 pandemic upon this informal economy, in which *The Economist* pointed out that the global lockdown had also shut down Cuba's economic lifeline ("Neither Mulas nor Moolah: The Pandemic Shuts Down a Lifeline for Cuba" 2020).

5 Santería is a syncretic religion practiced in Cuba and beyond, whose roots can be traced back to West Africa (among other places) via the slave trade. It arose through a process of syncretism between Yoruba religious practices in West Africa, Roman Catholicism, and Spiritism. The numbers of those practicing the religion, both in Cuba and overseas, has steadily increased, and it has been suggested that practitioners of Santería "greatly outnumber" those who practice Catholicism, Protestantism, or Judaism in the country (Wedel 2004, 2).

6 I should also note that these items then continue to circulate through society through preexisting networks of informal exchange on the island. Thus, while not all Cubans have procured items directly from the Mula Ring or paid a mula, the majority of material commodities originally will have entered the island this way at some point and are then redistributed locally.

7 Consider also the Cuban pun on *socio-lismo* and *socialismo*, i.e., a dependence upon *socios* (friends) to navigate socialism.

8 I generally found that my Cuban friends referred to other friends as *socios, amigos,* or, if they were more distant acquaintances, as *compañeros,* and when they referred to someone as a "brother" (*hermano/hermano-amigo*), it would be to correct me in my assumption that they were merely friends. "*Pero es como mi hermano, sabes?*" ("But he's like a brother, you know?") was a way of telling me a friend was so close, the relationship was unbreakable, and demanded a higher degree of reciprocal care than mere friendship. While in some cases, then, this was a figure of speech, I was also corrected various times for presuming that it merely demonstrated linguistic decoration.

9 Härkönen (2011a) provides an example of this in her ethnography of kinship in Havana. She describes how a daughter would not be "required" or perhaps even

Notes to Pages 102–108 · 215

expected to attend her own father's funeral if he had not financially provided for her fifteenth birthday party, which is considered a key rite of passage in Cuba and across much of Latin America. In other words, if he had not invested in her future, materially, in life, she would not be expected to do the same for him in death.

10 One female mula friend of mine had certainly had difficulties with this, as the hostels are not segregated by gender, and she shared a room with several unknown men. Thereafter she decided only to travel in groups with several other women and never stay on her own, but she was unusual in this regard, and most of the mulas who travel very regularly in "teams" or *equipos* (as opposed to on one-off trips) are young men hoping to make a name for themselves. Women are often considered to attract too much attention within teams, but some do make a successful living traveling on their own or in smaller, all-female groups.

11 At the time of fieldwork, Cuban nationals were permitted to import 120 pounds of merchandise each, per calendar year, on which they paid import tax in Cuban pesos (CUP). Thereafter their allowance lowered to 30lb per year, and taxes had to be paid in Cuban convertible pesos (CUC)—i.e., they were much more expensive. Larger items (like fridges) would need to be brought in openly and declared, or officials would need to be bribed to allow onward passage, while smaller items were typically easier to hide in luggage. In 2021 the Cuban government changed some of the custom regulations to ease the import of food and medicines during the pandemic, and also to reflect the change in currency ("Cuba Lifts Food, Medicine Customs Restrictions amid Protests" 2021).

12 It is worth explaining that in Havana (and across much of Cuba), many bars and cafes sell two versions of soft drinks: domestic and international. So, for example, one can buy a can of Coca-Cola for US$2, or one can buy a very similar tasting product called *tuKola* for US$1. So the choice to buy an imported soft drink is also a decision to display wealth and status, as such products generally cost roughly double the domestic version.

13 Property sales have been permitted in Cuba since 2011, and the new Cuban constitution (2019) has introduced further recognition of private ownership.

14 President Trump's reduction of the U.S. embassy services in Havana in 2018 caused great anxiety and would clearly have significant implications for many negociantes and mulas as their old five-year visas came closer to expiring and could not easily be renewed.

15 Both Panama and Guyana represent particularly dangerous options for Cuban mulas, and those that I observed there traveled around in large groups, tight-lipped and tense. However, for some, this has provided new opportunities, such as for Abu, who employed "security guards" to accompany shoppers on their trips.

16 This is akin to how I have heard the loans business works in Cuba's informal sector. As this is illegal, it is a world that operates on similar moral codes of "trust" and "honour," and given the obvious risks of moving in this world, my participants strongly advised me against seeking it out.

17 The José Martí Pioneer Organization (Organización de Pioneros José Martí) is a Cuban youth organization created in 1961 as a replacement for the banned Scouts

216 · Notes to Pages 117–153

Association. The initiation takes place with a traditional act of giving a neckerchief to the new member, blue or red depending on the student's level, and from that moment it forms a part of the scholastic uniform. Its motto is: "Pioneers for communism: Let us be like Che [Guevara]!"

Chapter 4. The "e-Mula Ring"

1 Betamax was an analogue cassette-recording device popular through the 1970s and 80s before the invention of VHS, which has latterly been replaced by DVDs and Blu-Ray technology.

2 For example, in the early 1980s, the U.S. government planned to create a radio station to be known as Radio Free Cuba, in the hope of hastening the fall of Fidel Castro. The station—renamed Radio Martí after Cuban independence fighter José Martí—was established in 1983 by President Ronald Reagan and continues running to the present day, along with a sister television station.

3 Willy Chirino (born 1947) is a Grammy-winning Cuban American singer who left Cuba as a child, and has had numerous hits in the Miami diaspora, including "Yo No Coopero Con La Dictadura" ("I Don't Cooperate with the Dictatorship").

4 It is worth noting that some of my participants had started pulling out of such contracts, as—given the number of paqueteros who cut materials out of the paquete, judging them not to be of interest to their local customers—it was becoming increasingly difficult to ensure the promotions would arrive on the end consumer's USB stick.

5 The use of the punctuation at the beginning is a common naming device in el paquete, as it moves folders to the top of a hard drive when ordered alphabetically.

6 Spanish from Spain pronounces "c" and "z" as in English "th," unlike most Latin American variants, and is the target of mockery from some Cubans.

Chapter 5. "Back to the Future"

1 "Ever onward to victory," Che Guevara's words of farewell to Fidel Castro, were later appropriated as a famous slogan of the 1959 Cuban revolution (Spencer 2007). The words have since been printed on t-shirts the world over, much to the ire of some of the interlocutors mentioned in this chapter.

2 Francisco was referring to how the symbolism of Martí's cause has been mobilized to different ideological ends by both Cubans on the island and those in the diaspora. For more on this, see Font and Quiroz (2006); Guerra (2005).

3 As of 2019, the University's new "Cuba House" (*CasaCuba*) presents itself as

a place to share and preserve Cuba's rich history and heritage; a global forum where top Cuban scholars and policymakers from around the world can meet and share their ideas; a vibrant education center where students and professionals will find learning resources and mentorship; a dynamic space to showcase Cuban arts and culture. CasaCuba is truly a home where we can all find our roots and envision a shared future as one people.

See https://casacuba.fiu.edu/

Notes to Pages 154–174 · 217

4 The Bacardí family's assets were nationalized when the revolution occurred, prompting the headquarters of the company to be set up in Bermuda, and the U.S. headquarters in Miami. The reference to Bacardí rum here, as opposed to Havana Club (which is still owned by the Cuban state), is symbolically potent among many Cubans residing in Miami (Gjelten 2008; Calvo Ospina 2002).

5 For a remarkably parallel case in Israel, see Kersel (2006).

Chapter 6. *Patria en Muerte*

1 Spanish: *"morir por la patria es vivir"*

2 Spanish: *"¡Patria o Muerte!"*

3 It is worth pointing out that *patria* is a difficult word to translate into English; many scholars translate it as "fatherland" (e.g., L. A. Pérez 2009), yet many of my research participants disliked that translation, insisting that while the word has clear etymological roots in *"patrius"* or *"pater"* (i.e., "of the father"), it is also a feminine word, and thus contains nurturing qualities of "motherland" as well. In one of the ethnographic vignettes discussed in this chapter, an advertisement placed by a Trinidadian man in a Cuban American newspaper where he used the English word "fatherland" to denote Cuba was met with scorn from several of my participants, and so in this chapter, I opt to use the Spanish word *patria*, or the more neutral translation "homeland." For extensive discussions of how *patria* arose as a concept across Latin America, and how it can be distinguished from *nación* or nation, see Bolívar (1999); N. Miller (2006); L. A. Pérez (2009).

4 Härkönen (2014) gives the example of internal Cuban migrants from the eastern provinces being returned to their place of birth for burial after dying in Havana. This was something I also observed during fieldwork in Havana, although for the purposes of this chapter I focus upon transnational flows, as opposed to domestic ones.

5 Very broadly speaking, Palo, Ifá and Santería are all syncretic religions practiced in Cuba (and beyond) whose roots can be traced back to West Africa (among other places) via the slave trade. Observance of these traditions has supposedly increased in Cuba since the revolution and decentralization of church power. I do not have space to do such practices justice here, and there is a lengthy literature exploring these religions. For an overview of the ways in which Santería continues to be (increasingly) transnational, see Beliso-De Jesús (2013); Delgado (2014); Espírito Santo (2018); Wirtz (2004).

6 Café Versailles is a long-standing café and restaurant in the heart of the Little Havana district that has been in business since the arrival of its founders from Cuba in 1971. It has become symbolic of the Cuban community in Havana and has consequently hosted various prominent (mostly Republican) politicians over the years as they have campaigned for votes among the Cuban diaspora in Florida.

7 Balseros, or rafters, were Cubans who fled the island on makeshift rafts with the hope of arriving on the shores of South Florida during the Special Period of economic hardship in Cuba in the 1990s.

8 To many of the exile generation who left for ideological reasons, the notion of be-

Notes to Pages 180–202

ing repatriated, at least before any substantive change in Cuban politics, would be offensive, and so recognizing to whom to offer such services demands considerable cultural acumen and sensitivity.

9 Victor, who was from Trinidad, was arguably rejecting a stigma against "other" mortuary practices from the Caribbean that is relatively common among a generation of white, middle/upper-class elites from the region. Tropes of alterity, such as "black magic," "sacrifice," and "witchcraft," dominated discussions of mortuary culture in the Caribbean for much of the nineteenth and twentieth centuries. For example, Fernando Ortiz, the Cuban lawyer and anthropologist, cited nineteenth-century armchair anthropologists' and missionaries' accounts of late-nineteenth century Africa for comparative examples of rituals and belief systems, evoking the contemporary anthropological notion of primitive society as a universal stage in cultural evolution. Ortiz's early work on Afro-Cuban religions "promoted the notion and politics of alterity by representing the sacrificing savage as temporally remote, inhabiting a primitive past rather than a civilized present" (Forde and Hume 2018, 6; see also Palmié 2002). This is relevant because there is an ongoing bias against such mortuary practices that is widely visible among Cuban funeral parlors in Miami. While Victor may have privately betrayed his thoughts to me, he was also unusual in running a business that explicitly accommodated the mortuary arrangements for these Afro-Cuban practices.

10 Pinar del Río is a province in Western Cuba known for its fertile (red) soil. It has historically been the centre of tobacco production in Cuba, and I heard people say on numerous occasions that this red soil imparted a distinctive taste to the tobacco grown there.

11 There were in fact six provinces in Cuba after the Ten Years War (1868–1878), created by the Spanish colonial government, and these remained in place until 1976, when the current government created the current 15 provinces and one "special sector." The reference to seven provinces in the memorial's sign is thus also a political statement, denying the newer reality imposed by Cuba's current government, but also adding Miami as a seventh province to the earlier formulation, thereby incorporating the diaspora in Miami into the Cuban nation.

Conclusion

1 See chapter 1 for a discussion of the connotations of *yuma*.

2 Catalan modernist architect Antoni Gaudí (1852–1926) developed a method of using broken shards of glazed ceramic and recomposing them into larger mosaic structures (*trencadís*), most notably in Barcelona's Parc Güell and the Passeig de la Glória.

Bibliography

Addo, Ping-Ann, and Niko Besnier. 2008. "When Gifts Become Commodities: Pawnshops, Valuables, and Shame in Tonga and the Tongan Diaspora." *Journal of the Royal Anthropological Institute* 14: 39–59.

Aguiar, José Carlos G. 2013. "Smugglers, Fayuqueros, Piratas: Transitory Commodities and Illegality in the Trade of Pirated CDs in Mexico." *PoLAR: Political and Legal Anthropology Review* 36, no. 2: 249–65.

Aja, Alan A. 2016. *Miami's Forgotten Cubans: Race, Racialization, and the Miami Afro-Cuban Experience.* New York: Springer Press.

Åkesson, Lisa. 2011. "Remittances and Relationships: Exchange in Cape Verdean Transnational Families." *Ethnos* 76, no. 3: 326–47.

Alonso, Andoni, and Pedro Oiarzabal, eds. 2010. *Diasporas in the New Media Age: Identity, Politics, and Community.* Reno: University of Nevada Press.

Alvarez, Johanna A. 2016. "A New Wave of Venezuelans on the Verge of Destitution Flees to Miami." *The Miami Herald,* 3 June 2016. https://www.miamiherald.com/news/local/immigration/article81578152.html. Accessed 8 June 2016.

Amuedo-Dorantes, Catalina, and Susan Pozo. 2006. "Remittances as Insurance: Evidence from Mexican Immigrants." *Journal of Population Economics* 19, no. 2: 227–54.

Anderson, Benedict. 1983. *Imagined Communities: Reflections on the Origin and Spread of Nationalism.* London: Verso.

Anderson, Patricia. 1986. "Conclusion: Women in the Caribbean." *Social and Economic Studies* 35, no. 2: 291–324.

Andrews-Swann, Jenna E. 2011. "Cafecitos Y Nostalgia: Building Transnational Landscapes in the Cuban Diaspora." *Anthropology News* 52, no. 3: 12.

Ang, Ien. 2011. "Unsettling the National: Heritage and Diaspora." In *Heritage, Memory and Identity,* edited by Helmut Anheier and Yudhishthir Raj Isar, 82–84. London: SAGE Publications.

Angé, Olivia, and David Berliner, eds. 2014. *Anthropology and Nostalgia.* New York: Berghahn Books.

Anzaldúa, Gloria. 1987. *Borderlands = La Frontera: The New Mestiza.* San Francisco: Aunt Lute Books.

Appadurai, Arjun, ed. 1986. *The Social Life of Things: Commodities in Cultural Perspective.* Cambridge: Cambridge University Press.

—. 1990. "Disjuncture and Difference in the Global Cultural Economy." *Theory, Culture & Society* 7, no. 2–3: 295–310.

—. 1991. "Global Ethnoscapes: Notes and Queries for a Transnational Anthropology." In *Recapturing Anthropology: Working in the Present*, edited by Richard Gabriel Fox, 191–210. Santa Fe: School of American Research.

—. 1996. *Modernity at Large: Cultural Dimensions of Globalization*. Minneapolis: University of Minnesota Press.

Appel, Hilary, and Mitchell A. Orenstein. 2018. *From Triumph to Crisis: Neoliberal Economic Reform in Postcommunist Countries*. Cambridge: Cambridge University Press.

Aranda, Elizabeth M., Sallie Hughes, and Elena Sabogal, eds. 2014. *Making a Life in Multiethnic Miami: Immigration and the Rise of a Global City*. Boulder, CO: Lynne Rienner Publishers.

Archibugi, Franco. 2008. "Between Neo-Capitalism and Post-Capitalism: A Challenging Turn for a Societal Reform." *International Review of Sociology—Revue Internationale de Sociologie* 18, no. 3: 505–17.

Arroyo-Martínez, Jossianna. 2018. "Cities of the Dead: Performing Life in the Caribbean." *Journal of Latin American Cultural Studies* 27, no. 3: 331–56.

Astley, Tom. 2016. "The People's Mixtape: Peer-to-Peer File Sharing without the Internet in Contemporary Cuba." In *Networked Music Cultures: Contemporary Approaches, Emerging Issues*, edited by Raphaël Nowak and Andrew Whelan, 13–30. London: Palgrave Macmillan.

Augé, Marc. 1995. *Non-Places: Introduction to an Anthropology of Supermodernity*. London: Verso.

Austin-Broos, Diane J. 1997. *Jamaica Genesis: Religion and the Politics of Moral Orders*. Chicago: University of Chicago Press.

Ayuso, Silvia. 2015. "Netflix Contra El 'Paquete' Cubano." *El País*, 15 February 2015. https://elpais.com/internacional/2015/02/15/actualidad/1423981072_014165.html. Accessed 2 April 2019.

Azenha, Gustavo S. 2006. "The Internet and the Decentralisation of the Popular Music Industry: Reflections on Technology, Concentration and Diversification." *Radical Musicology* 1: 125 pars.

Bach, Jonathan. 2002. "'The Taste Remains': Consumption, (N)Ostalgia, and the Production of East Germany." *Public Culture* 14, no. 3: 545–56.

—. 2015. "Collecting Communism: Private Museums of Everyday Life under Socialism in Former East Germany." *German Politics & Society* 33, no. 1/2: 135–45.

—. 2017. *What Remains: Everyday Encounters with the Socialist Past in Germany*. New York: Columbia University Press.

Baldassar, Loretta. 2008. "Missing Kin and Longing to Be Together: Emotions and the Construction of Co-Presence in Transnational Relationships." *Journal of Intercultural Studies* 29, no. 3: 247–66.

—. 2015. "Guilty Feelings and the Guilt Trip: Emotions and Motivation in Migration and Transnational Caregiving." *Emotion, Space and Society* 16: 81–89.

Baldassar, Loretta, Cora Vellekoop Baldock, and Raelene Wilding. 2007. *Families Caring across Borders: Migration, Ageing and Transnational Caregiving*. Basingstoke, U.K.: Palgrave Macmillan.

Barberia, Lorena. 2004. "Remittances to Cuba: An Evaluation of Cuban and U.S. Government Policy Measures." In *The Cuban Economy at the Start of the Twenty-First Century*, edited by Jorge Dominguez, Omar Everleny Pérez Villanueva, and Lorena Barberia, 353–412. Cambridge: Harvard University Press.

Barenboim, Deanna. 2018. "Reclaiming Tangible Heritage: Cultural Aesthetics, Materiality, and Ethnic Belonging in the Maya Diaspora." *Journal of Latin American and Caribbean Anthropology* 23, no. 1: 113–30.

Barnes, John. 1947. "The Collection of Genealogies." *Rhodes-Livingstone Journal* 5: 48–55.

Barragan, Yesenia. 2014. *Selling Our Death Masks: Cash-for-Gold in the Age of Austerity*. Alresford, U.K.: Zer0 Books.

Barthes, Roland. 1977. *Image, Music, Text*. Translated by Stephen Heath. New York: Fontana Press.

Bartlett, Christy. 2008. "A Tearoom View of Mended Ceramics." In *Flickwerk: The Aesthetics of Mended Japanese Ceramics*, 8–14. Münster: Museum für Lackkunst.

Basch, Linda G., Nina Glick Schiller, and Christina Szanton Blanc, eds. 1994. *Nations Unbound: Transnational Projects, Postcolonial Predicaments, and De-Territorialized Nation States*. Langhorne, PA: Gordon and Breach.

Bastian, Hope. 2018. *Everyday Adjustments in Havana: Economic Reforms, Mobility, and Emerging Inequalities*. Lanham: Lexington Books.

Bastide, Roger. 1973. "Le Principe D'individuation (Contribution À Une Philosophie Africaine)." *La notion de personne en Afrique Noir* 544: 33–43.

Baudrillard, Jean. 1981. *For a Critique of the Political Economy of the Sign*. St Louis: Telos.

Becker, Gaylene. 1997. *Disrupted Lives: How People Create Meaning in a Chaotic World*. Berkeley: University of California Press.

Beckett, Greg. 2020. "Unlivable Life: Ordinary Disaster and the Atmosphere of Crisis in Haiti." *Small Axe: A Caribbean Journal of Criticism* 24, no. 2: 78–95.

Behar, Ruth. 1991. "Death and Memory: From Santa María Del Monte to Miami Beach." *Cultural Anthropology* 6, no. 3: 346–84.

———. 1996. *The Vulnerable Observer: Anthropology That Breaks Your Heart*. Boston: Beacon.

Beliso-De Jesús, Aisha. 2013. "Religious Cosmopolitanisms: Media, Transnational Santería, and Travel between the United States and Cuba." *American Ethnologist* 40, no. 4: 704–20.

Belk, Russell. 2006. "Collectors and Collecting." In *Handbook of Material Culture*, edited by Christopher Tilley, Webb Keane, Susanne Kuechler-Fogden, Mike Rowlands, and Patricia Spyer, 534–45. London: SAGE Publications.

Benítez-Rojo, Antonio. 1996. *The Repeating Island: The Caribbean and the Postmodern Perspective*, edited by James E. Maraniss. Durham: Duke University Press.

222 · Bibliography

Berdahl, Daphne. 1999. *Where the World Ended: Re-Unification and Identity in the German Borderland*. Berkeley: University of California Press.

Berg, Mette Louise. 2011. *Diasporic Generations*. New York; Oxford: Berghahn Books.

———. 2014. "Cubans in Spain: Transnational Connections and Memories." In *Cuba in a Global Context: International Relations, Internationalism and Transnationalism*, 257–70. Gainesville: University Press of Florida.

Bernal, Victoria. 2014. *Nation as Network: Diaspora, Cyberspace & Citizenship*. Chicago & London: University of Chicago Press.

Bernstein, Peter L. 2000. *The Power of Gold: A History of an Obsession*. New York: John Wiley & Sons, Ltd.

Betancourt, Ernesto, and Sarah Blue. 2005. "Remittances to Cuba: A Survey of Methods and Estimates." *Cuba in Transition: Annual Proceedings of the ASCE* 15: 396–409.

Bhabha, Homi. 1994. *The Location of Culture*. New York: Routledge.

Birenbaum-Carmeli, Daphna. 2009. "The Politics of 'the Natural Family' in Israel: State Policy and Kinship Ideologies." *Social Science & Medicine* 69, no. 7: 1018–24.

Blok, Anton. 2001. "La Mafia D'un Village Sicilien." *Ethnologie Française* 31, no. 1: 61–67.

Blue, Sarah A. 2007. "The Erosion of Racial Equality in the Context of Cuba's Dual Economy." *Latin American Politics and Society* 49, no. 3: 35–68.

Blum, Martin. 2000. "Remaking the East German Past: Ostalgie, Identity, and Material Culture." *The Journal of Popular Culture* 34, no. 3: 229–53.

Bodernhorn, Barbara. 2000. "'He Used to Be My Relative': Exploring the Bases of Relatedness among Iñupiat of Northern Alaska.'" In *Cultures of Relatedness: New Approaches to the Study of Kinship*, edited by Janet Carsten, 128–48. Cambridge: Cambridge University Press.

Bolívar, Simón. 1999. "Inventing La Patria: Wars, Caudillismo, and Politics, 1810–1885." In *For La Patria: Politics and the Armed Forces in Latin America*, edited by Brian Loveman, 27–61. Wilmington: Scholarly Resources Incorporated.

Borneman, John. 1992. *Belonging in the Two Berlins: Kin, State, Nation*. Cambridge: Cambridge University Press.

Bosch, Tanja. 2010. "Piracy as Counter-Hegemony." *Communicare* 29, no. 2: 99–116.

Boudreault-Fournier, Alexandrine. 2017. "The Fortune of Scarcity: Digital Music in Circulation." In *The Routledge Companion to Digital Ethnography*, edited by Larissa Hjorth, Heather Horst, Anne Galloway, and Genevieve Bell, 344–53. London: Routledge.

———. 2019. "Social Imaginary, Memory Sticks, and Plastic Bags in Cuba." *American Anthropologist* 121, no. 3: 750–55.

Bourdieu, Pierre. 1972. *Esquisse D'une Théorie De La Pratique: Précédé De Trois Études D'ethnologie Kabyle*. Genève, Paris: Droz.

———. 1977. *Outline of a Theory of Practice*. Translated by Richard Nice. Cambridge: Cambridge University Press.

———. 1984. *Distinction: A Social Critique of the Judgement of Taste*. Translated by Richard Nice. Cambridge, MA: Harvard University Press.

———. 1986. "The Forms of Capital." In *Handbook of Theory and Research for the Sociology of Capital*, edited by J. G. Richardson, 241–58. New York: Greenwood Press.

Bourgois, Philippe. 1990. "Confronting Anthropological Ethics: Ethnographic Lessons from Central America." *Journal of Peace Research* 27, no. 1: 43–54.

———. 2003. *In Search of Respect: Selling Crack in El Barrio*. Cambridge: Cambridge University Press.

boyd, danah. 2011. "Social Networked Sites as Networked Publics: Affordance, Dynamics, and Implications." In *A Networked Self: Identity, Community, and Culture*, edited by Zizi Papacharissi, 39–58. New York: Routledge.

Boym, Svetlana. 2001. *The Future of Nostalgia*. New York: Basic Books.

Brah, Avtar. 2005. *Cartographies of Diaspora: Contesting Identities*. London: Routledge.

Brinkerhoff, Jennifer M. 2009. *Digital Diasporas: Identity and Transnational Engagement*. Cambridge: Cambridge University Press.

Brotherton, P Sean. 2008. "'We Have to Think Like Capitalists but Continue Being Socialists': Medicalized Subjectivities, Emergent Capital, and Socialist Entrepreneurs in Post-Soviet Cuba." *American Ethnologist* 35, no. 2: 259–74.

Brown, Bill. 2003. *A Sense of Things: The Object Matter of American Literature*. Chicago: University of Chicago Press.

Bruns, Bettina, and Judith Miggelbrink. 2011. *Subverting Borders: Doing Research on Smuggling and Small-Scale Trade*. Wiesbaden: VS Verlag für Sozialwissenschaften.

Burawoy, Michael, Joseph A. Blum, Sheba George, Zsuzsa Gille, Millie Thayer, Teresa Gowan, Lynne Haney, Maren Klawiter, Steve Lopez, and Sean O'Riain. 2000. *Global Ethnography: Forces, Connections, and Imaginations in a Postmodern World*. Berkeley: University of California Press.

Burawoy, Michael, and Verdery, Katherine, eds. 1999. *Uncertain Transition: Ethnographies of Change in the Postsocialist World*. Oxford: Lanham Press.

Burman, Jenny. 2006. "Migrant Remittances as Diasporic Communication." *The Journal of International Communication* 12, no. 2: 7–18.

Burrell, Kathy. 2008. "Managing, Learning and Sending: The Material Lives and Journeys of Polish Women in Britain." *Journal of Material Culture* 13, no. 1: 63–83.

———. 2017. "The Recalcitrance of Distance: Exploring the Infrastructures of Sending in Migrants' Lives." *Mobilities* 12, no. 6: 813–26.

Bush, Gregory W. 1999. "'Playground of the USA': Miami and the Promotion of Spectacle." *Pacific Historical Review* 68, no. 2: 153–72.

Bustamante, Michael J. 2021. "Cold War Paquetería: Snail Mail Services across and around Cuba's 'Sugar Curtain,' 1963–1969." *Journal of Latin American Cultural Studies* 30, no. 2: 215–31.

Buyandelgeriyn, Manduhai. 2007. "Dealing with Uncertainty: Shamans, Marginal Capitalism, and the Remaking of History in Postsocialist Mongolia." *American Ethnologist* 34, no. 1: 127–47.

———. 2008. "Post-Post-Transition Theories: Walking on Multiple Paths." *Annual Review of Anthropology* 37, no. 1: 235–50.

Byrne, Denis. 2016a. "Heritage Corridors: Transnational Flows and the Built Environment of Migration." *Journal Of Ethnic and Migration Studies* 42, no. 14: 2351–69.

———. 2016b. "The Need for a Transnational Approach to the Material Heritage of Migration: The China–Australia Corridor." *Journal of Social Archaeology* 16, no. 3: 261–85.

Byron, Margaret. 2005. "Expanding Narratives of Emigration and Return." In *Caribbean Narratives of Belonging: Fields of Relations, Sites of Identity,* edited by Jean Besson and Karen Fog Olwig, 206–21. Oxford: Macmillan Education.

Cabezas, Amalia L. 2004. "Between Love and Money: Sex, Tourism, and Citizenship in Cuba and the Dominican Republic." *Signs: Journal of Women in Culture and Society* 29, no. 4: 987–1015.

———. 2009. *Economies of Desire: Sex and Tourism in Cuba and the Dominican Republic.* Philadelphia: Temple University Press.

Calis, Irene. 2017. "Routine and Rupture: The Everyday Workings of Abyssal (Dis)Order in the Palestinian Food Basket." *American Ethnologist* 44, no. 1: 65–76.

Calvo Ospina, Hernando. 2002. *Bacardí: The Hidden War.* London; Sterling, VA: Pluto Press.

Campa, Roman de la. 2000. *Cuba on My Mind: Journeys to a Severed Nation.* London & New York: Verso.

Campkin, Ben. 2013. "Placing 'Matter out of Place': Purity and Danger as Evidence for Architecture and Urbanism." *Architectural Theory Review* 18, no. 1: 46–61.

Capó, Julio. 2017. *Welcome to Fairyland: Queer Miami before 1940.* Chapel Hill: University of North Carolina Press.

Carrier, James G. 1995. *Gifts and Commodities: Exchange and Western Capitalism since 1700.* London & New York: Routledge.

Carruthers, Bruce, and Sarah Babb. 1996. "The Color of Money and the Nature of Value: Greenbacks and Gold in Postbellum America." *American Journal of Sociology* 101, no. 6: 1556–91.

Carsten, Janet. 1995a. "The Politics of Forgetting: Migration, Kinship and Memory on the Periphery of the Southeast Asian State." *The Journal of the Royal Anthropological Institute* 1, no. 2: 317–35.

———. 1995b. "The Substance of Kinship and the Heat of the Hearth: Feeding, Personhood, and Relatedness among Malays in Pulau Langkawi." *American Ethnologist* 22, no. 2: 223–41.

———, ed. 2000. *Cultures of Relatedness: New Approaches to the Study of Kinship.* Cambridge: Cambridge University Press.

———. 2004. *After Kinship.* Cambridge: Cambridge University Press.

———. 2011. "Substance and Relationality: Blood in Contexts." *Annual Review of Anthropology* 40: 19–35.

———. 2013. "What Kinship Does—and How." *HAU: Journal of Ethnographic Theory* 3, no. 2: 245–51.

Caskey, John. 1991. "Pawnbroking in America: The Economics of a Forgotten Credit." *Journal of Money, Credit, and Banking* 23, no. 1: 85.

Castells, Manuel. 2018. *Rupture: The Crisis of Liberal Democracy.* Cambridge: Polity Press.

Cearns, Jennifer. 2019. "The 'Mula Ring': Material Networks of Circulation through the Cuban World." *The Journal of Latin American and Caribbean Anthropology* 24, no. 4: 864–90.

———. 2021a. "Connecting (to) Cuba: Transnational Digital Flows between Havana and the Cuban Diaspora." *Cuban Studies* 50, no. 1: 161–85.

———. 2021b. "Packaging Cuban Media: Communities of Digital Sharing in Cuba and Its Diaspora." *Cuban Studies* 50, no. 1: 99–110.

———. 2021c. "'A Una Cuba Alternativa': Digital Millennials, Social Influencing and Cuentapropismo in Havana." In *Cuba's Digital Revolution: Citizen Innovation and State Policy*, edited by Ted A. Henken and Sara Garcia Santamaria, 262–81. Gainesville: University Press of Florida.

Centeno, Miguel Angel, and Alejandro Portes. 2006. "The Informal Economy in the Shadow of the State." In *Out of the Shadows: Political Action and the Informal Economy in Latin America*, edited by Patricia Fernández-Kelly and Jon Shefner, 26–54. University Park: Pennsylvania State University Press.

Chang, Hsiao-Hung. 2004. "Fake Logos, Fake Theory, Fake Globalization." *Inter-Asia Cultural Studies* 5, no. 2: 222–36.

Chatters, Linda M., Robert Joseph Taylor, and Rukmalie Jayakody. 1994. "Fictive Kinship Relations in Black Extended Families." *Journal of Comparative Family Studies* 25, no. 3: 297–312.

Ciani Forza, Daniela M. 2006. "American-Cuban and Cuban-American: Hyphens of Identity." In *The Cuban Spirit: Transculturation, Mestizaje and Hybridism*, edited by Susanna Regazzoni, 53–80. Madrid: Iberoamericana.

Cieślewska, Anna. 2014. "From Shuttle Trader to Businesswomen: The Informal Bazaar Economy in Kyrgyzstan." In *The Informal Post-Socialist Economy: Embedded Practices and Livelihoods*, edited by Jeremy Morris and Abel Polese, 121–34. Abingdon: Routledge.

Cimpanu, Catalin. 2021. "Cuba Passes Internet Censorship and Cybersecurity Law." *The Record*, 25 August 2021. https://therecord.media/cuba-passes-internet-censorship-and-cybersecurity-law/. Accessed 19 February 2022.

City of Miami (@CityofMiami). 2018. "It's official! The unveiling of the beautiful #Little-Havana flag." *Twitter*, November 30, 2018. https://twitter.com/CityofMiami/status/1068554279986827264?s=20&t=z3V9ya1LEayvRXftMmAOdw.

Clarke, Edith. 1999. *My Mother Who Fathered Me: A Study of the Families in Three Selected Communities of Jamaica*. Kingston: University of West Indies Press.

Clifford, James. 1994. "Diasporas." *Cultural Anthropology* 9, no. 3: 302–38.

———. 1999. *Routes: Travel and Translation in the Late Twentieth Century*. Cambridge: Harvard University Press.

Cohen, Robin. 1996. "Diasporas and the Nation-State: From Victims to Challengers." *International Affairs* 72, no. 3: 507–20.

Coleman, Gabriella. 2012. *Coding Freedom: The Ethics and Aesthetics of Hacking*. Princeton: Princeton University Press.

Coleman, Gabriella, and Golub, Alex. 2008. "Hacker Practice: Moral Genres and the Cultural Articulation of Liberalism." *Anthropological Theory* 8, no. 3: 255–77.

226 · Bibliography

Colomer, Laia. 2020. "Feeling Like at Home in Airports: Experiences, Memories and Affects of Placeness among Third Culture Kids." *Applied Mobilities* 5, no. 2: 155–70.

Comaroff, Jean, and Comaroff, John L. 2001. "Millennial Capitalism: First Thoughts on a Second Coming." In *Millennial Capitalism and the Culture of Neoliberalism,* edited by Jean Comaroff and John L. Comaroff, 1–56. Durham: Duke University Press.

Commaerts, Bart. 2011. "Disruptive Sharing in a Digital Age: Rejecting Neoliberalism?" *Continuum* 25, no. 1: 47–62.

Commission for Assistance to a Free Cuba. 2004. *Report to the President.* https://www .american.edu/centers/latin-american-latino-studies/upload/bush-commission -report.pdf. Accessed 7 February 2023.

Concepción, Sunamis Fabelo. 2021. "Japón En Cuba: El Fenómeno Del Manga Y Otros Espacios De Cooperación En Materia Cultural." *Mirai. Estudios Japoneses* 5: 77–89.

Concepción, Yailenis Mulet. 2016. "Self-Employment in Cuba: Between Informality and Entrepreneurship—The Case of Shoe Manufacturing." *Third World Quarterly* 37, no. 9: 1713–29.

Congdon, Venetia. 2015. "The 'Lone Female Researcher': Isolation and Safety Upon Arrival in the Field." *Journal of the Anthropological Society of Oxford* 7, no. 1: 15–24.

Connerton, Paul. 2006. "Cultural Memory." In *Handbook of Material Culture,* edited by Christopher Tilley, Webb Keane, Susanne Kuechler-Fogden, Mike Rowlands, and Patricia Spyer, 315–24. London: SAGE Publications.

———. 2017. "Seven Types of Forgetting." *Memory Studies* 1, no. 1: 59–71.

"The Constabulary Ranks Are Harassing Cuban Shoppers." 2017. *Kaieteur News,* 14 September 2017. https://www.kaieteurnewsonline.com/2017/09/14/the-constabulary -ranks-are-harassing-cuban-shoppers/. Accessed 19 February 2022.

Copeman, Jacob, and Giovanni da Col, eds. 2018. *Fake: Anthropological Keywords.* Chicago: Hau Books.

Cordero, Mónica, Constanza Gallardoy, and Alma Sacasa. 2017. "Cómo Funcionan los Préstamos de Barrio entre los Latinos de Nueva York." *Univision,* 5 June 2017. https:// www.univision.com/noticias/citylab-vida-urbana/los-prestamistas-de-barrio-el -costoso-ultimo-recurso-de-los-latinos. Accessed 16 August 2019.

Creed, Gerald W. 1995. "An Old Song with a New Voice: Decollectivization in Bulgaria." In *East European Communities: The Struggle for Balance in Turbulent Times,* edited by D. A. Kideckel, 25–46. Boulder, CO: Westview Press.

Cromwell, Jesse. 2018. *The Smugglers' World: Illicit Trade and Atlantic Communities in Eighteenth-Century Venezuela.* Williamsburg: Omohundro Institute of Early American History and Culture.

Crowdy, Denis. 2015. "When Digital Is Physical and Ethnomusicologists Are File Sharers." *Journal of World Popular Music* 2, no. 1: 61–77.

"Cuba Lifts Food, Medicine Customs Restrictions amid Protests." 2021. *Al Jazeera,* 15 July 2021. https://www.aljazeera.com/news/2021/7/15/cuba-lifts-food-medicine -restrictions-amid-protests. Accessed 3 February 2022.

"Cuba: Freedom on the Net 2021 Country Report." 2021. Freedom House. https:// freedomhouse.org/country/cuba/freedom-net/2021. Accessed 16 February 2022.

Cubas, Mario Anthony. 2007. "Performing Cubanidad: Identity and Expressive Culture in Cuban Miami." PhD thesis, University of Wisconsin-Madison.

Current, Cheris Brewer. 2008. "Normalizing Cuban Refugees: Representations of Whiteness and Anti-Communism in the USA During the Cold War." *Ethnicities* 8, no. 1: 42–66.

Dalakoglou, Dimitris. 2012. "'The Road from Capitalism to Capitalism': Infrastructures of (Post)Socialism in Albania." *Mobilities* 7, no. 4: 1–16.

Dalakoglou, Dimitris, and Penelope Harvey. 2012. "Roads and Anthropology: Ethnographic Perspectives on Space, Time and (Im)Mobility." *Mobilities* 7, no. 4: 1–7.

Das, Veena. 1995. "National Honour and Practical Kinship: Unwanted Women and Children." In *Conceiving the New World Order: The Global Politics of Reproduction*, edited by Faye D. Ginsburg and Rayna Rapp, 213–33. Berkeley: University of California Press.

Dawdy, Shannon Lee. 2016. *Patina: A Profane Archaeology*. Chicago: University of Chicago Press.

de la Fuente, Alejandro. 1995. "Race and Inequality in Cuba, 1899–1981." *Journal of Contemporary History* 30, no. 1: 131–68.

———. 2016. "Race and Income Inequality in Contemporary Cuba." *NACLA Report on the Americas* 44, no. 4: 30–33.

"Decreto Oficial Trabajo Por Cuenta Propia." 2021. *Gaceta Oficial De La República De Cuba, Ministerio De Justicia*.

Del Real, Patricio, and Anna Cristina Pertierra. 2008. "Inventar: Recent Struggles and Inventions in Housing in Two Cuban Cities." *Buildings & Landscapes* 15, no. 1: 78–92.

Deleuze, Gilles, and Felix Guattari. 1987. *A Thousand Plateaus: Capitalism and Schizophrenia*. London: Athlone Press.

———. 1994. *What Is Philosophy?* Translated by Graham Burchell and Hugh Tomlinson. London: Verso.

Delgado, Kevin M. 2014. "Santeria Commerce and the Unofficial Networks of Interpersonal Internationalism." In *Cuba in a Global Context: International Relations, Internationalism and Transnationalism*, edited by Catherine Krull, 144–59. Gainesville: University Press of Florida.

Dent, Alexander S. 2012. "Piracy, Circulatory Legitimacy, and Neoliberal Subjectivity in Brazil." *Cultural Anthropology* 27, no. 1: 28–49.

Desilver, Drew. 2015. "What We Know About Cuba's Economy." *Pew Research Center*, 28 May 2015. https://www.pewresearch.org/fact-tank/2015/05/28/what-we-know-about-cubas-economy/. Accessed 16 April 2018.

Di Leonardo, Micaela. 1987. "The Female World of Cards and Holidays: Women, Families, and the Work of Kinship." *Signs* 12, no. 3: 440–53.

Díaz-Briquets, Sergio, and Jorge Pérez-López. 2002. "Combating Corruption in Post-Castro Cuba." *Cuba in Transition: Annual Proceedings of the ASCE* 12: 145–157.

———. 2006. *Corruption in Cuba: Castro and Beyond*. Austin: University of Texas Press.

Dijck, José van. 2007. *Mediated Memories in the Digital Age*. Stanford: Stanford University Press.

228 · Bibliography

Douglas, Mary. 1991. *Purity and Danger: An Analysis of the Concepts of Pollution and Taboo*. London: Routledge.

Douglas, Mary, and Baron Isherwood, eds. 1979. *The World of Goods: Towards an Anthropology of Consumption*. New York: Basic Books.

Driscoll, Jesse, and Caroline Schuster. 2018. "Spies Like Us." *Ethnography* 19, no. 3: 411–30.

Duany, Jorge. 1997. "From the Cuban Ajiaco to the Cuban-American Hyphen: Changing Discourses of National Identity on the Island and in the Diaspora." *Cuban Studies Association Occasional Papers* 2, no. 8. https://scholarship.miami.edu/discovery/fulldisplay/alma991031447976002976/01UOML_INST:ResearchREpository. Accessed 29 May 2019.

———. 1999. "Cuban Communities in the United States: Migration Waves, Settlement Patterns and Socioeconomic Diversity." *Pouvoirs dans la Caraïbe: Revue du Centre de recherche sur les pouvoirs locaux dans la Caraïbe* 11: 69–103.

———. 2002. *The Puerto Rican Nation on the Move: Identities on the Island and in the United States*. Chapel Hill & London: University of North Carolina Press.

———. 2007. "Networks, Remittances, and Family Restaurants: The Cuban Diaspora from a Transnational Perspective." In *Cuba: Idea of a Nation Displaced*, edited by Andrea O'Reilly Herrera, 161–75. Albany: State University of New York Press.

———. 2010. "To Send or Not to Send: Migrant Remittances in Puerto Rico, the Dominican Republic, and Mexico." *The Annals of the American Academy of Political and Social Science* 630, no. 1: 205–23.

Duncan, Carol. 1995. *Civilizing Rituals: Inside Public Art Museums*. London: Taylor & Francis.

Dye, Alan, and Sicotte, Richard. 2004. "The US Sugar Program and the Cuban Revolution." *The Journal of Economic History* 64, no. 3: 673–704.

Ebaugh, Helen Rose, and Mary Curry. 2000. "Fictive Kin as Social Capital in New Immigrant Communities." *Sociological Perspectives* 43, no. 2: 189–209.

Eckstein, Susan. 1986. "The Impact of the Cuban Revolution: A Comparative Perspective." *Comparative Studies in Society and History* 28, no. 3: 502–34.

———. 2003. "Diasporas and Dollars: Transnational Ties and the Transformation of Cuba." The Rosemarie Rogers Working Paper Series, Boston. https://core.ac.uk/download/pdf/78062818.pdf. Accessed 29 May 2019.

———. 2006. "Transnational Family Based Social Capital: Remittances and the Transformation of Cuba." *International Journal of Sociology of the Family* 32, no. 2: 141–71.

———. 2009. *The Immigrant Divide: How Cuban Americans Changed the Us and Their Homeland*. New York, London: Routledge.

———. 2010. "Remittances and Their Unintended Consequences in Cuba." *World Development* 38, no. 7: 1047–55.

———. 2014. "Cubans without Borders: From the Buildup to the Breakdown of a Socially Constructed Wall across the Florida Straits." In *Cuba in a Global Context: International Relations, Internationalism and Transnationalism*, edited by Catherine Krull, 287–301. Gainesville: University Press of Florida.

Eckstein, Susan, and Lorena Barberia. 2002. "Grounding Immigrant Generations in History: Cuban Americans and Their Transnational Ties." *International Migration Review* 36, no. 3: 799–837.

Eckstein, Susan, and Mette Louise Berg. 2015. "Cubans in the United States and Spain: The Diaspora Generational Divide." *Diaspora: A Journal of Transnational Studies* 18 (1–2): 159–83.

Edwards, Brent Hayes. 2001. "The Uses of 'Diaspora.'" *Social Text* 19, no. 1: 45–73.

Edwards, Jeanette, and Marilyn Strathern. 2000. "Including Our Own." In *Cultures of Relatedness: New Approaches to the Study of Kinship*, edited by Janet Carsten, 149–66. Cambridge: Cambridge University Press.

Eire, Carlos M. N. 2010. *Learning to Die in Miami: Confessions of a Refugee Boy*. New York: Free Press.

Eltringham, Nigel. 2004. *Accounting for Horror: Post-Genocide Debates in Rwanda*. London: Pluto Press.

"Envío De Remesas a Cuba Cayó El 54,14 % En 2020, Según Expertos." 2020. *OnCuba News*, 24 November 2020. https://oncubanews.com/cuba/envio-de-remesas-a-cuba -cayo-el-5414-en-2020-segun-expertos/. Accessed 16 February 2022.

Escobar, Luz. 2017. "El 'Paketito,' Un Rival Clandestino Para El 'Paquete'—14ymedio." *14ymedio*, 5 May 2017. https://www.14ymedio.com/cienciaytecnologia/paketito -rival-clandestino-paquete_0_2211978784.html. Accessed 16 February 2022.

Espírito Santo, Diana. 2018. "Telegraph Spirits and Muertos Chinos: Technologies of Proximity and Distance in the Material Commemoration of the Dead in Cuba." *Journal of Africana Religions* 6, no. 2: 208–31.

Evans, Anya. 2017. "The Ethnographer's Body Is Gendered." *The New Ethnographer*. https://thenewethnographer.com/the-new-ethnographer/2017/02/14/gendered -bodies-2. Accessed 8 February 2022.

Evans-Pritchard, Edward Evan. 1940. *The Nuer: A Description of the Modes of the Livelihood and Political Institutions of a Nilotic People*. Oxford: Clarendon Press.

———. 1976. *Witchcraft, Oracles, and Magic among the Azande*, edited by Eva Gillies. Oxford: Clarendon Press.

———. 1990. *Kinship and Marriage among the Nuer*. Oxford: Clarendon Press.

Farrell, Michelle Leigh. 2021. "Disrupting the Algorithm: The Streaming Platforms in the Cuban Audiovisual Landscape: El Paquete Semanal, Netflix, and Mi Mochila." *Cuban Studies* 50, no. 1: 186–204.

Faubion, James D. 1996. "Kinship Is Dead. Long Live Kinship. A Review Article." *Comparative Studies in Society and History* 38, no. 1: 67–91.

Fazekas, David, and Serena Marshall. 2016. "The Package (El Paquete) Is Illegal but It's Cuba's No. 1 Employer." *ABC News*, 21 March 2016. https://abcnews.go.com/ International/package-el-paquete-illegal-cubas-number-employer/story?id= 33279812. Accessed 3 June 2017.

Featherstone, Mike. 2001. "Postnational Flows, Identity Formation and Cultural Space." In *Identity, Culture and Globalization: The Annals of the International Institute of Sociology, Volume 8*, edited by Yitzhak Sternberg and Eliezer Ben-Rafael, 483–526. Boston: Brill.

Feeley-Harnik, Gillian. 1984. "The Political Economy of Death: Communication and Change in Malagasy Colonial History." *American Ethnologist* 11, no. 1: 1–19.

Fehérváry, Krisztina. 2011. "The Materiality of the New Family House in Hungary: Postsocialist Fad or Middle-Class Ideal?" *City & Society* 23, no. 1: 18–41.

———. 2013. *Politics in Color and Concrete: Socialist Materialities and the Middle Class in Hungary.* Bloomington: Indiana University Press.

Feinberg, Richard. 2017. "Bienvenida—Maybe: Cuba's Gradual Opening to World Markets." *Social Research* 84, no. 2: 305–30.

Fernandes, Sujatha. 2017. "Cuban Connectivity: Cuba Enters the Digital Age." *Cultural Anthropology*, 27 March 2017. https://culanth.org/fieldsights/cuban-connectivity-cuba-enters-the-digital-age. Accessed 3 April 2017.

Fernandez, Alexander. 2014. "Odú in Motion: Afro-Cuban Orisha Hermeneutics and Embodied Scholarship, Life Reflections of a Lukumí Priest." PhD thesis, Florida International University.

Fernández, Damián J, ed. 2005. *Cuba Transnational.* Gainesville: University Press of Florida.

———. 2000. *Cuba and the Politics of Passion.* Austin: University of Texas Press.

Fernández, Gastón A. 2007. "Race, Gender, and Class in the Persistence of the Mariel Stigma Twenty Years after the Exodus from Cuba." *International Migration Review* 41, no. 3: 602–22.

Fernández, Miguel A. 2001. "The Spanish Navy and the Spanish-American War." In *Theodore Roosevelt, the U.S. Navy, and the Spanish-American War,* edited by Edward J. Marolda, 19–29. New York: Palgrave Macmillan US.

Fernandez, Nadine T. 2010. *Revolutionizing Romance: Interracial Couples in Contemporary Cuba.* New Brunswick, NJ; London: Rutgers University Press.

Fisher, Berenice, and Joan C. Tronto. 1990. "Toward a Feminist Theory of Caring." In *Circles of Care,* edited by Emily K. Abel and Margaret K. Nelson. Albany: State University of New York Press.

Foner, Philip S. 1972. *The Spanish-Cuban-American War and the Birth of American Imperialism 1895–1902. Volume 1: 1895–1898.* New York: New York University Press.

Font, Mauricio A., and Alfonso W. Quiroz, eds. 2006. *The Cuban Republic and José Martí: Reception and Use of a National Symbol.* Lanham, MD: Lexington Books.

Forde, Maarit, and Yanique Hume, eds. 2018. *Passages and Afterworlds: Anthropological Perspectives on Death in the Caribbean.* Durham: Duke University Press.

Foster, Robert J. 1995. *Social Reproduction and History in Melanesia: Mortuary Ritual, Gift Exchange, and Custom in the Tanga Islands.* Cambridge: Cambridge University Press.

———. 2006. "Tracking Globalization: Commodities and Value in Motion." In *Handbook of Material Culture,* edited by Christopher Tilley, Webb Keane, Susanne Kuechler-Fogden, Mike Rowlands, and Patricia Spyer, 285–302. London: SAGE Publications.

———. 2008a. *Coca-Globalization: Following Soft Drinks from New York to New Guinea.* New York: New York University Press.

———. 2008b. "Commodities, Brands, Love and Kula." *Anthropological Theory* 8, no. 1: 9–25.

Foucault, Michel. 1979. *Discipline and Punish: The Birth of the Prison*. New York: Vintage Books.

———. 2002. *The Order of Things: An Archaeology of the Human Sciences*. London: Routledge.

Fouratt, Caitlin. 2017. "Love for the Land: Remittances and Care in a Nicaraguan Transnational Community." *Latin American Research Review* 52, no. 5: 792–806.

Fowler, Víctor. 2019. "'El Paquete': Internet in Cuba." In *The Cuba Reader: History, Culture, Politics,* edited by Aviva Chomsky, Barry Carr, Alfredo Prieto, and Pamela Maria Smorkaloff, 667–71. New York: Duke University Press.

Freeman, Dena. 2017. "Affordances of Rupture and Their Enactment: A Framework for Understanding Christian Change." *Suomen Antropologi* 42, no. 4: 3–24.

Fulger, Diana. 2012. "The Colors of the Cuban Diaspora: Portrayal of Racial Dynamics among Cuban-Americans." *Annual Proceedings,* FIAR: Forum for Inter-American Research 5, no. 2: 21–36.

Gaceta Oficial de la República de Cuba. 2021. "Ordinaria No. 94." https://www.gacetaoficial.gob.cu/es/gaceta-oficial-no-94-ordinaria-de-2021. Accessed 1 February 2023.

Gámez Torres, Nora. 2012. "Hearing the Change: Reggaeton and Emergent Values in Contemporary Cuba." *Latin American Music Review / Revista de Música Latinoamericana* 33, no. 2: 227–60.

García, María Cristina. 2007. "The Cuban Population of the United States: An Introduction María Cristina García." In *Cuba: Idea of a Nation Displaced,* edited by Andrea O'Reilly Herrera, 75–89. Albany: State University of New York Press.

García Martínez, Antonio. 2017. "Inside Cuba's D.I.Y. Internet Revolution." *Wired,* 26 July 2017. https://www.wired.com/2017/07/inside-cubas-diy-internet-revolution/. Accessed 15 October 2018.

Gardner, Katy. 1993. "Desh-Bidesh: Sylheti Images of Home and Away." *Man* 28, no. 1: 1–15.

———. 2002. *Age, Narrative and Migration: The Life Course and Life Histories of Bengali Elders in London*. London: Bloomsbury Publishing.

Gartman, David. 1991. "Culture as Class Symbolization or Mass Reification? A Critique of Bourdieu's Distinction." *American Journal of Sociology* 97, no. 2: 421–47.

Gell, Alfred. 1992. "Inter-Tribal Commodity Barter and Reproductive Gift-Exchange in Old Melanesia." In *Barter, Exchange and Value: An Anthropological Approach,* edited by Caroline Humphrey and Stephen Hugh-Jones, 142–68. Cambridge: Cambridge University Press.

Girard, Chris, Guillermo J. Grenier, and Hugh Gladwin. 2012. "Exile Politics and Republican Party Affiliation: The Case of Cuban Americans in Miami." *Social Science Quarterly* 93, no. 1: 42–57.

Gjelten, Tom. 2008. *Bacardi and the Long Fight for Cuba: The Biography of a Cause*. New York: Viking.

Gladwell, Malcolm. 2010. "Small Change: Why the Revolution Will Not Be Tweeted." *The New Yorker,* 27 September 2010. https://www.newyorker.com/magazine/2010/10/04/small-change-malcolm-gladwell. Accessed 16 September 2020.

González, Nancie. 1996. "Rethinking the Consanguineal Household and Matrifocality." In *Family in the Caribbean: Themes and Perspectives*, 149–59. Kingston: Ian Randle Publishers.

González-Corzo, Mario A, and Justo, Orlando. 2017. "Private Self-Employment under Reform Socialism in Cuba." *The Journal of Private Enterprise* 32, no. 2: 45–82.

Gordy, Katherine. 2006. "'Sales + Economy + Efficiency = Revolution'? Dollarization, Consumer Capitalism, and Popular Responses in Special Period Cuba." *Public Culture* 18, no. 2: 383.

Gregory, Chris A. 1997. *Savage Money: The Anthropology and Politics of Commodity Exchange*. Amsterdam: Harwood Academic Publishers.

Grenier, Guillermo, and Hugh Gladwin. 2016. *Cuba Poll*. FIU Cuban Research Institute. https://cri.fiu.edu/research/cuba-poll/cuba-poll-powerpoint.pdf. Accessed 3 December 2019.

———. 2018. *Cuba Poll*. FIU Cuban Research Institute. https://cri.fiu.edu/research/cuba-poll/2018-fiu-cuba-poll.pdf. Accessed 3 December 2019.

Grenier, Guillermo. 2006. "The Creation and Maintenance of the Cuban American 'Exile Ideology' in Miami." *Circunstancia* 10: 1–14.

Grenier, Guillermo, and Alex Stepick, eds. 1992. *Miami Now! Immigration, Ethnicity, and Social Change*. Gainesville: University Press of Florida.

Guerra, Lillian. 2005. *The Myth of José Martí: Conflicting Nationalisms in Early Twentieth-Century Cuba*. Chapel Hill, NC: University of North Carolina Press.

Guzzo, Paul. 2017. "Tiny Park Presents Political Challenge in Bid to Honor Cuba's José Martí." *Tampa Bay Times*, 11 June 2017. https://www.tampabay.com/news/humaninterest/tiny-park-presents-political-challenge-in-bid-to-honor-cubas-jos233-mart237/2326726/. Accessed 12 May 2022.

Hale, Charles R. 1996. "Mestizaje, Hybridity, and the Cultural Politics of Difference in Post-Revolutionary Central America." *Journal of Latin American Anthropology* 2, no. 1: 34–61.

Halebsky, Sandor, and John Kirk, eds. 1992. *Cuba in Transition: Crisis and Transformation*. Boulder, CO: Westview Press.

Hall, Stuart. 2015. "Creolité and the Process of Creolization." In *Creolizing Europe: Legacies and Transformations*, edited by Encarnación Gutiérrez Rodríguez and Shirley Anne Tate, 12–25. Liverpool: Liverpool University Press.

Hallam, Elizabeth, and Jenny Hockey, eds. 2001. *Death, Memory and Material Culture*. Oxford: Berg.

Handler, Richard. 2002. "What Is New About Culture in the Postnational World?" *National Identities* 4, no. 1: 69–75.

Hannerz, Ulf. 1997. "Flows, Boundaries and Hybrids: Keywords in Transnational Anthropology." *Mana* 3, no. 1: 7–39.

Hansen, Karen V. 2005. *Not-So-Nuclear Families: Class, Gender, and Networks of Care*. Piscataway, NJ: Rutgers University Press.

Hansen, Karen V., and Anita Ilta Garey, eds. 1998. *Families in the Us: Kinship and Domestic Politics*. Philadelphia: Temple University Press.

Hansing, Katrin. 2015. "Racial Inequality in the New Cuba." *Cuba Counterpoints*, 18

October 2015. https://cubacounterpoints.com/archives/2454.html. Accessed 22 April 2017.

———. 2018. "Race and Rising Inequality in Cuba." *Current History* 117 (796): 69–72.

Hansing, Katrin, and Bert Hoffmann. 2020. "When Racial Inequalities Return: Assessing the Restratification of Cuban Society 60 Years after Revolution." *Latin American Politics and Society* 62, no. 2: 29–52.

Hansing, Katrin, and Manuel Orozco. 2014. *The Role and Impact of Remittances on Small Business Development During Cuba's Current Economic Reforms*. International Research Network on Interdependent Inequalities in Latin America (Berlin). https://d-nb.info/1049416406/34. Accessed 22 April 2021.

Harboe Knudsen, Ida, and Martin Demant Frederiksen, eds. 2015. *Ethnographies of Grey Zones in Eastern Europe: Relations, Borders and Invisibilities*. London: Anthem Press.

Härkönen, Heidi. 2011a. "Funerals in Socialist Cuba." In *Cuba Futures: Politics and Civil Society in Contemporary Cuba*, 267–81. New York: City University of New York.

———. 2011b. "Girls' 15-Year Birthday Celebration as Cuban Women's Space Outside of the Revolutionary State." *ASA Online Journal: Association of Social Anthropologists of the UK and Commonwealth* 1, no. 4: 1–41.

———. 2014. "Kinship, Love, and Life Cycle in Contemporary Havana, Cuba: To Not Die Alone." PhD thesis, University of Helsinki.

———. 2015. "Negotiating Wealth and Desirability: Changing Expectations on Men in Post-Soviet Havana." *Etnográfica* 19, no. 2: 367–88.

———. 2018. "Money, Love, and Fragile Reciprocity in Contemporary Havana, Cuba." *Journal of Latin American and Caribbean Anthropology* 24: 370–87.

Harvey, David. 2007. "Neoliberalism as Creative Destruction." *The Annals of the American Academy of Political and Social Science* 610, no. 1: 21–44.

Hass, Jeffrey Kenneth. 2011. *Rethinking the Post Soviet Experience: Markets, Moral Economies and Cultural Contradictions of Post Socialist Russia*. Basingstoke, U.K.: Palgrave Macmillan.

Hearn, Adrian H. 2016. *Diaspora and Trust: Cuba, Mexico, and the Rise of China*. Durham: Duke University Press.

Hecht, Tobias. 2006. *After Life: An Ethnographic Novel*. Durham: Duke University Press.

Heidegger, Martin. 2010. *Ontology: The Hermeneutics of Facticity*. Translated by John van Buren. Bloomington: Indiana University Press.

Heinze, Andrew R. 1990. *Adapting to Abundance: Jewish Immigrants, Mass Consumption, and the Search for American Identity*. New York: Columbia University Press.

Helft, Miguel. 2015. "No Internet? No Problem. Inside Cuba's Tech Revolution." *Forbes*, 1 July 2015. https://www.forbes.com/sites/miguelhelft/2015/07/01/no-internet-no-problem-inside-cubas-tech-revolution/. Accessed 16 October 2018.

Helmreich, Stefan. 1992. "Kinship, Nation, and Paul Gilroy's Concept of Diaspora." *Diaspora* 2, no. 2: 243–49.

Henderson, George. 2013. *Value in Marx: The Persistence of Value in a More-Than-Capitalist World*. Minnesota: University of Minnesota Press.

Henig, David, and Nicolette Makovicky, eds. 2017. *Economies of Favour after Socialism*. Oxford: Oxford University Press.

234 · Bibliography

Henken, Ted A. 2005. "Entrepreneurship, Informality, and the Second Economy: Cuba's Underground Economy in Comparative Perspective." *Cuba in Transition: Annual Proceedings of the ASCE* 15: 360–75.

———. 2017. "Cuba's Digital Millennials: Independent Digital Media and Civil Society on the Island of the Disconnected." *Social Research* 84, no. 2: 429–56.

Henken, Ted A., and Archibald R. M. Ritter. 2014. "Self-Employment in Today's Cuba: Quantitative Expansion Amid Qualitative Limitation." *Cuba in Transition: Annual Proceedings of the ASCE* 24: 288–96.

Hernández Tapia, Lidia. 2017. "El Paquete Semanal Comes to New York." *Cuban Art News,* 31 October 2017. https://cubanartnewsarchive.org/2017/10/31/el-paquete-semanal-comes-to-new-york/. Accessed 5 April 2019.

Hernandez-Reguant, Ariana. 2004. "Copyrighting Che: Art and Authorship under Cuban Late Socialism." *Public Culture* 16, no. 1: 1–29.

———, ed. 2009. *Cuba in the Special Period: Culture and Ideology in the 1990s.* Basingstoke, U.K.: Palgrave Macmillan.

Herrera, Andrea O'Reilly, ed. 2007a. *Cuba: Idea of a Nation Displaced.* Albany: State University of New York Press.

———. 2007b. "The Politics of Mis-Remembering: History, Imagination, and the Recovery of the Lost Generation." In *Cuba: Idea of a Nation Displaced,* edited by Andrea O'Reilly Herrera, 176–93. Albany: State University of New York Press.

Hertz, Robert. 1960. "A Contribution to the Study of the Collective Representation of Death." In *Death and the Right Hand,* translated by Rodney and Claudia Needham, 29–86. Glencoe, IL: The Free Press.

Hirschfeld Davis, Julie. 2017. "Trump Reverses Pieces of Obama-Era Engagement with Cuba." *New York Times,* 16 June 2017. https://www.nytimes.com/2017/06/16/us/politics/cuba-trump-engagement-restrictions.html. Accessed 2 June 2020.

Ho, Cheuk-Yuet. 2015. *Neo-Socialist Property Rights: The Predicament of Housing Ownership in China.* Lanham: Lexington Books.

Ho, Christine G. T. 1999. "Caribbean Transnationalism as a Gendered Process." *Latin American Perspectives* 26, no. 5: 34–54.

Ho, Elaine L-E, Mark Boyle, and Brenda S. A. Yeoh. 2015. "Recasting Diaspora Strategies through Feminist Care Ethics." *Geoforum* 59: 206–14.

Hobsbawm, Eric. 2000. *Bandits.* London, Weidenfeld & Nicolson.

Hockey, Jenny, Carol Komaromy, and Kate Woodthorpe, eds. 2010. *The Matter of Death: Space, Place and Materiality.* Basingstoke, U.K.: Palgrave Macmillan.

Hockey, Jenny, Leonie Kellaher, and David Prendergast. 2011. "Sustaining Kinship: Ritualization and the Disposal of Human Ashes in the United Kingdom." In *Remember Me: Constructing Immortality—Beliefs on Immortality, Life, and Death,* edited by Margaret Mitchell, 45–60. London: Routledge.

Hodge, Derrick G. 2001. "Colonization of the Cuban Body: Growth of Male Sex Work in Havana." *NACLA Report on the Americas* 34, no. 5: 20–44.

Hoffmann, Bert. 2001. "Transformation and Continuity in Cuba." *Review of Radical Political Economics* 33, no. 1: 1–20.

Holbraad, Martin. 2007. "The Power of Powder: Multiplicity and Motion in the Divinatory Cosmology of Cuban Ifá (or Mana, Again)." In *Thinking through Things: Theorising Artefacts Ethnographically,* edited by Amiria J. M. Henare, Martin Holbraad, and Sari Wastell, 189–225. London: Routledge.

———. 2010. "The Whole Beyond Holism: Gambling, Divination and Ethnography." In *Experiments in Holism: Theory and Practice in Contemporary Anthropology,* edited by Nils Bubandt and Ton Otto, 67–86. Malden, MA: Wiley-Blackwell.

———. 2014a. "Revolución O Muerte: Self-Sacrifice and the Ontology of Cuban Revolution." *Ethnos* 79, no. 3: 365–87.

———. 2014b. "The Values of Money: Economies of Need in Contemporary Cuba." *Suomen Antropologi: Journal of the Finnish Anthropological Society* 39, no. 2: 5–19.

———. 2017. "Money and the Morality of Commensuration: Currencies of Poverty in Post-Soviet Cuba." *Social Analysis* 61, no. 4: 81–97.

Holbraad, Martin, Bruce Kapferer, and Julia F. Sauma. 2019. "Introduction: Critical Ruptures." In *Ruptures: Anthropologies of Discontinuity in Times of Turmoil,* edited by Martin Holbraad, Bruce Kapferer, and Julia F. Sauma, 1–27. London: University College London Press.

Holly, Jessica. 2018. "Miami City Commissioner Met with Controversy over Little Havana Event." *WSVN News Miami,* November 30, 2018. https://wsvn.com/news/local/miami-city-commissioner-met-with-controversy-over-little-havana-event/. Accessed 12 August 2022.

Horst, Heather A. 2010. "Keeping the Link: ICTs and Jamaican Migration." In *Diasporas in the New Media Age: Identity, Politics, and Community,* edited by Andoni Alonso and Pedro J. Oiarzabal, 136–50. Reno: University of Nevada Press.

———. 2011a. "Appropriation and Resistance of New Media Technologies in Brazil." *International Journal of Communication* 5: 437–62.

———. 2011b. "Reclaiming Place: The Architecture of Home, Family and Migration." *Anthropologica* 53, no. 1: 29–39.

Hoshino, Kanehiro. 1973. "Fictive Kinship in Semi-National Criminal Gangs." *Reports of the National Research Institute of Police Science* 14, no. 1: 13–27.

Humphrey, Caroline. 2002. *The Unmaking of Soviet Life: Everyday Economies after Socialism.* New York: Cornell University Press.

———. 2018. "Reassembling Individual Subjects: Events and Decisions in Troubled Times." In *Recovering the Human Subject: Freedom, Creativity and Decision,* edited by James Laidlaw, Barbara Bodenhorn, and Martin Holbraad, 24–50. Cambridge: Cambridge University Press.

Humphreys, Laura-Zoë. 2021. "Loving Idols: K-Pop and the Limits of Neoliberal Solidarity in Cuba." *International Journal of Cultural Studies* 24, no. 6: 1009–26.

Huntington, Richard, and Peter Metcalf, eds. 1979. *Celebrations of Death: The Anthropology of Mortuary Rituals.* Cambridge: Cambridge University Press.

Hutchinson, Sharon Elaine. 1996. *Nuer Dilemmas: Coping with Money, War, and the State.* Berkeley: University of California Press.

———. 2000. "Identity and Substance: The Broadening Bases of Relatedness among the Nuer of Southern Sudan." In *Cultures of Relatedness: New Approaches to the Study of Kinship,* edited by Janet Carsten, 55–72. Cambridge: Cambridge University Press.

Ingham, Geoffrey. 2001. "Fundamentals of a Theory of Money: Untangling Fine, Lapavitsas and Zelizer." *Economy and Society* 30, no. 3: 304–23.

Ingold, Tim. 1996. *Key Debates in Anthropology*. London: Routledge.

———. 2008. "Bindings against Boundaries: Entanglements of Life in an Open World." *Environment and Planning* 40: 1796–1810.

Iordanova, Dina. 2003. *Cinema of the Other Europe: The Industry and Artistry of East Central European Film*. London: Wallflower.

Iten, Charly. 2008. "Ceramics Mended with Lacquer—Fundamental Aesthetic Principles, Techniques and Artistic Concepts." In *Flickwerk: The Aesthetics of Mended Japanese Ceramics*, 18–24. Münster: Museum für Lackkunst.

Jameson, Fredric. 1991. *Postmodernism, or, the Cultural Logic of Late Capitalism*. Durham: Duke University Press.

Jamieson, Mark. 1999. "The Place of Counterfeits in Regimes of Value: An Anthropological Approach." *Journal of the Royal Anthropological Institute*: 1–11.

Jansen, Stefaan. 2015. *Yearnings in the Meantime: "Normal Lives" and the State in a Sarajevo Apartment Complex*. New York: Berghahn Books.

John, Mauricia. 2019. "Venezuelan Economic Crisis: Crossing Latin American and Caribbean Borders." *Migration and Development* 8, no. 3: 437–47.

Johnson, Mark. 1997. "At Home and Abroad: Inalienable Wealth, Personal Consumption and the Formulations of Femininity in the Southern Philippines." In *Material Cultures: Why Some Things Matter*, edited by Daniel Miller, 215–38. London: University College London Press.

Johnstone, Lindsey. 2019. "Mobile Internet Rings the Changes in Cuba." *Reuters/euronews*, 22 February 2019. https://www.euronews.com/2019/02/22/watch-mobile-internet-rings-the-changes-in-cuba. Accessed 4 April 2019.

Jones, Gareth A., and Dennis Rodgers. 2019. "Ethnographies and/of Violence." *Ethnography* 20, no. 3: 297–319.

Judt, Tony. 1992. "The Past Is Another Country: Myth and Memory in Postwar Europe." *Daedalus* 121, no. 4: 83–118.

Kahn, Jeffrey S. 2019a. *Islands of Sovereignty: Haitian Migration and the Borders of Empire*. Chicago: University of Chicago Press.

———. 2019b. "Smugglers, Migrants, and Demons: Cosmographies of Mobility in the Northern Caribbean." *American Ethnologist* 46, no. 4: 470–81.

Kammen, Michael. 2012. *American Culture, American Tastes: Social Change and the 20th Century*. New York: Knopf Press.

Kaneff, Deema. 2002. "The Shame and Pride of Market Activity: Morality, Identity and Trading in Postsocialist Rural Bulgaria." In *Markets and Moralities: Ethnographies of Postsocialism*, edited by Caroline Humphrey and Ruth Mandel, 33–51. New York; Oxford: Berg.

Karjanen, David. 2014. "When Is an Illicit Taxi Driver More Than a Taxi Driver? Case Studies from Transit and Trucking in Post-Socialist Slovakia." In *The Informal Post-Socialist Economy: Embedded Practices and Livelihoods*, edited by Jeremy Morris and Abel Polese, 102–18. Abingdon, U.K.: Routledge.

Kasbarian, Sossie. 2009. "The Myth and Reality of 'Return'—Diaspora in the 'Homeland.'" *Diaspora: A Journal of Transnational Studies* 18, no. 3: 358–81.

Keane, Webb. 2001. "Money Is No Object: Materiality, Desire, and Modernity in an Indonesian Society." In *The Empire of Things: Regimes of Value and Material Culture*, edited by Fred R Myers, 65–90. Santa Fe, NM: Oxford: School of American Research Press.

Kearney, Michael. 1995. "The Local and the Global: The Anthropology of Globalization and Transnationalism." *Annual Review of Anthropology* 24, no. 1: 547–65.

Kellaher, Leonie, David Prendergast, and Jenny Hockey. 2005. "In the Shadow of the Traditional Grave." *Mortality* 10, no. 4: 237–50.

Kellaher, Leonie, and Ken Worpole. 2016. "Bringing the Dead Back Home: Urban Public Spaces as Sites for New Patterns of Mourning and Memorialisation." In *Deathscapes: Spaces for Death, Dying, Mourning and Remembrance*, edited by James D. Sidaway, 179–98. Farnham: Ashgate.

Kelty, Christopher. 2008. *Two Bits: The Cultural Significance of Free Software*. Durham: Duke University Press.

Kersel, Morag M. 2006. "From the Ground to the Buyer: A Market Analysis of the Trade in Illegal Antiquities." In *Archaeology, Cultural Heritage, and the Antiquities Trade*, edited by Neil Brodie, Morag Kersel, Christina Luke, and Kathryn Walker Tubb, 188–205. Gainesville: University Press of Florida.

Keulemans, Guy. 2016. "The Geo-Cultural Conditions of Kintsugi." *The Journal of Modern Craft* 9, no. 1: 15–34.

Khan, Aisha. 2001. "Journey to the Center of the Earth: The Caribbean as Master Symbol." *Cultural Anthropology* 16, no. 3: 271–302.

King, Russell, and Julie Vullnetari. 2009. "The Intersections of Gender and Generation in Albanian Migration, Remittances and Transnational Care." *Geografiska Annaler: Series B, Human Geography* 91, no. 1: 19–38.

Knauer, Lisa Maya. 2009. "Audiovisual Remittances and Transnational Subjectivities." In *Cuba in the Special Period: Culture and Ideology in the 1990s*, edited by Ariana Hernandez-Reguant, 159–78. New York: Palgrave Macmillan.

Knepper, Wendy. 2006. "Colonization, Creolization, and Globalization: The Art and Ruses of Bricolage." *Small Axe: A Caribbean Journal of Criticism* 10, no. 3: 70–86.

Knopper, Steve. 2009. *Appetite for Self-Destruction: The Spectacular Crash of the Record Industry in the Digital Age*. London: Simon Schuster.

Knudsen, Ida Harboe. 2015. "Fighting the Shadows: Lithuania's Informal Workers and the Financial Crisis." In *Informal Economies in Post-Socialist Spaces: Practices, Institutions and Networks*, edited by Jeremy Morris and Abel Polese, 70–94. Basingstoke, U.K.: Palgrave Macmillan.

Köhn, Steffen. 2019. "Unpacking El Paquete: The Poetics and Politics of Cuba's Offline Data-Sharing Network." *Digital Culture & Society* 5, no. 1: 105–24.

Kopytoff, Igor. 1986. "The Cultural Biography of Things: Commoditization as Process." In *The Social Life of Things: Commodities in Cultural Perspective*, edited by Arjun Appadurai, 64–91. Cambridge: Cambridge University Press.

Koselleck, Reinhart. 2006. "Crisis." *Journal of the History of Ideas* 67: 357–400.

Krull, Catherine, ed. 2014. *Cuba in a Global Context: International Relations, Internationalism, and Transnationalism.* Gainesville: University Press of Florida.

Kummels, Ingrid. 2014. "Love in the Time of Diaspora. Global Markets and Local Meanings in Prostitution, Marriage and Womanhood in Cuba." *Iberoamericana* 5, no. 20: 7–26.

Laguna, Albert Sergio. 2017. *Diversion: Play and Popular Culture in Cuban America.* New York: New York University Press.

Lambek, Michael. 2011. "Kinship as Gift and Theft: Acts of Succession in Mayotte and Israel." *American Ethnologist* 38, no. 1: 2–16.

Lankauskas, Gediminas. 2014. "Missing Socialism Again? The Malaise of Nostalgia in Post-Soviet Lithuania." In *Anthropology and Nostalgia,* edited by Olivia Angé and David Berliner, 35–60. New York: Berghahn Books.

Larkin, Brian. 2004. "Degraded Images, Distorted Sounds: Nigerian Video and the Infrastructure of Piracy." *Public Culture* 16, no. 2 (43): 289–314.

Leach, Edmund. 1970. *Political Systems of Highland Burma a Study of Kachin Social Structure,* edited by American Council of Learned Societies. London: Athlone Press.

Ledeneva, Alena V. 2017. "Russia's Economy of Favours: Blat, Networking, and Informal Exchange." In *Economies of Favour after Socialism,* edited by David Henig and Nicolette Makovicky, 21–49. Cambridge: Cambridge University Press.

Lee, Benjamin, and Edward LiPuma. 2002. "Cultures of Circulation: The Imaginations of Modernity." *Public Culture* 14, no. 1: 191–213.

Lee, Catherine. 2013. *Fictive Kinship: Family Reunification and the Meaning of Race and Nation in American Immigration.* New York: Russell Sage Foundation.

Lemon, Alaina. 1998. "'Your Eyes Are Green Like Dollars': Counterfeit Cash, National Substance, and Currency Apartheid in 1990s Russia." *Cultural Anthropology* 12, no. 1: 22–55.

LeoGrande, William M. 2017. "Updating Cuban Socialism: The Politics of Economic Renovation." *Social Research* 84, no. 2: 353–82.

Lessig, Lawrence. 2004. *Free Culture: How Big Media Uses Technology and the Law to Lock Down Culture and Control Creativity.* New York: Penguin.

Lévi-Strauss, Claude. 1966. *The Savage Mind.* London: Weidenfeld and Nicholson.

Levine, Mike. 2020. "Sounding El Paquete: The Local and Transnational Routes of an Afro-Cuban Repartero." *Cuban Studies* 50: 139–60.

Levitt, Peggy. 1998. "Social Remittances: Migration Driven Local-Level Forms of Cultural Diffusion." *The International Migration Review* 32, no. 4: 926–48.

———. 2001. *The Transnational Villagers.* Berkeley: University of California Press.

Levitt, Peggy, and Deepak Lamba-Nieves. 2011. "Social Remittances Revisited." *Journal of Ethnic and Migration Studies* 37: 1–22.

Lindley, Anna. 2009. "The Early-Morning Phonecall: Remittances from a Refugee Diaspora Perspective." *Journal of Ethnic and Migration Studies* 35, no. 8: 1315–34.

Lindquist, Galina. 2006. *Conjuring Hope: Magic and Healing in Contemporary Russia.* New York: New York.

Lins Ribeiro, Gustavo. 2019. "Cuba: Anthropological Imaginaries, Flows, and Comparisons." *American Anthropologist* 121, no. 3: 764–66.

Liosi, Marianna. 2017. "The Digital Revolution in Havana: Between Liberation and Submission." *openDemocracy,* 27 July 2017. https://www.opendemocracy.net/en/digitaliberties/digital-revolution-in-havana-between-liberation-and-submission/. Accessed 11 October 2018.

Lohmeier, Christine, and Christian Pentzold. 2014. "Making Mediated Memory Work: Cuban-Americans, Miami Media and the Doings of Diaspora Memories." *Media, Culture & Society* 36, no. 6: 1–14.

Lorenzi, Jane, and Jeanne Batalova. 2022. "Caribbean Immigrants in the United States." *Migration Policy Institute.* https://www.migrationpolicy.org/article/caribbean-immigrants-united-states. Accessed 7 July 2022.

"Los 'Cuentapropistas' Representan El 13% De Los Trabajadores Cubanos." 2019. *14ymedio,* 11 February 2019. https://www.14ymedio.com/economia/cuentapropistas-representan-poblacion-cubana_0_2600139962.html. Accessed 3 April 2019.

Lowenthal, David. 1985. *The Past Is a Foreign Country.* Cambridge: Cambridge University Press.

Lundgren, Silje. 2011. "Heterosexual Havana: Ideals and Hierarchies of Gender and Sexuality in Contemporary Cuba." PhD thesis, Uppsala University.

MacCannell, Dean. 2013. *The Tourist: A New Theory of the Leisure Class.* Berkeley: University of California.

Madianou, Mirca. 2017. "'Doing Family' at a Distance: Transnational Family Practices in Polymedia Environments." In *The Routledge Companion to Digital Ethnography,* edited by Larissa Hjorth, Heather Horst, Anne Galloway, and Genevieve Bell, 128–37. London: Routledge.

Madianou, Mirca, and Daniel Miller, eds. 2012. *Migration and New Media: Transnational Families and Polymedia.* London: Routledge.

Maigret, Nicolas, and Maria Roszowska, eds. 2015. *The Pirate Book.* Ljubljana: Aksioma—Institute for Contemporary Art.

Maleuvre, Didier. 1999. *Museum Memories: History, Technology, Art.* Stanford CA: Stanford University Press.

Malinowski, Bronisław. 1922. *Argonauts of the Western Pacific.* Prospect Heights: Waveland Press.

Malkki, Liisa H. 2012. *Purity and Exile: Violence, Memory, and National Cosmology among Hutu Refugees in Tanzania.* Chicago: University of Chicago Press.

———. 2007. "Tradition and Improvisation in Ethnographic Field Research." In *Improvising Theory: Process and Temporality in Ethnographic Fieldwork,* edited by Allaine Cerwonka and Liisa H. Malkki, 162–88. Chicago: University of Chicago Press.

Mandel, Ruth, and Caroline Humphrey, eds. 2002. *Markets and Moralities: Ethnographies of Postsocialism.* Oxford: Berg.

Manuel, Peter. 2014. "The Regional North Indian Popular Music Industry in 2014: From Cassette Culture to Cyberculture." *Popular Music* 33, no. 3: 389–412.

Marcus, George E. 1995. "Ethnography in/of the World System: The Emergence of Multi-Sited Ethnography." *Annual Review of Anthropology* 24: 95–117.

Markham, Annette. 2012. "Fabrication as Ethical Practice: Qualitative Inquiry in Ambiguous Internet Contexts." *Information, Communication, and Society* 15, no. 3: 334–53.

Marsh, Sarah, and Elizabeth Culliford. 2021. "Faced with Rare Protests, Cuba Curbs Social Media Access, Watchdog Says." https://www.reuters.com/world/americas/cuba-curbs-access-facebook-messaging-apps-amid-protests-internet-watchdog-2021-07-13/. Accessed 16 February 2022.

Marshall, Kimberly Jenkins. 2016. *Upward, Not Sunwise: Resonant Rupture in Navajo Neo-Pentecostalism*. Lincoln: University of Nebraska Press.

Marsters, Evelyn, Nick Lewis, and Wardlow Friesen. 2006. "Pacific Flows: The Fluidity of Remittances in the Cook Islands." *Asia Pacific Viewpoint* 47, no. 1: 31–44.

Martínez, Samuel. 2007. *Decency and Excess: Global Aspirations and Material Deprivation on a Caribbean Sugar Plantation*. Boulder, CO: Paradigm Press.

———. 2009. "Toward an Anthropology of Excess: Wanting More (While Getting Less) on a Caribbean Global Periphery." In *Empirical Futures Anthropologists and Historians Engage the Work of Sidney W. Mintz*, edited by George Baca, Aisha Khan, and Stephan Palmié, 205–35. Chapel Hill: University of North Carolina Press.

Marx, Karl. 2020. *Capital*. edited by David McLellan. Oxford: Oxford University Press.

Mattelart, Tristan. 2009. "Audio-Visual Piracy: Towards a Study of the Underground Networks of Cultural Globalization." *Global Media and Communication* 5, no. 3: 308–26.

Maurer, Bill. 2006. "The Anthropology of Money." *Annual Review of Anthropology* 35: 15–36.

Mauss, Marcel. 1954. *The Gift: Forms and Functions of Exchange in Archaic Societies*. London: Cohen & West.

McClure, Rosemary. 2008. "Miami Is the Epicenter for Conspicuous Consumption." https://www.sfgate.com/travel/article/Miami-is-the-epicenter-for-conspicuous-consumption-3210984.php. Accessed 14 August 2019.

McKay, Deirdre. 2007. "'Sending Dollars Shows Feeling'—Emotions and Economies in Filipino Migration." *Mobilities* 2, no. 2: 175–94.

Mejía Estévez, Silvia. 2009. "Is Nostalgia Becoming Digital? Ecuadorian Diaspora in the Age of Global Capitalism." *Social Identities* 15, no. 3: 393–410.

Méndez Rodenas, Adriana. 2007. "Cuban Culture at the Crossroads." In *Cuba: Idea of a Nation Displaced*, edited by Andrea O'Reilly Herrera, 143–60. Albany: State University of New York Press.

Merleau-Ponty, Maurice. 1964. *Signs*. Evanston: Northwestern University Press.

Mesa-Lago, Carmel. 1981. *The Economy of Socialist Cuba: A Two-Decade Appraisal*. Albuquerque: University of New Mexico Press.

Metcalf, Peter. 1981. "Meaning and Materialism: The Ritual Economy of Death." *Man* 16, no. 4: 563–78.

Miles, Douglas. 1965. "Socio-Economic Aspects of Secondary Burial." *Oceania* 35, no. 3: 161–74.

Miller, Daniel. 1987. *Material Culture and Mass Consumption*. Oxford: Basil Blackwell.

———. 1997a. "Coca-Cola: A Black Sweet Drink from Trinidad." In *Material Cultures: Why Some Things Matter,* edited by Daniel Miller, 169–89. London: University College London Press.

———, ed. 1997b. *Material Cultures: Why Some Things Matter.* London: University College London Press.

———. 2001. *The Dialectics of Shopping.* Chicago: Chicago University Press.

———. 2008. "The Uses of Value." *Geoforum* 39, no. 3: 1122–32.

Miller, Daniel, and Heather A. Horst, eds. 2012. *Digital Anthropology.* New York: Berg.

Miller, Jade. 2012. "Global Nollywood: The Nigerian Movie Industry and Alternative Global Networks in Production and Distribution." *Global Media and Communication* 8, no. 2: 117–33.

Miller, Nicola. 2006. "The Historiography of Nationalism and National Identity in Latin America." *Nations and Nationalism* 12, no. 2: 201–21.

Mintz, Sidney Wilfred. 1956. "The Role of the Middleman in the Internal Distribution System of a Caribbean Peasant Economy." *Human Organization* 15, no. 2: 18–23.

———. 1986. *Sweetness and Power: The Place of Sugar in Modern History.* New York: Penguin Books.

Mintz, Sidney Wilfred, and Richard Price, eds. 1976. *An Anthropological Approach to the Afro-American Past: A Caribbean Perspective.* Philadelphia: Institute for the Study of Human Issues.

Mitford, Jessica. 1963. *The American Way of Death.* Greenwich: Fawcett Publications.

Mitra, Subrata K., ed. 2013. *Citizenship as Cultural Flow Structure, Agency and Power.* Berlin: Springer.

Moghaddam, Fathali M., Donald M. Taylor, Wallace E. Lambert, and Amy E. Schmidt. 1995. "Attributions and Discrimination: A Study of Attributions to the Self, the Group, and External Factors among Whites, Blacks, and Cubans in Miami." *Journal of Cross-Cultural Psychology* 26, no. 2: 209–20.

Momsen, Janet Henshall, ed. 1993. *Women and Change in the Caribbean: A Pan-Caribbean Perspective.* London: James Currey.

Mónica, Lizabel. 2017. "El Paquete's Art Gallery." *Cuba Counterpoints.* https://cubacounterpoints.com/archives/5121.html. Accessed 12 March 2020.

Moors, Annelies. 1998. "Wearing Gold." In *Border Fetishisms: Material Objects in Unstable Spaces,* edited by Patricia Spyer, 208–23. New York: Routledge.

Morales, Emilio. 2013. "Cuba: $2.6 Billion in Remittances in 2012." *Havana Times,* 11 June 2013. https://havanatimes.org/features/cuba-2-6-billion-in-remittances-in-2012/. Accessed 27 November 2018.

———. 2017. "Analysis: Cuba Remittances and the Shifting Pattern of Cuban Emigration." *Cuba Trade,* 27 April 2017.

———. 2018. "Remittances to Cuba Diversify and Heat up the Payment Channels." *The Havana Consulting Group.* http://www.thehavanaconsultinggroup.com/enUS/Articles/Article/63. Accessed 12 July 2019.

Morales, Emilio, and Joseph L. Scarpaci. 2012. *Marketing without Advertising: Brand Preference and Consumer Choice in Cuba.* New York: Routledge.

242 · Bibliography

Moreno, Sarah. 2017. "Quiénes Son En Realidad Los 'Balseros' Cubanos Recién Llegados a Miami." *El Nuevo Herald,* 13 December 2017. https://www.elnuevoherald.com/noticias/sur-de-la-florida/article189491034.html. Accessed 14 August 2019.

———. 2018. "Thousands of Cuban Exiles Are Exploring an Unusual Option: Returning to Cuba to Live." *WLRN,* 12 March 2018. https://www.wlrn.org/news/2018-03-12/thousands-of-cuban-exiles-are-exploring-an-unusual-option-returning-to-cuba-to-live. Accessed 22 September 2018.

Morin Aguado, Vincente. 2015. "The Strange Case of Cuba's Gilbert Man." *Havana Times,* 14 February 2015. https://havanatimes.org/features/the-strange-case-of-cubas-gilbert-man/. Accessed 3 April 2019.

Morozov, Evgeny. 2011. *The Net Delusion: How Not to Liberate the World.* London: Allen Lane.

Morris, Jeremy, and Abel Polese, eds. 2014. *The Informal Post-Socialist Economy: Embedded Practices and Livelihoods.* London: Routledge.

Mulich, Jeppe. 2020. *In a Sea of Empires: Networks and Crossings in the Revolutionary Cuba.* Cambridge: Cambridge University Press.

Munn, Nancy D. 1977. "The Spatiotemporal Transformations of Gawa Canoes." *Journal de la Société des océanistes* 54–55, no. 33: 39–53.

———. 1987. *The Fame of Gawa: A Symbolic Study of Value Transformation in a Massim (Papua New Guinea) Society.* Cambridge: Cambridge University Press.

Murawski, Michał. 2018. "Actually-Existing Success: Economics, Aesthetics, and the Specificity of (Still-)Socialist Urbanism." 60, no. 4: 907–37.

Narotzky, Susana, and Niko Besnier. 2014. "Crisis, Value and Hope: Rethinking the Economy. An Introduction to Supplement 9." *Current Anthropology* S9: S4–S16.

Navaro-Yashin, Yael. 2007. "Make-Believe Papers, Legal Forms and the Counterfeit: Affective Interactions between Documents and People in Britain and Cyprus." *Anthropological Theory* 7, no. 1: 79–98.

"Neither Mulas nor Moolah: The Pandemic Shuts Down a Lifeline for Cuba." 2020. *The Economist,* 2 July 2020. https://www.economist.com/the-americas/2020/07/02/the-pandemic-shuts-down-a-lifeline-for-cuba. Accessed 12 June 2021.

Nelson, Anne. 2016. *Cuba's Parallel Worlds: Digital Media Crosses the Divide.* Washington: Center for International Media Assistance.

Nijman, Jan. 2011. *Miami: Mistress of the Americas.* Philadelphia: University of Pennsylvania Press.

Nora, Pierre. 1989. "Between Memory and History: Les Lieux De Mémoire." *Representations* 26: 7–24.

Notar, Beth E. 2006. "Authenticity Anxiety and Counterfeit Confidence: Outsourcing Souvenirs, Changing Money, and Narrating Value in Reform-Era China." *Modern China* 32, no. 1: 64–98.

Nygren, Katarina Giritli, and Katarina L. Gidlund. 2016. "The Pastoral Power of Technology. Rethinking Alienation in Digital Culture." In *Marx in the Age of Digital Capitalism,* edited by Christian Fuchs and Vincent Mosco, 396–412. Boston: Brill.

"Obama Visitó a Panfilo." 2016. *Vivir del Cuento.* Video. YouTube. https://www.youtube.com/watch?v=CTZGaskdU3I. Accessed 20 February 2021.

Ochoa, Ana Maria. 2003. *Musicas Locales En Tiempos De Globalización*. Bogotá: Norma SA Editorial.

Ochoa, Todd Ramón. 2010. *Society of the Dead: Quita Manaquita and Palo Praise in Cuba*. Berkeley: University of California Press.

Oeltjen, Jarret C. 1996. "Florida Pawnbroking: An Industry in Transition." *Florida State University Law Review* 23, no. 4: 995–1042.

Oglesby, Elizabeth. 1995. "Myrna Mack." In *Fieldwork under Fire: Contemporary Studies of Violence and Survival*, edited by Carolyn Nordstrom and Antonius C.G.M. Robben, 253–59. Berkeley: University of California Press.

Olwig, Karen Fog. 1993. *Global Culture, Island Identity: Continuity and Change in the Afro-Caribbean Community of Nevis*. Chur: Harwood Academic Publishers.

———. 2007. *Caribbean Journeys: An Ethnography of Migration and Home in Three Family Networks*. Durham: Duke University Press.

———. 2012. "The 'Successful' Return: Caribbean Narratives of Migration, Family, and Gender." *Journal of the Royal Anthropological Institute* 18, no. 4: 828–45.

Ong, Aihwa. 1999. *Flexible Citizenship: The Cultural Logics of Transnationality*. Durham: Duke University Press.

Orozco, Manuel. 2009. "On Remittances, Markets, and the Law: The Cuban Experience in Present Times." https://cri.fiu.edu/cuban-america/remittance/remittance-manual-orozco.pdf. Accessed 28 February 2018.

Ortega, Luis. 1998. *Cubanos En Miami*. La Habana: Editorial de Ciencias Sociales.

Ortiz, Fernando. 1940. "Los Factores Humanos De La Cubanidad." *Revista Bimestre Cubana* 21: 161–86.

———. 1947. *Cuban Counterpoint: Tobacco and Sugar*. Translated by Harriet de Onís. New York: Alfred A. Knopf.

Ortner, Sherry B. 2003. *New Jersey Dreaming: Capital, Culture, and the Class of '58*. Durham: Duke University Press.

Otero, Gerardo, and Janice O'Bryan. 2002. "Cuba in Transition? The Civil Sphere's Challenge to the Castro Regime." *Latin American Politics and Society* 44, no. 4: 29–57.

Padrón Cueto, Claudia. 2020. "Con Tecnología China Y Muchos Recursos, El Gobierno Cubano Intensifica La Censura En Internet." *14ymedio*, 7 December 2020. https://www.14ymedio.com/cienciaytecnologia/tecnologia-recursos-Gobierno-intensifica-internet_0_2999100065.html. Accessed 16 February 2022.

Padrón Hernández, Maria. 2012. "Beans and Roses: Everyday Economies and Morality in Contemporary Havana, Cuba." PhD thesis, University of Gothenburg.

Paerregaard, Karsten. 2014. *Return to Sender: The Moral Economy of Peru's Migrant Remittances*. Washington: Woodrow Wilson Center Press.

Palmié, Stephan. 2002. *Wizards and Scientists: Explorations in Afro-Cuban Modernity and Tradition*. Durham, NC: Duke University Press.

———. 2006. "Creolization and Its Discontents." *Annual Review of Anthropology* 35: 433–56.

———. 2013. *The Cooking of History: How Not to Study Afro-Cuban Religion*. Chicago: University of Chicago Press.

244 · Bibliography

Parish, Nick. 2018. "Inside El Paquete, Cuba's Social Network." https://withintent
.uncorkedstudios.com/inside-el-paquete-cubas-social-network-2fa6c99660ee. Accessed 4 March 2020.

Parry, Jonathan. 1994. *Death in Banaras*. Cambridge: Cambridge University Press.

Parry, Jonathan, and Maurice Bloch. 1989. *Money and the Morality of Exchange*. Cambridge: Cambridge University Press.

Pascual, Margalida Mulet. 2020. "'Être D'ici Et De Là-Bas'. La Circulation Transnationale Et Transgénérationnelle De La Famille Vázquez." *Problemes d'Amerique latine* 117, no. 2: 67–90.

Pedraza-Bailey, Silvia. 1985. "Cuba's Exiles: Portrait of a Refugee Migration." *International Migration Review* 19, no. 1: 4–34.

Peletz, Michael. 2000. "Ambivalence in Kinship since the 1940s." In *Relative Values: Reconfiguring Kinship Studies,* edited by Sarah Franklin and Susan McKinnon. Durham: Duke University Press.

Pentón, Mario J. 2018. "Llueven Las Críticas a La Nueva Bandera De La Pequeña Habana." *El Nuevo Herald,* 7 December 2018. https://www.cibercuba.com/noticias/2018-12-07-u1-e129488-s27061-llueven-criticas-nueva-bandera-pequena-habana. Accessed 14 March 2020.

Pérez, Louis A., Jr. 1991. "Cuba and the United States: Origins and Antecedents of Relations, 1760s–1860s." *Cuban Studies* 21: 57–82.

———. 1999. *On Becoming Cuban: Identity, Nationality, and Culture*. Chapel Hill: University of North Carolina.

———. 2009. "Thinking Back on Cuba's Future: The Logic of Patria." *NACLA Report on the Americas* 42, no. 2: 12–17.

Pérez Firmat, Gustavo. 1995. *Next Year in Cuba: A Cubano's Coming of Age in America*. Houston: Arte Publico Press.

———. 1997. "A Willingness of the Heart: Cubanidad, Cubaneo, Cubanía." *Cuban Studies Association Occasional Papers* 8.

———. 2012. *Life on the Hyphen: The Cuban-American Way*. Austin: University of Texas Press.

Pérez-López, Jorge. 1995. *Cuba's Second Economy*. New York: Routledge.

Pertierra, Anna Cristina. 2008. "En Casa: Women and Households in Post-Soviet Cuba." *Journal of Latin American Studies* 40, no. 4: 743–67.

———. 2011. *Cuba: The Struggle for Consumption*. Pompano Beach: Caribbean Studies Press.

———. 2012. "The More Things Change, the More They Stay the Same: Rice and Beans in Modern Cuba." In *Rice and Beans: A Unique Dish in a Hundred Places,* edited by Richard Wilk and Livia Barbosa, 35–60. New York: Berg.

Peters, Amos. 2017. *Estimating the Size of the Informal Economy in Caribbean States*. Inter-American Development Bank: Washington. https://publications.iadb.org/en/estimating-size-informal-economy-caribbean-states#:~:text=The%20findings%20suggest%20that%20the,percent%20in%20Trinidad%20and%20Tobago. Accessed 19 August 2020.

Pine, Francis. 2002. "Dealing with Money: Zlotys, Dollars and Other Currencies in the Polish Highlands." In *Markets and Moralities: Ethnographies of Postsocialism*, edited by Ruth Mandel and Caroline Humphrey, 75–97. Oxford: Berg.

———. 2015. "Living in the Grey Zones: When Ambiguity and Uncertainty Are the Ordinary." In *Ethnographies of Grey Zones in Eastern Europe: Relations, Borders and Invisibilities*, edited by Ida Harboe Knudsen and Martin Demant Frederiksen, 25–41. London: Anthem Press.

Pinheiro-Machado, Rosana. 2017. *Counterfeit Itineraries in the Global South: The Human Consequences of Piracy in China and Brazil*. Abingdon, U.K.: Routledge.

Piot, Charles. 2010. *Nostalgia for the Future: West Africa after the Cold War*. Chicago: University of Chicago Press.

Polese, Abel. 2008. "'If I Receive It, It Is a Gift; If I Demand It, Then It Is a Bribe': On the Local Meaning of Economic Transactions in Post-Soviet Ukraine." *Anthropology in Action* 15, no. 3: 47–60.

Porter, Amy L. 2008. "Fleeting Dreams and Flowing Goods: Citizenship and Consumption in Havana Cuba." *PoLAR: Political and Legal Anthropology Review* 31, no. 1: 134–49.

Portes, Alejandro. 1983. "The Informal Sector: Definition, Controversy, and Relation to National Development." *Review* 7, no. 1: 151–74.

———. 1984. "The Rise of Ethnicity: Determinants of Ethnic Perceptions among Cuban Exiles in Miami." *American Sociological Review*: 383–97.

———. 1987. "The Social Origins of the Cuban Enclave Economy of Miami." *Sociological Perspectives* 30, no. 4: 340–72.

———. 1999. "Globalization from Below: The Emergence of Transnational Communities." *Actes de la recherche en sciences sociales* 129: 15–25.

Portes, Alejandro, and Alex Stepick, eds. 1993. *City on the Edge: The Transformation of Miami*. Berkeley; London; Los Angeles: University of California Press.

Potter, David M. 2009. *People of Plenty: Economic Abundance and the American Character*. Chicago: University of Chicago Press.

Povrzanovic Frykman, Maja. 2016. "Conceptualising Continuity: A Material Culture Perspective on Transnational Social Fields." *Ethnologia Fennica* 43: 43–56.

Powell, Kathy. 2008. "Neoliberalism, the Special Period and Solidarity in Cuba." *Critique of Anthropology* 28, no. 2: 177–97.

Prendergast, David, Jenny Hockey, and Leonie Kellaher. 2006. "Blowing in the Wind? Identity, Materiality, and the Destinations of Human Ashes." *Journal of the Royal Anthropological Institute* 12, no. 4: 881–98.

Press, Larry. 2015. "El Paquete Update—Cuba's Largest Private Employer?" *The Internet in Cuba* (blog). September 14, 2015. http://laredcubana.blogspot.com/2015/09/el -paquete-update-cubas-largest-private.html.

———. 2021. "The Past, Present, and Future of the Cuban Internet." In *Cuba's Digital Revolution: Citizen Innovation and State Policy*, edited by Ted Henken and Sara Garcia Santamaria, 29–49. Gainesville: University Press of Florida.

Puri, Shalini. 2004. *The Caribbean Postcolonial: Social Equality, Post/Nationalism, and Cultural Hybridity*. New York: Palgrave Macmillan.

246 · Bibliography

Ranger, Terence. 1983. "The Invention of Tradition in Colonial Africa." In *The Invention of Tradition*, edited by Eric J. Hobsbawm and Terence Ranger, 211–62. Cambridge: Cambridge University Press.

Rausenberger, Julie. 2018. "Importing Modernity: Foreign Fashion, Black Markets and Identity Making in Urban Cuba." *Voces del Caribe* 10, no. 1: 800–55.

Rausing, Sigrid. 2002. "Re-Constructing the 'Normal': Identity and the Consumption of Western Goods in Estonia." In *Markets and Moralities: Ethnographies of Postsocialism*, edited by Caroline Humphrey and Ruth Mandel, 127–42. New York: Berg.

Réjouis, Rose. 2014. "Dark Horse Poetics: Lévi-Strauss, Benítez-Rojo, and Caribbean Epistemology." *Small Axe: A Caribbean Journal of Criticism* 18, no. 1: 103–13.

"Rest, Relaxation & Digital Detox." 2019. *Captivating Cuba*. https://captivatingcuba .com/corona-virus-info/. Accessed 4 June 2021.

Reyes, Mario Luís. 2016. "Danys: El Hombre Detrás De El Paquete." *Universo Centro*, December 2016. https://www.universocentro.com/NUMERO82/ ElhombredetrasdeElPaquete.aspx. Accessed 4 April 2019.

Rhys-Taylor, Alex. 2013. "The Essences of Multiculture: A Sensory Exploration of an Inner-City Street Market." *Ethnography, Diversity and Urban Space* 20, no. 4: 393–406.

Ribeiro, Darcy. 2000. *The Brazilian People: The Formation and Meaning of Brazil*, edited by Gregory Rabassa. Gainesville: University Press of Florida.

Rieff, David. 1993. *The Exile: Cuba in the Heart of Miami*. New York: Simon Schuster.

Ries, Nancy. 2002. "'Honest Bandits' and 'Warped People': Russian Narratives About Money, Corruption and Moral Decay." In *Ethnography in Unstable Places: Everyday Lives in Contexts of Dramatic Political Change*, edited by C. J. Greenhouse, Elizabeth Mertz, and Kay B. Warren, 276–315. Durham, NC, and London: Duke University Press.

Ritter, Archibald R. M. 2005. "Survival Strategies and Economic Illegalities in Cuba." *Cuba in Transition: Annual Proceedings of the ASCE* 15: 342–59.

———. 2014. "Economic Illegalities and the Underground Economy in Cuba." In *A Contemporary Cuba Reader: The Revolution under Raúl Castro*, edited by Philip Brenner, Marguerite Rose Jiménez, John M. Kirk, and William M. LeoGrande, 203–30. Lanham: Rowman & Littlefield.

———. 2017. "Private and Cooperative Enterprise in Cuba's Economic Future." *Social Research* 84, no. 2: 277–303.

Rivera, Fredo. 2019. "Precarity and Excess in the Latinopolis: Miami as Erzulie." *Cultural Dynamics* 31, no. 1–2: 62–80.

Rivera, Mario A. 1998. "Second Economy, Second Society, and Political Control in Cuba: Perspectives from Network Institutional Economics." *Cuba in Transition: Annual Proceedings of the ASCE* 8: 102–13.

Robbins, Joel. 2003. "On the Paradoxes of Global Pentecostalism and the Perils of Continuity Thinking." *Religion* 33, no. 3: 221–31.

———. 2007. "Continuity Thinking and the Problem of Christian Culture. Belief, Time, and the Anthropology of Christianity." *Current Anthropology* 48, no. 1: 5–38.

———. 2018. "Afterword: Some Reflections on Rupture." In *Ruptures: Anthropologies of*

Discontinuity in Times of Turmoil, edited by Martin Holbraad, Bruce Kapferer, and Julia F. Sauma, 218–32. London: University College London Press.

Rodgers, Dennis. 2019. "From 'Broder' to 'Don': Methodological Reflections on Longitudinal Gang Research in Nicaragua." In *Ethnography as Risky Business: Field Research in Violent and Sensitive Contexts,* edited by Kees Koonings, Dirk Kruijt, and Dennis Rodgers, 123–38. Lanham: Lexington Books.

Rofel, Lisa. 1999. *Other Modernities: Gendered Yearnings in China after Socialism.* Berkeley: University of California Press.

Roitman, Janet. 2014. *Anti-Crisis.* Durham: Duke University Press.

Ros, Adela. 2010. "Interconnected Immigrants in the Information Society." In *Diasporas in the New Media Age: Identity, Politics, and Community,* edited by Andoni Alonso and Pedro J Oiarzabal, 19–38. Reno: University of Nevada Press.

Rosenblum, Beth Tamar. 2013. "From 'Special Period' Aesthetics to Global Relevance in Cuban Art: Tania Bruguera, Carlos Garaicoa, and Los Carpinteros." PhD dissertation, UCLA. https://escholarship.org/uc/item/67x720hp. Accessed 21 April 2020.

Rosendahl, Mona. 1997. *Inside the Revolution: Everyday Life in Socialist Cuba.* Ithaca and London: Cornell University Press.

———. 2001. "Household Economy and Morality During the Special Period." In *Globalization and Third-World Socialism,* edited by Claes Brundenius and John Weeks, 88–101. London: Palgrave Macmillan.

Rubinov, Igor. 2014. "Migrant Assemblages: Building Postsocialist Households with Kyrgyz Remittances." *Anthropological Quarterly* 87, no. 1: 183–215.

Ryer, Paul. 2017. "The Rise and Decline of La Yuma: Global Symbols, Local Meanings, and Remittance Circuits in Post-Soviet Cuba." *The Journal of Latin American and Caribbean Anthropology* 22, no. 2: 276–97.

———. 2018. *Beyond Cuban Waters: Africa, La Yuma, and the Island's Global Imagination.* Nashville: Vanderbilt University Press.

Rytter, Mikkel. 2010. "'The Family of Denmark' and 'the Aliens': Kinship Images in Danish Integration Politics." *Ethnos* 75, no. 3: 301–22.

Safa, Helen. 1995. *The Myth of the Male Breadwinner: Women and Industrialization in the Caribbean.* Boulder, CO: Westview Press.

———. 2008. "The Matrifocal Family and Patriarchal Ideology in Cuba and the Caribbean." *Journal of Latin American Anthropology* 10, no. 2: 314–38.

Sahlins, Marshall. 2011a. "What Kinship Is (Part One)." *Journal of the Royal Anthropological Institute* 17, no. 1: 2–19.

———. 2011b. "What Kinship Is (Part Two)." *Journal of the Royal Anthropological Institute* 17, no. 2: 227–42.

Sahlins, Marshall, and Graeber, David. 2017. *On Kings.* Chicago: HAU Books.

Sahlins, Peter. 1991. *Boundaries: The Making of France and Spain in the Pyrenees.* Berkeley: University of California Press.

Salomon, Gisela. 2020. "Miami Sees a Return to Cold War Cultural Hard Line on Cuba." *AP News,* 4 February 2020. https://apnews.com/article/entertainment-latin-america-cuba-elections-miami-2ec5402e74c5904246b4db88b5dd8501. Accessed 4 April 2020.

Salter, Paul S., and Robert C. Mings. 1972. "The Projected Impact of Cuban Settlement on Voting Patterns in Metropolitan Miami, Florida." *The Professional Geographer* 24, no. 2: 123–31.

Samuels-Wortley, Kanika. 2021. "To Serve and Protect Whom? Using Composite Counter-Storytelling to Explore Black and Indigenous Youth Experiences and Perceptions of the Police in Canada." *Crime and Delinquency* 67, no. 8: 1137–64.

San Pedro, Emilio. 2015. "Cuban Internet Delivered Weekly by Hand." *BBC News*, 10 August 2015. https://www.bbc.co.uk/news/technology-33816655. Accessed 21 March 2019.

Sasunkevich, Olga. 2014. "'Business as Casual': Shuttle Trade on the Belarus-Lithuania Border." In *The Informal Post-Socialist Economy: Embedded Practices and Livelihoods*, edited by Jeremy Morris and Abel Polese, 135–51. Abingdon, U.K.: Routledge.

———. 2016. *Informal Trade, Gender and the Border Experience: From Political Borders to Social Boundaries*. London: Routledge.

Scarpaci, Joseph L. 2014. "Material and Cultural Consumption in Cuba: New Reference Groups in the New Millennium." *Journal of Cultural Geography* 31, no. 3: 257–79.

———. 2015. "A Tale of Two Cities: Hialeah's Economic Ties with Havana." *Focus on Geography* 58, no. 2: 49–58.

Schiller, Nina Glick, and Georges Eugene Fouron. 2001. *Georges Woke up Laughing: Long-Distance Nationalism and the Search for Home*. Durham: Duke University Press.

Schoenberger, Erica. 2011. "Why Is Gold Valuable? Nature, Social Power and the Value of Things." *Cultural Geographies* 18, no. 1: 3–24.

Schoon, Allette. 2016. "Distributing Hip-Hop in a South African Town: From the Digital Backyard Studio to the Translocal Ghetto Internet." *AfriCHI'16: Proceedings of the First African Conference on Human Computer Interaction* 104–113. https://doi.org/10.1145/2998581.2998592. Accessed 15 May 2020.

Schumpeter, Joseph A. 1992. *Capitalism, Socialism and Democracy*, edited by Richard Swedberg and William Margulies. London: Routledge.

Schwenkel, Christina. 2013. "Post/Socialist Affect: Ruination and Reconstruction of the Nation in Urban Vietnam." *Cultural Anthropology* 28, no. 2: 252–77.

Scott, David. 2004. "Modernity That Predated the Modern: Sidney Mintz's Caribbean." *History Workshop Journal* (58): 191–210.

Semple, Abigail. 2016. "Cuban Shoppers Helping to Keep Guyana's Economy Afloat." *Demerara Waves*, 27 October 2016. https://demerarawaves.com/2016/10/27/cuban-shoppers-helping-to-keep-guyanas-economy-afloat/. Accessed 6 August 2019.

Settle, Heather. 2008. "The Coca-Cola of Forgetting: Reflections on Love and Migration in a Post-Castro Age." *Transforming Anthropology* 16, no. 2: 173–75.

Silot Bravo, Eva. 2016. "Reimagining Cubanidad: Transnational and Alternative Spaces in Contemporary Cuban Cultural Production." PhD thesis, University of Miami. https://scholarship.miami.edu/esploro/outputs/99103144756910297. Accessed 4 February 2019.

Simmel, Georg. 1957. "Fashion." *American Journal of Sociology* 62, no. 6: 541–58.

———. 1990. *The Philosophy of Money*. Translated by Tom Bottomore and David Frisby. London: Routledge.

Simoni, Valerio. 2012. "Dancing Tourists: Tourism, Party and Seduction in Cuba." In *Emotion in Motion: Tourism, Affect and Transformation*, edited by David Pickard and Mike Robinson, 267–82. Farnsham: Ashgate.

Singh, Supriya, Anuja Cabraal, and Shanthi Robertson. 2010. "Remittances as a Currency of Care: A Focus on 'Twice Migrants' among the Indian Diaspora in Australia." *Journal of Comparative Family Studies* 41, no. 2: 245–63.

Skaine, Rosemarie. 2004. *The Cuban Family: Custom and Change in an Era of Hardship*. Jefferson, NC: McFarland & Co.

Skop, Emily H. 2001. "Race and Place in the Adaptation of Mariel Exiles." *International Migration Review* 35, no. 2: 449–71.

Smith, Cheryl A. 2005. *Market Women: Black Women Entrepreneurs, Past, Present, and Future*. Westport: Praeger Publishers.

Smith, Raymond T. 1988. *Kinship and Class in the West Indies: A Genealogical Study of Jamaica and Guyana*. Cambridge: Cambridge University Press.

———. 1996. *The Matrifocal Family: Power, Pluralism, and Politics*. New York: Routledge.

Söderberg, Johan. 2002. "Copyleft vs. Copyright: A Marxist Critique." *First Monday* 7, no. 3.

Speakman, Maile. 2021. "'Hay Muchísimo Poder En La Oscuridad': Black Cuir Cinema Clubs in Contemporary Havana." *Revista Periódicus* 1, no. 15: 40–62.

Speck, Mary. 2005. "Prosperity, Progress, and Wealth: Cuban Enterprise During the Early Republic, 1902–1927." *Cuban Studies* 36: 50–86.

Spencer, Anthony T. 2007. "Hasta La Victoria Siempre: The Ongoing Rhetorical Revolution in Cuba." *Texas Speech Communication Journal* 31, no 1: 16–23.

Spiegel, Frances Alia. 2004. "Cuban Americans on Remittances and the Embargo." PhD thesis, Florida International University. https://cri.fiu.edu/cuban-america/remittance/remittance-frances-spiegel.pdf. Accessed 20 March 2020.

St. John, Rachel. 2011. *Line in the Sand: A History of the Western U.S.-Mexico Border*. Princeton; Oxford: Princeton University Press.

Statista. 2019. "Largest Cuban-American Population Groups in the United States, by County." https://www.statista.com/statistics/234931/us-cuban-population-by-county/. Accessed 21 March 2021.

Steingo, Gavin. 2015. "Sound and Circulation: Immobility and Obduracy in South African Electronic Music." *Ethnomusicology Forum* 24, no. 1: 102–23.

Stepick, Alex. 1994a. "Miami: Capital of Latin America." In *Newcomers in the Workplace: Immigrants and the Restructuring of the U.S. Economy*, edited by Guillermo Grenier, Louise Lamphere, and Alex Stepick, 129–44. Philadelphia: Temple University Press.

———. 1994b. "Miami: Capital of Latin America." In *Newcomers in the Workplace: Immigrants and the Restructuring of the U.S. Economy*, edited by Louise Lamphere, Alex Stepick, and Guillermo Grenier, 129–44. Philadelphia: Temple University Press.

Stepick, Alex, Guillermo Grenier, Max Castro, and Marvin Dunn, eds. 2003. *This Land Is Our Land: Immigrants and Power in Miami*. Berkeley: University of California Press.

250 · Bibliography

Stepick, Alex, and Carol Dutton Stepick. 2002. "Power and Identity: Miami Cubans." In *Latinos: Remaking America,* edited by Marcelo Suarez-Orozco and Mariela M Paez, 75–92. Berkeley: University of California Press.

Stern, Monika. 2014. "'Mi Wantem Musik Blong Mi Hemi Blong Evriwan' ['I Want My Music to Be for Everyone']. Digital Developments, Copyright and Music Circulation in Port Vila, Vanuatu." *First Monday* 19, no. 10. https://firstmonday.org/ojs/index .php/fm/article/view/5551. Accessed 18 March 2020.

Sterne, Jonathan. 2016. "The Mp3 as Cultural Artifact." *New Media & Society* 8, no. 5: 825–42.

Stobart, Henry. 2010. "Rampant Reproduction and Digital Democracy: Shifting Landscapes of Music Production and 'Piracy' in Bolivia." *Ethnomusicology Forum* 19, no. 1: 27–56.

Stoner, K. Lynn. 1991. *From the House to the Streets: The Cuban Woman's Movement for Legal Reform, 1898–1940.* Durham: Durham University Press.

Stout, Noelle. 2014a. *After Love: Queer Intimacy and Erotic Economies in Post-Soviet Cuba.* Durham: Duke University Press.

———. 2014b. "Bootlegged: Unauthorized Circulation and Digital Age." *Visual Anthropology Review* 30, no. 2: 177–87.

———. 2015. "When a Yuma Meets Mama: Commodified Kin and the Affective Economies of Queer Tourism in Cuba." *Anthropological Quarterly* 88, no. 3: 665–91.

Strathern, Marilyn. 1988. *The Gender of the Gift: Problems with Women and Problems with Society in Melanesia.* Berkeley: University of California Press.

———. 1992. *After Nature: English Kinship in the Late Twentieth Century.* Cambridge: Cambridge University Press.

Stubbs, Jean. 2014. "Transnationalism and the Havana Cigar: Commodity Chains, Networks, and Knowledge Circulation." In *Cuba in a Global Context: International Relations, Internationalism and Transnationalism,* edited by Catherine Krull, 227–42. Gainesville: University Press of Florida.

Sutton, Constance. 1992. "Some Thoughts on Gendering and Internationalizing Our Thinking About Transnational Migrations." *Annals of the New York Academy of Sciences* 645, no. 1: 241–49.

Sweig, Julia E., and Michael J. Bustamante. 2013. "Cuba after Communism: The Economic Reforms That Are Transforming the Island." *Foreign Affairs* 92, no. 4: 101–14.

Taussig, Michael T. 1992. *The Nervous System.* London: Routledge.

Taylor, Georgina, Jane Wangaruro, and Irena Papadopoulos. 2012. "'It Is My Turn to Give': Migrants' Perceptions of Gift Exchange and the Maintenance of Transnational Identity." *Journal of Ethnic and Migration Studies* 38, no. 7: 1085–1100.

Theodossopoulos, Dimitrios. 2013. "Introduction: Laying Claim to Authenticity: Five Anthropological Dilemmas." *Anthropological Quarterly* 86, no. 2: 337–60.

Thomas, Deborah A. 2019. "Crisis, Epochal Shifts, and Conceptual Disenchantment." *American Anthropologist* 121, no. 3: 549–53.

Thomas, Hugh. 1987. "Cuba: The United States and Batista, 1952–58." *World Affairs* 149, no. 4: 169–76.

Tilly, Charles. 1990. "Transplanted Networks." In *Immigration Reconsidered: History, Sociology, and Politics,* edited by Virginia Yans-McLaughlin. New York: Oxford University Press.

Torres-Queral, Maria del Carmen. 1998. "Living-on-the-Hyphen: An Exploration of the Phenomenon of Being Cuban-American." PhD thesis, University of Maryland.

"Trade in Goods with Cuba." 2022. *United States Census Bureau.* https://www.census.gov/foreign-trade/balance/c2390.html. Accessed 28 March 2022.

Trouillot, Michel-Rolph. 1992. "The Caribbean Region: An Open Frontier in Anthropological Theory." *Annual Review of Anthropology* 21, no. 1: 19–42.

———. 2002. "Culture on the Edges: Caribbean Creolization in Historical Context." In *From the Margins: Historical Anthropology and Its Futures,* edited by Brian K. Axel, 189–210. Durham: Duke University Press.

———. 2020. "The Odd and the Ordinary: Haiti, the Caribbean and the World." *Vibrant: Virtual Brazilian Anthropology* 17: 1–7.

Tsang, Martin. 2015. "Con La Mocha Al Cuello: From Canton to Havana, the Emergence and Negotiation of Afro-Chinese Religion in Cuba." PhD thesis, Florida International University. https://digitalcommons.fiu.edu/etd/1247/. Accessed 12 June 2020.

Tsing, Anna Lowenhaupt. 2011. *Friction: An Ethnography of Global Connection.* Princeton: Princeton University Press.

Turner, Terence. 2008. "Marxian Value Theory: An Anthropological Perspective." *Anthropological Theory* 8, no. 1: 43–56.

Tweed, Thomas A. 1997. *Our Lady of the Exile: Diasporic Religion at a Cuban Catholic Shrine in Miami.* New York; Oxford: Oxford University Press.

Vann, Elizabeth F. 2006. "The Limits of Authenticity in Vietnamese Consumer Markets." *American Anthropologist* 108, no. 2: 286–96.

Veblen, Thorstein. 1899. *The Theory of the Leisure Class,* edited by Martha Banta. New York: New America Library.

Veenis, Milena. 2012. *Material Fantasies: Expectations of the Western Consumer World among the East Germans,* edited by Stichting Historie der Techniek. Amsterdam: Amsterdam University Press.

Venegas, Cristina. 2007. "Shared Dreams and Red Cockroaches: Cuba and Digital Culture." *Hispanic Review* 75, no. 4: 399–414.

Verdery, Katherine. 1996. *What Was Socialism, and What Comes Next?* Princeton: Princeton University Press.

———. 2003. *The Vanishing Hectare: Property and Value in Postsocialist Transylvania.* Ithaca, NY: Cornell University Press.

Vigh, Henrik. 2008. "Crisis and Chronicity: Anthropological Perspectives on Continuous Conflict and Decline." *Ethnos* 73, no. 1: 5–24.

Viveiros de Castro, Eduardo. 2009. "The Gift and the Given: Three Nano-Essays on Kinship and Magic." In *Kinship and Beyond: The Genealogical Model Reconsidered,* edited by Sandra Bamford and James Leach, 237–68. New York: Berghahn Books.

Vuletin, Guillermo. 2008. *Measuring the Informal Economy in Latin America and the Caribbean.* International Monetary Fund. https://www.imf.org/external/pubs/ft/wp/2008/wp08102.pdf. Accessed 14 August 2019.

Wacquant, Loïc J. D. 2005. "Habitus." In *International Encyclopedia of Economic Sociology*, edited by Jens Beckert and Milan Zafirovski, 316. London: Routledge.

Wade, Peter. 2005. "Rethinking Mestizaje: Ideology and Lived Experience." *Journal of Latin American Studies* 37, no. 2: 239–57.

Wagner, Mathias. 2011. *Die Schmugglergesellschaft: Informelle Ökonomien an Der Ostgrenze Der Europäischen Union. Eine Ethnographie*. Bielefeld: transcript Verlag.

Wagner, Roy. 1977. "Analogic Kinship: A Daribi Example." *American Ethnologist* 4, no. 4: 623–42.

Walcott, Derek. 1993. "The Antilles, Fragments of Epic Memory: The 1992 Nobel Lecture." *World Literature Today* 67, no. 2: 261.

Waltorp, Karen, and Steffen Jensen. 2019. "Awkward Entanglements: Kinship, Morality and Survival in Cape Town's Prison–Township Circuit." *Ethnos* 84, no. 1: 41–55.

Ward, Marianne, and John Devereux. 2012. "The Road Not Taken: Pre-Revolutionary Cuban Living Standards in Comparative Perspective." *Journal of Economic History* 72, no. 1: 104–32.

Wardle, Huon. 2002. "Ambiguation, Disjuncture, Commitment: A Social Analysis of Caribbean Cultural Creativity." *The Journal of the Royal Anthropological Institute* 8, no. 3: 493–508.

Wedel, Johan. 2004. *Santería Healing: A Journey into the Afro-Cuban World of Divinities, Spirits, and Sorcery*. Gainesville: University Press of Florida.

Weiner, Annette. 1992. *Inalienable Possessions: The Paradox of Keeping-While-Giving*. Berkeley: University of California Press.

Weinreb, Amelia. 2009. *Cuba in the Shadow of Change: Daily Life in the Twilight of the Revolution*. Gainesville: University Press of Florida.

Werbner, Richard. 2011. "The Charismatic Dividual and the Sacred Self." *Journal of Religion in Africa* 41, no. 2: 180–205.

Weston, Kath. 2005. "Families in Queer States: The Rule of Law and the Politics of Recognition." *Radical History Review* (93): 122–41.

Whitehead, Laurence, and Bert Hoffman, eds. 2016. *Debating Cuban Exceptionalism*. New York: Palgrave Macmillan.

Whynacht, Ardath. 2009. "Raperas of the Neorevolución: Young Women, Capitalism and Cuban Hip Hop Culture." *Girlhood Studies* 2, no. 2: 119–38.

Wile, Rob. 2019. "Census: Miami Immigration Evolves; Cubans Dominate." *Miami Herald*, 5 August 2019. Accessed 26 August 2020.

Wilk, Richard. 1995. "Consumer Goods as Dialogue About Development: Colonial Time and Television Time in Belize." In *Consumption and Identity*, edited by Jonathan Friedman, 97–118. Chur: Harwood Academic Publishers.

Williams, Bianca C. 2009. "'Don't Ride the Bus!' and Other Warnings Women Anthropologists Are Given During Fieldwork." *Transforming Anthropology* 17, no. 2: 155–58.

Willis, Rebecca. 2019. "The Use of Composite Narratives to Present Interview Findings." *Qualitative Research* 19, no. 4: 471–80.

Wilson, Marisa. 2014. *Everyday Moral Economies: Food, Politics and Scale in Cuba*. Chichester: Wiley Blackwell.

Wilson, Peter J. 1969. "Reputation and Respectability: A Suggestion for Caribbean Ethnology." *Man* 4, no. 1: 70–84.

———. 1995. *Crab Antics: A Caribbean Case Study of the Conflict between Reputation and Respectability*. Prospect Heights: Waveland Press.

Wirtz, Kristina. 2004. "Santeria in Cuban National Consciousness: A Religious Case of the Doble Moral." *Journal of Latin American Anthropology* 9, no. 2: 409–38.

———. 2017. "Race in the Cuban Revolution: '¿Y Mi Cuba Negra?'" *Cultural Anthropology*, 27 March 2017. https://culanth.org/fieldsights/race-in-the-cuban-revolution-y-mi-cuba-negra. Accessed 28 February 2019.

Wolseth, Jon M. 2013. *Life on the Malecón: Children and Youth on the Streets of Santo Domingo*. New Brunswick: Rutgers University Press.

Woltman, Kelly, and K. Bruce Newbold. 2009. "Of Flights and Flotillas: Assimilation and Race in the Cuban Diaspora." *The Professional Geographer* 61, no. 1: 70–86.

World Bank. 2021. "Personal Remittances, Received (% of GDP)—Latin America & Caribbean." World Development Indicators. https://data.worldbank.org/indicator/BX.TRF.PWKR.DT.GD.ZS?locations=ZJ. Accessed 1 February 2023.

Wyndham, Marivic, and Peter Read. 2010. "The Cemetery, the State and the Exiles: A Study of Cementerio Colón, Havana, and Woodlawn Cemetery, Miami." *PORTAL: Journal of Multidisciplinary International Studies* 8, no. 1.

Yeh, Rihan. 2017. "Visas, Jokes, and Contraband: Citizenship and Sovereignty at the Mexico-U.S. Border." *Comparative Studies in Society and History* 59, no. 1: 154–82.

Yelvington, Kevin. 2001. "The Anthropology of Afro-Latin America and the Caribbean: Diasporic Dimensions." *Annual Review of Anthropology* 30: 227–60.

Yúdice, George. 2005. "Miami: Images of a Latinopolis." *NACLA Report on the Americas* 39, no. 3: 35–39.

Yurchak, Alexei. 2005. *Everything Was Forever, Until It Was No More: The Last Soviet Generation*. Princeton: Princeton University Press.

Zavodny, Madeline. 2003. "Race, Wages, and Assimilation Among Cuban Immigrants." *Population Research and Policy Review* 22, no. 3: 201–19.

Zelizer, Viviana A. 1994. *The Social Meaning of Money: Pin Money, Paychecks, Poor Relief and Other Currencies*. Princeton: Princeton University Press.

———. 2005. *The Purchase of Intimacy*. Princeton: Princeton University Press.

Zontini, Elisabetta. 2004. "Immigrant Women in Barcelona: Coping with the Consequences of Transnational Lives." *Journal of Ethnic and Migration Studies* 30, no. 6: 1113–44.

Zuboff, Shoshana. 2019. *The Age of Surveillance Capitalism: The Fight for the Future at the New Frontier of Power*. London: Profile Books.

Index

Abundance, 36, 43–46, 50–54, 150

Acoustic attacks, 7, 49

Advertising: billboards and posters, 2, 35, 51, 64, 106, 120, 132–133, 174–175, 183, 190–191; private (*see* Brand); revenue from, 28, 112–117

Aesthetics, 44, 52–54, 109–110, 135, 162–164, 202–204

Airports, 17; Havana airport, 125; Miami airport, 1, 58, 68, 180–181, 207–209; security, 58, 68, 100–102, 118

Ajiaco, 13

Anderson, Benedict, 203

Antiques, 39–40, 145–153, 155–157, 162–166

Anzaldúa, Gloria, 33

Appadurai, Arjun: on globalization, 8, 198; on *habitus*, 200; on "regimes of value," 42, 90, 98, 163 (*see also* Value); on "social lives of things," 54–55

Arroyo-Martínez, Jossianna, 170

Artists in Cuba, 49, 119, 124–125, 133–136

Austin-Broos, Diane J., 205

Authenticity, 160, 164–166, 188; in anthropology, 19; and authorship, 123, 139; and tourism, 48, 164, 192

Bach, Jonathan, 145, 151–153, 204

Baldassar, Loretta, 77, 81

Barthes, Roland, 125

Basch, Linda G., 132

Baseball, 137, 163, 181

Bastide, Roger, 77

Baudrillard, Jean, 52

Beckett, Greg, 19

Behar, Ruth, 8, 170

Benítez Rojo, Antonio, 19, 93, 203

Berdahl, Daphne, 160

Berg, Mette Louise, 11, 159, 165

Biden, Joe, 7

Bling, 40, 45, 50–52

Bloch, Maurice, 212

Borders, 212n2; border "culture" and zones, 33, 134; border guards, 2, 100, 215n11; crossing borders, 48–49, 62, 75–76, 106, 180, 199; internalized borders, 8–9; and nation, 60, 80; reification of, 3, 144

Borneman, John, 80

Boudreault-Fournier, Alexandrine, 114, 124

Boym, Svetlana, 144, 153, 160

Brand: consumer, 28, 44–45, 50–52, 90, 102, 105, 108, 130, 145; personal, 26–27, 127–132

Burawoy, Michael, 199, 205

Burial, 137, 149, 167–176, 180–181, 185–186, 217n4; secondary burial, 169–170, 181

Bush, George W., 6, 37, 44, 62, 80

Bustamante, Michael J., 61, 96

Byrne, Denis, 161

Café Versailles (business), 172, 191, 217n6

Capitalism, 16–17, 45, 130–131, 205

Capitol building, Havana, 147, 163

Capó, Julio, 54

Caribbean, 203–205; and (post)colonialism, 89, 96, 170, 205; diasporas, 33, 37; economies, 94; kinship/gender, 71–73, 97; migration, 12–13; remittances, 62; representations, 19, 131; sociality, 110

Carrier, James G., 90

Cars, 23, 150

256 · Index

Carsten, Janet, 59–60, 75, 82, 145
Casa/calle division, 107
Castells, Manuel, 206
Castro, Fidel, 7, 36, 163; death of, 95, 196; policy, 10, 61, 188; portraits, 151, 158; quotations, 216n1
Catholic church, 169–170, 174, 212n6, 214n5
Cell phones, 1–2, 44, 95, 130; access to, 113–117, 136–137; applications, 99, 112; credit/data, 35, 63–64
Cemeteries, 170, 182; Cementerio de Colón (Havana), 169; Woodlawn Park Cemetery (Miami), 173, 186
Censorship, 113–116, 123, 128; self-censorship, 114–115, 123
Centeno, Miguel Angel, 89, 113
Chino/a (as description), 35, 94, 135
Chisme (gossip), 108, 110
Churchill, Winston, 44
Cinema, 116, 121–122, 136
Citizenship, 58, 80, 105, 199
Class, 73, 200; classism, 38, 46–50, 52–53, 192–193; and the Cuban Revolution, 9–14; in the diaspora, 12–14, 34, 53–55, 146, 188; emerging class stratification in Cuba, 46–50, 88, 105–110
Clifford, James, 138, 187, 190
Clinton, Bill, 211n2
Clothing: for the dead, 169, 178–179; production and sale of, 66, 107, 150; sent to Cuba, 1, 28, 64, 95, 99–102, 181; as status symbol, 48, 51, 99, 169; wholesale, 35, 107–108, 135
Coca-Cola, 45, 130, 147, 215n12
Coffee, 47, 118, 178, 191, 193–194, 208
Coffin, 149, 171, 173, 178–179, 187
Coins. *See* Currency
Cold War, 3, 6, 8, 80
Colombia, 93
Colonialism: and burial practices, 170; and Caribbean history, 19, 73, 93, 107, 189, 205; and corporate capitalism, 16, 132–134
Comedy, 52, 135–138
Commodity, 5, 55, 74, 82, 127–129, 139, 163–166; commodity fetishism, 44–48, 90, 145

Confianza, 38, 97, 99, 107–111, 177, 181
Connerton, Paul, 145, 152, 164
Consumer culture: and the American Dream, 68; collecting, 157–159, 166; in Cuban diaspora, 52; decommoditization, 129; emerging in (post)socialist Cuba, 44, 62; history of in Cuba, 44–45, 96
Consumption, 43–53, 59, 89–91, 96, 113, 132–134, 159–168
Copyright, 28, 130–133, 136
Corpse, 171, 178
Corruption, 2, 146
Creole, 14, 19, 203
Criminality, 10–11, 26–27, 38, 91, 109, 130, 158, 197
Crisis, 19–20, 117, 203–204. *See also* Rupture
Cuban Adjustment Act, 12. *See also* U.S.–Cuba relations: wet foot/dry foot policy
Cuban Missile Crisis, 6, 9
Cuban Revolution (1959), 8–10, 43, 167
Cubanness (*cubanía* or *cubanidad*), 13–15, 35–36, 45–46, 201–204; as ideology, 7–9, 89, 149, 186; ingredients of, 14, 183; interpretations and performativity of, 15, 22–23, 159, 196–197; in material/digital culture, 46, 131–134, 147. *See also ajiaco*
Cuentapropismo, 12, 24, 89, 109, 113, 213
Currency, 51, 62, 106, 211n1, 212n7, 213n1; coins, 157–157
Customs. *See* Borders: border guards

Dawdy, Shannon Lee, 160–164
Deleuze, Gilles, 202
Diaspora, 135–139, 167, 187; *balseros*, 11–12, 52, 174, 182, 192; exile generation, 9–10, 13–16, 37, 60–63, 144–154, 172–176, 188, 211; *marielitos*, 10–11, 61; Ybor City, 167–168; "New Cubans," 36–43, 48, 53–55
Digital media: alienation and sociality, 29, 114, 124; digital content, 113, 124, 128; digital detox, 27, 130; materiality of, 29, 125–126, 134, 152; and piracy, 129–132; as public sphere (*see* Public sphere); and research methods, 22. *See also* Social media
"Distinction" (Bourdieu). *See* Taste
Dominican Republic, 26, 50, 184

Dominoes, 137, 147
Douglas, Mary, 52, 170–171
Duany, Jorge, 11, 36, 62–63, 76, 95, 197–199

Eckstein, Susan, 10, 37, 60–65, 75, 95, 110
Education: cost of, 39, 109–110; as ideological
   in diaspora, 9, 148–150, 216n3; as marker
   of success, 46–47; and salary in Cuba, 65; in
   socialist ideology, 43, 121–122; university,
   24–25
Edwards, Jeanette, 75–76
El paquete, 112–113, 116–124, 127–128, 131–
   133, 135–139, 200
El tema (expression), 192
Embargo (*bloqueo*): circumventing of, 104,
   155–158, 175–183, 208; and economic
   struggle in Cuba, 56, 112; history of, 6,
   60–61
Embassies, 6–7, 49, 106, 215n14
Estefan, Gloria, 172
Ethnicity. *See* Race
Evans-Pritchard, Edward Evan, 81
Exceptionalism, 197
Excess. *See* Abundance
Exchange: and gender, 72–74, 108; Kula
   exchange circuits (*see* Kula Ring); and
   research methods, 24, 22; across socioeco-
   nomic systems, 42, 47, 51; and space (see
   Casa/calle division); versus production and
   consumption, 21
Exchange value. *See* Marxian theory
Exile politics, 9–16, 36, 147–151, 155–159,
   167, 176–177, 188–189, 211n4, 217n6

Fame, 55–56, 88, 92, 128
Fashion, 44, 47, 54, 108, 110
Fernández, Damián J., 99, 113, 197
Fieldwork, 4, 7, 22–28, 196
Flag, 35, 186, 188–199
Food, 35; from Cuban soil, 95; and kinship
   (substance), 59, 76–81; and nostalgia/
   cultural identity, 105, 147, 155–156, 182; as
   remittances, 1, 28, 61, 64
Foster, Robert J., 16, 55, 98, 143, 212
Foucault, Michel, 203
Fouron, Georges Eugene, 80

Freedom (*libertad*), 16, 46–47, 115, 188;
   Freedom Flights, 9–10, 66; of the press (*see*
   Censorship)
Frontier zone, 13, 56, 129, 144, 212n2. *See also*
   Borders

Gardner, Katy, 182–183
Gaudí, Antoni, 202–203
Gell, Alfred, 98
Gender, 20, 88, 176; and fieldwork, 25; role of
   men, 25, 102; role of women, 29, 71–77,
   107–114, 215n10
Gift, 55, 97–98, 130, 147; "spirit of the," 81. *See*
   also Mauss, Marcel
Globalization, 17–18, 73, 98, 110, 131–134,
   198–205
Gold, 175; and colonialism, 51; jewelry or
   clothing, 1–2, 39–43, 48, 50–52, 104, 179;
   repair, 201–202 (see also *Kintsugi*); value of,
   40–42 (*see also* Value). *See also* Bling
Graffiti, 78, 154
Greater Miami, 33–34, 44, 54, 212n4; Hialeah,
   11–15, 34–38, 50–53, 63, 135–137; Little
   Havana, 7–10, 146, 172, 186, 188–190; Mi-
   ami Beach, 34, 50; Westchester, 14, 154, 173
Grenier, Guillermo, 12, 46, 188
Guattari, Félix, 202
Guevara, Che, 145, 155–156, 215n17, 216n1
Guyana, 93, 100–107, 215

Habitus, 197–203
Haiti, 19, 22, 46, 50, 80, 93–94, 108
Hall, Stuart, 19
Hansing, Katrin, 63–65
Härkönen, Heidi, 47, 56, 73–79, 107, 169–172
Havana, 22; El Cerro, 115–121; Cojímar, 99;
   La Cuevita, 106–107; Habana Vieja, 107,
   114, 162–163; El Malecón, 154; Necrópolis
   Cristóbal Colón (*see also* Cemeteries);
   Playa, 48–50; El Vedado, 44, 138, 163, 117;
   La Víbora, 162–163
Heidegger, Martin, 168
Henken, Ted A., 88, 113
Heritage, 144–149, 160–161, 165–166, 176
Hernández-Reguant, Ariana, 133–134
Hockey, Jenny, 180–182

258 · Index

Holbraad, Martin, 4, 34, 43–44, 65, 91
Homeland, 80, 131, 134, 138, 145–146, 155; *patria*, 167, 217n3, 182–184
Homosexuality, 10, 49, 120
Horst, Heather A., 48, 122, 129, 139, 199
Hotel Havana Libre (Havana), 117
Hotel Nacional (Havana), 44
Hurricane, 1, 40
Hutchinson, Sharon Elaine, 59, 81
Hybridity, 14, 19, 82, 88, 20, 203

Ideology: competing, 13, 27, 155–160, 180–185; counter ideological, 36–37, 52, 67, 177; hegemonic, 4, 9, 30, 46, 71, 145–151, 172, 188; socialist, 16–17, 139, 170
Informal economy: and ethnographic fieldwork, 22; and remittances to Cuba, 62–65, 70; and smuggling, 156, 163, 177–178; and socialism, 88–91, 96–97, 113–114, 132, 139; and women, 107–110
Intellectual property. *See* Private ownership
Internet in Cuba, 112–118, 122–128, 139, 156
Invento (inventiveness), 56, 112, 128, 131, 163, 167, 179, 205
Instituto Superior de las Artes (Higher institute of Arts, ISA), 136

Jameson, Fredric, 205
Judaism, 182, 214
Judt, Tony, 144

Kahn, Jeffrey S., 4, 96
Key West, 183–184
Khan, Aisha, 14, 19, 89, 203
Kinship: in anthropology, 80–82; in the Caribbean, 97; and death, 169, 173–176; diagram, *72*; and material culture, 24, 41, 52–53, 74; and national identity/symbolism, 145–146, 176, 183, 187 (see also *ajiaco*); as patronage, 88, 93, 109–111, 183; and transnational remittances, 58–62, 70–77
Kintsugi, 201–204
Kopytoff, Igor, 98, 144, 159
Kula Ring, 3, 29, 55–56, 87–88, 91–99, 110–111, 128, 135, 201

La comunidad (expression), 149
Labor, 55, 61, 77–78, 82, 109, 133
Laguna, Albert Sergio, 117, 123, 136–138
Lee, Benjamin, 98, 206
Lévi-Strauss, Claude, 82, 88, 149
Levitt, Peggy, 37, 60, 64
LiPuma, Edward, 98, 206
Los Van Van (musical group), 38

Maleuvre, Didier, 146
Malinowski, Bronisław, 87, 91–92, 98
Marcus, George E., 8, 23
Martí, José, 151, 167
Marx, Karl, 212
Marxian theory, 28, 41–42, 55, 90
Materiality, 42, 50–51, 59, 74, 81, 122, 128, 168–169, 196
Maurer, Bill, 42, 212
Mauss, Marcel, 81, 91, 98
McDonald's (restaurant), 105
McKay, Deirdre, 74
Medicine, 1, 35, 64, 67, 181, 211n2, 215n11
Memory, 42, 144–149, 152–153, 160, 166
Mercado negro (black market). *See* Informal economy
Merleau-Ponty, Maurice, 202
Mestizaje, 19, 33
Mexico, 3, 22, 61, 67, 92–93, 100–101, 109, 128, 174
Migration, 190, 198–199; economic, 36, 75; generations migrating from Cuba, 7–13; return migration, 37, 43, 48–53, 62–63, 94, 166–168, 182, 208
Miller, Daniel, 76; on consumption and material culture, 16, 59, 82; on digital media, 122, 129, 139; on value, 41, 45
Mintz, Sidney Wilfred, 18, 52, 93, 94–96, 108, 205
Modernity, 47, 122, 151, 165, 198, 205, 212
Motherhood, 20, 49, 66–71, 76–79, 83
Mula Ring, 3, 29, 87–88, 92–97, 105–109, 131, 200–201, 206
Mulas, 49, 126; activities of, 92–94, 99–107; appearance of, 58, 192; and gender, 25, 215n10; and legality, 28; as social portals, 62–63, 180–182

Munn, Nancy D., 29, 60, 95; on "intersubjective spacetime," 55, 99; on personhood, 92, 110, 128 (*see also* Fame); on value creation, 41, 55–56, 91

Museums, 95, 148, 151–153, 159, 162–163; American Museum of the Cuban Diaspora (Miami), 153; Casa Cuba (Miami), 153; Cuban Heritage Collection (Miami), 146, 152–153; Queens Museum (New York), 125–127, 131

Music, 49, 51, 113–119, 130–133, 194

Nationalism, 13–14, 129–130, 134, 148–151, 155–156, 160, 187, 189

Neoliberalism, 17, 133–134, 170, 205–206

New Man (*hombre nuevo*), 43

New York, 22, 93, 125–126, 194–195

Nicaragua, 39, 174, 183

¡Ñooo! que barato (store), 35, 138, 192

Nora, Pierre, 146

Nostalgia, 135, 144–148, 153–157, 160–166, 191; Cuba Nostalgia Fair, 153–159

Obama, Barack, 6–7, 12, 37, 62–65, 95, 136–137, 195–196

Olwig, Karen Fog, 19, 48, 71, 95–96, 199–205

Ong, Aihwa, 198

Operation Peter Pan, 9

Organización de Pioneros José Martí, 108, 215n17

Ortiz, Fernando, 13–14, 82, 131, 218

Palmié, Stephan, 13–14, 82, 89, 131, 203, 218

Panama, 3, 22, 92–94, 100–107, 215n15

Pánfilo (TV character), 135–137

Parabolic antennas, 117

Parry, Jonathan, 180–181, 212

Partido Comunista Cubano (Cuban Communist Party), 61, 150, 118

Passports, 1–2, 13, 24, 62, 67, 93, 109, 113, 208

Patria o muerte (expression), 167

Pawnshops, 28, 35, 38–43, 46–47, 51, 139, 163, 196

Pérez Firmat, Gustavo, 8, 35, 189–190, 193, 197, 204

Pérez Jr., Louis A., 44

Pertierra, Anna Cristina, 44, 48, 96–97, 107–108, 113, 162, 197

Photography (selfies), 43, 105, 138, 146–148, 154

Plastic wrap, 2, 102, 107, 137

Por la izquierda (expression), 109, 214n3

Portes, Alejandro, 9, 46, 89, 113, 132, 188–190

Postsocialism, 45, 98–99, 110, 145, 153, 199; transition, 16–18, 153

Prestamista (loanshark), 38

Prison, 10, 67, 109

Private ownership, 28, 56, 87, 139; and the American Dream, 34–35, 46; and exile, 156; of home, 110; and inalienability, 166; in Cuba, 117, 130–131, 169; intellectual property, 129–134; versus shared ownership, 47, 123

Provinces of Cuba, 168, 180, 183, 186, 217–218

Public sphere, 29, 71, 108, 110, 113, 139

¿Qué Pasa, USA? (TV show), 190–193

Race, 146; in Cuba, 10–11, 24–25, 65, 105–107, 120, 186, 218n9; racism, 11, 146; in United States diaspora, 9–15, 24, 35, 106, 174, 188

Radio, 117, 180, 216n2

Radio bemba (expression), 128

Reagan, Ronald, 216n2

Remittances, 35–37, 67–70, 117–118, 164; and class, 95, 110; as substance of kinship, 72, 80–82; reverse direction, 157; social, 60–65

Repatriation, 13, 173–176, 180, 217n8

Republican Party (U.S.), 7, 12, 155, 217n6

Robbins, Joel, 18, 204–205

Rupture, 7, 18–21; and cultural identity, 184, 189–190, 201–206; "dual aspect" of, 3–4, 34, 111; and mobility, 80–82, 87–90

Russia, 22, 93–94, 100–102, 164

Ryer, Paul, 44–45, 90, 105

Safa, Helen, 108–110

Sahlins, Marshall, 59, 73, 77, 81

Saint Lazarus, 40–42, 185

Santería, 95, 170, 174, 179–180, 184, 215n5, 217n5

Scarcity, 36, 45, 52, 58, 62, 88–90, 112–113

260 · Index

Schiller, Nina Glick, 80
Schumpeter, Joseph A., 4
Seeds, 30, 182–185
Self-employment. See *Cuentapropismo*
Simmel, Georg, 42, 52, 212
Siré, Nestor, 26, 116, 124–126, 130–134
Slavery, 73, 189, 205, 214n5
Social media, 2, 122–126; and politics, 155, 188; and reputation, 43, 128. *See also* Censorship
Socialism, 2, 15–19, 96–99, 197–198; cultural policy, 121–123, 132–134; historical background in Cuba, 42–45; imagined other, 56 (see also *Yuma*); leftism, 214n3; material scarcity (*see* Scarcity); "postsocialism," 45, 145, 199, 213n8; "reform socialism" in Cuba, 89–91
Soil (*tierra*), 167–168, 180–186
Soviet Union, 6, 11, 19, 90, 107
Spain, 22, 158, 164–165; citizenship for Cubans, 105; colonization of South America, 50; occupation of Cuba, 4–5; transfers to Cuba via, 61, 67, 99
Special Period (*Período Especial*), 6, 51, 96, 117; and capitalism, 45 (see also *Yuma*); and gender roles, 107; and struggle, 36 (*see also* Scarcity; Struggle); as crisis, 111; as referent to hardship, 40–41, 211n3
Spying, 23, 208, 156, 193, 123
Strathern, Marilyn, 59–60, 75–77
Street Network (SNET), 115
Struggle, 38–42, 53, 80–81, 202–205; and agency, 21, 34; as discourse ('*la lucha*'), 211n3; as resistance, 45, 81, 130–132
Substance (in kinship), 13, 29, 73, 77, 81
Success, 110–111, 122, 175–179; definition of, 37–38, 46; and *invento*, 90, 198, 179, 56, 131; performance of, 42–44, 48–53
Sugar, 4–6, 52, 64, 147

Taste ("distinction"), 38, 44–45, 50–56
Tax, 107, 215n11, 211n1, 213n1
Theatre, 190–193

Tobacco, 4, 64, 95, 183, 218n10
Tourism, 158; to Cuba, contemporary, 24–27, 48–49, 96, 104–105, 162–165; to Cuba, historic, 5, 117; enabling material transfers, 126; to Miami, 44
Travel restrictions, 7, 13, 37, 93–95, 106
Trencadís, 203–204
Trouillot, Michel-Rolph, 19, 89, 203–205
Trump, Donald, 7, 70, 94, 155, 106, 215n14
Tsing, Anna Lowenhaupt, 21, 54, 199, 206

U.S.–Cuba relations, 4–8, 16, 80; commercial flights, 7, 96, 125, 162, 174, 208; diplomatic relations, 7, 49, 196; history of, 44; trade, 6–8; wet foot/dry foot policy, 12, 24
USB sticks, 112, 122, 128, 117

Valsan (store), 138, 192
Value: affective, 40–41, 158–163; alternative systems of, 39–42, 47–48, 132–134; creation of, 87–94, 98–99, 200–201 (*see also* Marxian theory); material value, 50–51; regimes of value, 42, 47, 90, 98, 109, 163, 203–204 (*see also* Appadurai, Arjun); symbolic, 51–55
Veblen, Thorstein, 52
Venezuela, 39, 50, 90, 93, 96, 114, 192–193, 196
Verdery, Katherine, 96
Video, 51, 112, 118, 121, 135–138
Viveiros de Castro, Eduardo, 59

Wacquant, Loïc J. D., 200
Wagner, Roy, 59
Walcott, Derek, 201–202
Weiner, Annette, 42, 60, 166, 163
Western Union, 7, 63
Wilk, Richard, 48
Wilson, Peter J., 72, 97

Yuma (expression), 45, 54–56, 192

Zelizer, Viviana A., 60, 74, 212

Jennifer Cearns is currently a postdoctoral research fellow at the Department of Anthropology, University College London. She completed her PhD in anthropology at UCL in 2020 and was appointed one of the inaugural Leach Fellows in Public Anthropology at the Royal Anthropological Institute of Great Britain and Ireland. Her research has won the Arthur Maurice Hocart Prize (Royal Anthropological Institute of Great Britain and Ireland) and the Roseberry Nash Award (Society for Latin American and Caribbean Anthropology). She lives in London, where she also works as a professional classical soprano.

New World Diasporas

Edited by Kevin A. Yelvington

This series seeks to stimulate critical perspectives on diaspora processes in the New World. Representations of race and ethnicity, the origins and consequences of nationalism, migratory streams and the advent of transnationalism, the dialectics of homelands and diasporas, trade networks, gender relations in immigrant communities, the politics of displacement and exile, and the utilization of the past to serve the present are among the phenomena addressed by original, provocative research in disciplines such as anthropology, history, political science, and sociology.

International Editorial Board
Herman L. Bennett, Rutgers University
Gayle K. Brunelle, California State University at Fullerton
Jorge Duany, Universidad de Puerto Rico
Sherri Grasmuck, Temple University
Daniel Mato, Universidad Central de Venezuela
Kyeyoung Park, University of California at Los Angeles
Richard Price, College of William and Mary
Sally Price, College of William and Mary
Vicki L. Ruiz, Arizona State University
John F. Stack Jr., Florida International University
Mia Tuan, University of Oregon
Peter Wade, University of Manchester

More Than Black: Afro-Cubans in Tampa, by Susan D. Greenbaum (2002)
Carnival and the Formation of a Caribbean Transnation, by Philip W. Scher (2003)
Dominican Migration: Transnational Perspectives, edited by Ernesto Sagás and Sintia E. Molina (2004)
Salvadoran Migration to Southern California: Redefining El Hermano Lejano, by Beth Baker-Cristales (2004)
The Chrysanthemum and the Song: Music, Memory, and Identity in the South American Japanese Diaspora, by Dale A. Olsen (2004)
Andean Diaspora: The Tiwanaku Colonies and the Origins of South American Empire, by Paul S. Goldstein (2005)
Migration and Vodou, by Karen E. Richman (2005; first paperback edition, 2008; second paperback edition, 2018)
True-Born Maroons, by Kenneth M. Bilby (2005)
The Tears of Hispaniola: Haitian and Dominican Diaspora Memory, by Lucía M. Suárez (2006)
Dominican-Americans and the Politics of Empowerment, by Ana Aparicio (2006)
Nuer-American Passages: Globalizing Sudanese Migration, by Dianna J. Shandy (2006)
Religion and the Politics of Ethnic Identity in Bahia, Brazil, by Stephen Selka (2007)
Reconstructing Racial Identity and the African Past in the Dominican Republic, by Kimberly Eison Simmons (2009)
Haiti and the Haitian Diaspora in the Wider Caribbean, edited by Philippe Zacaïr (2010)
From Douglass to Duvalier: U.S. African Americans, Haiti, and Pan Americanism, 1870–1964, by Millery Polyné (2010)
New Immigrants, New Land: A Study of Brazilians in Massachusetts, by Ana Cristina Braga Martes (2010)
Yo Soy Negro: Blackness in Peru, by Tanya Maria Golash-Boza (2011; first paperback edition, 2012)
Trance and Modernity in the Southern Caribbean: African and Hindu Popular Religions in Trinidad and Tobago, by Keith E. McNeal (2011; first paperback edition, 2015)

Kosher Feijoada and Other Paradoxes of Jewish Life in São Paulo, by Misha Klein (2012; first paperback edition, 2016)

African-Brazilian Culture and Regional Identity in Bahia, Brazil, by Scott Ickes (2013; first paperback edition, 2015)

Islam and the Americas, edited by Aisha Khan (2015; first paperback edition, 2017)

Building a Nation: Caribbean Federation in the Black Diaspora, by Eric D. Duke (2016; first paperback edition, 2018)

Tampa: Impressions of an Emigrant, by Wenceslao Gálvez y Delmonte, Translation by Noel M. Smith, Introduction and Notes by Noel M. Smith and Andrew T. Huse (2020)

Blackness in Mexico: Afro-Mexican Recognition and the Production of Citizenship in the Costa Chica, by Anthony Russell Jerry (2023)

Circulating Culture: Transnational Cuban Networks of Exchange, by Jennifer Cearns (2023)